THE GRAPEVINE

Books by Jess Stearn

The Grapevine
The Door to the Future
The Sixth Man
The Wasted Years
Sisters of the Night

THE GRAPEVINE

JESS STEARN

Doubleday & Company, Inc.
Garden City, New York
1964

Library of Congress Catalog Card Number 63-18029

CONTENTS

THE GRAPEVINE

THE GRAPEVINE

While I was writing a recent book on male homosexuality, many people suggested that I also deal with the female homosexual—the lesbian. However, lesbianism did not seem a comparable problem to me at that time, and it wasn't until I was nearing the end of my research that I began to suspect that lesbianism might be just as rampant as male homosexuality, only far more secretive. I was very much aware that the lesbian would not speak of her lesbianism with the same candor as the male homosexual, nor was she as readily accessible. And, anyway, from my few cursory experiences with lesbians, in the process of putting together my book on male homosexuality, I had also gained the impression that lesbians were a harshly unattractive and one-sided group. "They combine the worst features of both sexes," a male homosexual had told me, his voice edged with contempt. "They're horrible."

But all this was long before I was invited to a national convention of lesbians, and began to realize for the first time that lesbians, perhaps even more so than male homosexuals, were a formidable cross-section of the general population.

It was following this realization—and my invitation to the lesbian convention—that I eventually decided to write this book. Meanwhile, because of a surprising response among lesbians to my book *The Sixth Man*, which had resulted in my invitation to the convention in the first place, I suddenly found myself a welcome figure in the strange, forbidden world of lesbianism. Even more so than the male homosexuals, lesbians, who had maintained their secrecy vigilantly for years, wanted to challenge the picture I had drawn of the homosexual. And some were positively livid about the brief references I had made to the lesbian. Suddenly I found many doors opening that had been previously closed to the independent researcher. And where lesbianism had once seemed too much of an enigma for any outsider to crack, I was now encouraged by many lesbians to embark on my new project.

Even so, I had no open sesame, for lesbianism, by its very nature, flourished best in secrecy. Some lesbians managed their secret so well that many unhappy husbands, unwittingly married to lesbians, never suspected why their marriages didn't work. In the same way, many parents fretted over lovely daughters who showed no inclination to marry, and many a frustrated suitor developed a sex complex over the indifference of a girl he had been ardently courting.

It soon became apparent to me, as I got on with my research, that my original view of the lesbian, which was shared by so many males, had been completely erroneous. Where I had thought of lesbians as mannish, hostile figures, I soon discovered that some of the loveliest women in the world were lesbians, and were, ironically, appealing sex symbols on stage and screen to millions of unsuspecting males who didn't even begin to realize they were worshiping at a false shrine.

It was relatively easy for a lesbian to keep her secret, since nobody thought anything of two women kissing, embracing, or dancing together. "They get away with murder," male homosexuals told me resentfully. "There are just as many of them, but nobody ever bothers them."

Only a small minority of the lesbian underground, I found, frankly proclaimed their lesbianism, and it was from this stereotype that casual observers got their impression of the lesbian as a harshly hostile figure with a short masculine haircut, coarse skin, nasty vocabulary, and rough male clothing. Some of these obvious stereotypes tried so hard to be masculine that they even wore male underwear—jockey shorts, in some cases—and instead of bras, they fastened leather straps under their men's shirts to minimize their female characteristics.

Actually, there were all types of lesbians, and the masculine stereotype, known as the "butch" or "dike," had many variations —the "bull-dagger," the "bull-dike," the "big diesel," the "stompin' butch," and the "baby butch," the latter the confused teen-ager who was not sure what she was.

For every butch, of course, there was a feminine counterpart— the "femme" or "doll"—though the butches, I soon learned, were not averse to indoctrinating attractive non-lesbians who showed any sign of being interested.

But, butch or femme, the majority of lesbians, though they might slightly modify their dress or hair-do in deference to their inclinations, were indistinguishable from the majority of women who were normally sexed. Like the male homosexual, the lesbian crowded the publishing, theatrical, and modeling fields, and studied the arts and sciences. But they were also cabbies, truck drivers, clerks, engineers, stenographers, teachers, and nurses—certainly a representative cross-section.

Even with lesbian co-operation, it was often difficult to find out what made the lesbian tick and learn how she managed to live with herself and society. I visited literally hundreds of lesbians in their homes as well as in shops, bars, and recreation grounds, observed them at play and work, and checked, too, with the few outside observers who knew anything about them—the police, sociologists, psychologists, male homosexuals, and the lesbian aficionados, the male Johns who got their "kicks" out of lesbian prostitutes.

More than once my own motivations were subjected to question. At a cocktail party, a sociologist, informed of my new project, remarked sourly, "Isn't it strange that you should have written first about male homosexuality—and now lesbians?"

"Not at all," I answered lightly, ignoring the obvious innuendo. "I have lesbian tendencies."

He had the grace to retreat.

Nevertheless, the stigma of lesbianism was so great that it discouraged needed research by trained sociologists, who were afraid some of the stigma would rub off on them. "I wouldn't dare embark on such a study," observed a distinguished female professor who had done a comparable male study. "What would people think?"

As a reporter intent on thoroughly researching this project, I was more concerned with the questions that went teeming through my mind than with what others might think.

For instance, how many lesbians were there? If the male homosexual comprised one sixth of the nation's adult male population, as some authorities maintained, could it be considered that the lesbian population, though definitely more hidden, was comparably large?

How large a part did the rising aggressiveness of women play in the development of masculine qualities that seemed a symptom of lesbianism?

Also, if the lesbian really hated men, as so many observers assumed, why then did she so frequently imitate the very figure she hated?

Why, too, incongruously, did so many apparently feminine women who were besieged by male admirers reach out instead for the clandestine love of other women?

Lesbians obviously had a problem in adjusting to a society that condemned them as lesbians. And yet, though I was to meet many teen-age lesbians who were already prostitutes and drug addicts, many adult women seemed to have found happiness in the mature love of another woman.

Often, too, the boundaries of female homosexuality were so vague that many women slipped into lesbianism without realizing they were lesbians. "Lesbianism," as one lesbian pointed out, "is often only an extension of woman's natural affection."

In a figurative—if not literal—sense, lesbians made strange bedfellows. Cultivated, refined women, fearful of exposure in their own decorous circles, haunted dirty, dingy bars in search of companions who would satisfy their restless yearnings; it was commonplace for a celebrated intellectual or a film personality to pay court to girls they would ordinarily disdain as maids.

Bisexuality was common. And the woman of position, mindful first of her security, often fell back on marriage and maternity as a cover for her relationships with other women. Still other women had married in good faith, only to discover later that what they had considered an exaggerated fear of sex was in fact a more vital deviation from the sexual norm.

As I continued to delve into the problem, I was impressed by the attempts of many lesbians to maintain their secrecy. Lesbians who were admittedly homosexual in their own circles were nevertheless determined to keep their secret from other intimates—friends, relatives, co-workers. Many were part of a vast, sprawling grapevine, with a secret code of their own.

On Thursdays, for instance, multitudes of lesbians throughout the country wore a special color dress to identify themselves to other secret lesbians. In New York, Los Angeles, and San Francisco, the cognoscenti wore green; in Chicago, they chose yellow; in Connecticut, it was pink. The day itself was known as Sweet Thursday.

Many lesbians even had a special vernacular. The phrase "coming out" ironically indicated a lesbian's sexual debut; being "brought out" reflected the same result. A "lez" was a friendly diminutive for lesbian; "being gay" denoted female as well as male homosexuality. A "straight" was a heterosexual, a straight attitude "jam" and a "swinger," an object of admiration, could handle any lesbian situation, from an unwanted overture to making an overture herself. "Kiki" (pronounced *ky-ky*) was a fundamental reversal in the femme-butch role.

Like the male homosexual, the lesbian was often a heavy

drinker, insecure emotionally, and quick to blame society for her insecurity. And yet, with it all, she frequently felt superior to men. "I don't have to ask any man what I do," lesbians told me coolly, "and I don't need any man to do it with."

Yet wincing at the very word "lesbian," many preferred to be known as deviates, variants, homophiles—anything but the lesbians they were.

The teen-age lesbian seemed to be a problem by herself, and her lesbianism at times appeared more symptomatic of juvenile delinquency than anything else. One pretty teen-ager clad in leather jacket and riding boots, reading as she rode the New York City subways, casually leafed through the pages of a book with a razor-sharp switchblade. "I was raped once," she said grimly, "and I'm not taking any more chances."

More than any other group, lesbians seemed to express themselves artistically—in writing, painting, and song. Turning themselves over, they revealed the pangs and loneliness of their torment and love, just as the followers of the poetess Sappho had some twenty-five hundred years before on the Grecian island of Lesbos which gave lesbians their name.

And it soon became apparent, as I went along, that lesbianism was by no means the province of the big cities alone. I met lesbians from virtually every state in the union, and from every walk of life. However, as with the male homosexuals, there was a tendency for female homosexuals to lose themselves in the anonymity and excitement of a teeming metropolis.

The rise in lesbianism was noticeably obvious. And the American Psychoanalytic Association, at an unprecedented symposium on lesbians, decided that women might be compensating for a burgeoning male homosexuality which was up some six hundred per cent in England alone since World War II. And lesbianism was clearly more prevalent among the younger set, suggesting that the sexuality of the rising generation might be significantly changing.

In Hollywood, long famed for beauty and ennui, the homosexuality of many leading male and female stars was calmly accepted, though the rest of the country, hearing these famous names, would only gasp incredulously. Still, because of a curious grapevine, many teen-age lesbians around the country, hanging pictures of their favorite feminine stars above their beds, seemed very much aware of the lesbian stars. "It takes two to tango," a baby butch told me carelessly, accounting for the lack of secrecy.

In Hollywood, as in other cities, there were lesbian prostitutes, their names confided to secret Betty Books. And on the other end of the scale, in the semblance of utmost respectability, many women were living comfortably together as "man and wife," their relationship secretly reinforced by mock marriage ceremonies.

Reasonably free from public scrutiny, on the beaches, at house parties, and in office klatches, lesbians quietly carried on the bittersweet work of conversion. And while many office managers became aware of the undefinable lack of femininity in their office staffs, few could put their finger on the specific problem.

It was at play, generally, that the lesbian revealed herself, but only, as a rule, when she was confident that she ran no risk of exposure or reprisal. Lesbian vacation paradises were well-known to the informed—Long Island's fashionable Hamptons, Fire Island, the California beaches, and the lush tropical islands of the Caribbean, Jamaica and the Virgin Islands. The international set flourished on the Riviera, in Switzerland, Paris, and Rome. And the subway set fared equally well at New York's Riis Park, not far from Coney Island, where hundreds of lesbians gathered via their grapevine at the extreme left end of the broad beach without thousands of other bathers suspecting for a moment what was going on.

While it was virtually impossible to tell how many lesbians there were in the country, it seemed reasonable that the social forces inducing homosexuality were similarly effective for men and women. "As the old song goes," one homosexual wag slyly observed, "you can't have the one without the other."

Lesbianism was nothing new. Long before Sappho's time, lesbians had left their impact on the cultures of ancient Egypt and

Persia. Later they were common in imperial Rome, the Elizabethan era in England, when good Queen Bess herself was suspect, and in the French court of Marie Antoinette, who was accused of "unnaturalness" by the revolutionary mob which detested her more than they did the King.

More recently I discovered that sociologists and psychologists were suggesting that two world wars, raising havoc with the personal lives of men and women, have apparently given homosexuality a strong forward thrust. And no group is more aware of this upsurge than the homosexuals themselves. In the Agony Columns of one nationally distributed newspaper—of a sensational turn— I noticed many advertisements which reflected this growing "togetherness."

One ad read: "Loving brunette, twenty-six, 38–26–34, neat, attractive, would welcome hearing from women with like interests. No men; no prudes. Photo a must. Only those who can speak sincerely. Will make all replies."

To capitalize on this growing awareness of lesbians for one another, some unscrupulous book and magazine publishers have actually invented lesbian case studies to reach an audience newly alive to the scope of their own problem—and their own kind.

Also because of this growing awareness, lesbian groups have sprung up across the country, and lesbians have for the first time dared to meet openly with other lesbians to work out their common problem as best they can.

It was for this reason, I was formally advised, that the Daughters of Bilitis, a predominantly lesbian group, was staging a national convention in Los Angeles, and wondered if I—the author of *The Sixth Man*—would participate in their convention program.

"We hope," the D.O.B. invitation went, "that you will be able to join us and learn more of the subject which you have already covered very well so far as your study went."

The aims of the D.O.B. were mentioned briefly. "The Daughters of Bilitis," reported Los Angeles chapter president Jean Nathan (a pseudonym) "is a nonprofit organization dedicated to strengthening the bond between the homosexual and society. This does not mean that we adhere to any particular point of view regarding homosexuality or that we are attempting to swell our ranks by recruitment. Rather, we feel that there is a need for such a group of women who have made an adjustment to the social system and who have learned self-acceptance to be of assistance to others who face these problems."

While it seemed a worth-while cause, the idea of lesbians banding together for any purpose was a source of amusement to many. "You mean," one of my editors observed incredulously, "that they have a union?"

As it developed, it was a union, and a good one. But long before I flew out for the convention, I had begun my investigation of lesbianism in America.

And, conservatively speaking, it was my most unique assignment in twenty-five years of reporting the unique.

2

THE FOURTH SEX

Many have written of a third sex—the male homosexual.

But if there is a third sex, there is certainly a fourth, for the female homosexual is no more like the male homosexual than she is like other women. Only in being socially taboo does the lesbian closely resemble the male homosexual. But, even so, theirs is an uneasy alliance, with no real bond of mutual respect.

Though often the fairer, the lesbian is hardly the weaker sex. At times, indeed, she seems the strongest. While she thinks directly and to the point, like the man, she has the endurance and resilience of the female. Her masculinity is often so formidable that it alienates not only the casual male but the very femme she is trying to influence.

Far more so than the male homosexual, lesbians have experimented with the so-called opposite sex before turning hopefully to their own. Taking a head count of a representative group of lesbians, I discovered that some five out of six had sexual relationships with men, and some acknowledged enjoying these relationships physically, if in no other way. But essentially the emotional response was not the same as with women. There was not the same sense of delightful anticipation, the same flights of fancy, or the same emotional reaction. "With a man," a lesbian told me, "I felt emotionally let down, not only at the conclusion, but during the act."

Even the genesis of homosexuality was often quite different between the sexes. The female, thinking of herself as a woman, usually turned to women only after failing to find satisfaction with the male. But the ambivalent male homosexual generally experimented homosexually first and then sought out women, often in the slim hope of redeeming himself.

As a rule, men had homosexual experiences earlier, between eleven and fifteen, while more women "came out" between sixteen and twenty, when, presumably, their first sorties into heterosexuality had proven unsatisfactory. For women who never evinced any curiosity in men, the transition was even simpler. "I was always a tomboy, playing with boys," a butch-type lesbian confided, "and when the boys started playing with girls, so did I."

Unlike the male homosexual, the lesbian seldom considered herself an aggrieved minority. When a young firebrand representing the Homosexual League of America called on a lesbian meeting in New York to knock on publishers' doors in a crusade to gain equal rights for homosexuals, most lesbians present were singularly unimpressed. "He's going to knock on doors," one commented wryly, "until somebody knocks on his door—and takes him away."

And they were equally unmoved by male homosexual movements to crystallize a homosexual vote in the battle of power politics, ridiculing a claim by the Homosexual Voters' Advisory Service of Denver, Colorado, that it could muster twelve million homosexual votes for legal reforms.

Unlike their male counterpart, many lesbians have an esoteric sense of humor about themselves, and are amused by male attempts to treat homosexuality as the heaven-sent answer to the current population explosion. "What the gay set forget," a middle-aged lesbian observed wryly, "is that total homosexuality would put an end to homosexuals, too."

There was often a tenderness between lesbians which few male relationships could match. When her love for a younger, prettier woman was spurned after two years of intimacy—and sacrifice— an aging butch lyrically toasted the femme who had spurned her for another: "Having loved you once, I will never love again nor thrill to the soft sweet kisses of another's lips, for their kisses would be a bitter thing, and my own lips could not respond. No other voice could ever make me feel the tingling sensation throughout my being. Their voices, though the words be sweet, would rasp against my nerves."

However, unrequited love can quickly turn to hate—and violence. "Fate hath no fury like the butch scorned," a battered femme reported ruefully. "This one butch kept me with her for two years, threatening to shoot me." Only by finding another butch even more fearsome did she win her freedom, or, rather, exchange masters. "My new butch," she said proudly, "was ready to fight a duel for me."

Though no statistics are directly available, homosexual suicides over broken romances seem inordinately high, and may account, some observers think, for the extraordinarily high suicide rate in San Francisco, where the homosexual population is numerous enough to be a voting factor.

Lesbians stay together longer, as a rule, than their male counterpart and are not anywhere near as promiscuous. "Basically," lesbians told me, "we want a home life." A survey made by lesbians of some one hundred and fifty lesbians revealed a singular togetherness. The largest number had lived with the same partner for four and five years; one couple had managed for twenty years. Ten years under the same roof—with the same woman was not uncommon. Many, of course, lasted but a few weeks or months, and some bull-dikes, like the Don Juan homosexual, prided themselves on transitory conquests spun out from one-night stands to a few weeks at the most.

In her hope to establish a permanent relationship, the lesbian often tried to simulate the heterosexual marriage. Rings were exchanged, property acquired jointly, wills made out in each other's favor. In California, with its community-property law, this stress on joint living often had an ironic twist. One lesbian couple had acquired six cats, which they fondly regarded as their little family. When they split up after three years, the cats, too, were split down the middle—three apiece.

When promiscuous, the lesbian—generally the butch—frequently pandered to men to support her lesbian life, with the butchiest butch often fraternizing for money with males to whom they would ordinarily be indifferent. "The biggest butches," one femme told me contemptuously, "can hardly wait till the sailors come to town."

Even so, the lesbian prided herself on the chastity of the lesbian group as compared to the male homosexual, and it was not unusual for lesbians to remain true to one woman. "Like other women," a lesbian told me, "we think in terms of a monogamous ideal, even when we don't practice it."

This difference in attitude—if not always performance—was reflected in even the most bizarre circumstances. One male homosexual responding to the lesbian survey *proudly* reported five thousand separate homosexual contacts; whereas a correspondingly promiscuous lesbian *sheepishly* reported several hundred contacts.

The lesbian seems to have a greater instinct for self-preservation than the male homosexual, and will often zealously protect her job and professional status. Two eminent college educators, sharing campus living quarters, nevertheless steadfastly refused all invitations to attend the same educational conferences. "We never," one stressed, "allow our two worlds to cross."

Even when they think like men, lesbians, except for the butch stereotype, generally enjoy the trappings of womanhood, and happily shop for clothes that set off their femininity. Some wide-awake shops in New York and Los Angeles feature smart slacks and shirts for the swank butch, while others stock the pointed ankle-strap half-length boots currently favored by the sharp set. The butch herself likes her femme in clothes that set her figure off to advantage. "My butch," one femme told me proudly, "picks out the sheerest negligees for me."

Because her homosexuality is so easily veiled, the lesbian mingles congenially in conventional society when she chooses. And quite often she is so much above suspicion that she can afford herself the perverse luxury of mocking the very respectability that she resentfully clings to. "When I get real bitchy," a Los Angeles businesswoman told me, "I tell some of my customers—particularly the ones I don't like—that I'm a lesbian, but"—she shrugged —"I know they won't believe me. I guess it's just a way of compensating for not having the courage to shout what I am to the tree tops."

Once committed to lesbianism, the lesbian does not seem to be troubled by the same guilt feelings that plague the male homosexual. "How can I be upset about some girl I adore," one pretty teen-ager pointed out, "when my mother married six men she didn't love?"

Though their deviation ostensibly stems from an underlying hostility to men, many lesbians apparently enjoy the male so long as "he keeps his place." Many baby butches, often seeming more delinquent than lesbian, have taken temporary refuge with older males when they had no place to go. "Usually," a baby butch confided, "this arrangement is good for a few days to a week, depending on the shelterer's age and vigor, before sex rears its ugly head."

As homebodies fundamentally, lesbians frequently marry and stay married, even when the marriage is unsatisfactory. As the passive partner in matrimony, they can easily disguise their indifference. And staying home all day, they can make friends among other housewives without stirring suspicion. "Why leave my husband?" a lesbian housewife observed. "He's a good provider, and I can still see my girl-friends whenever I want."

Lesbians pride themselves on their individuality, and many insist that no two lesbians have exactly the same problem or react the same way. However, even though their thinking may vary, the problems themselves seem similar:

How to find somebody they could love who loved them?

How to avoid giving unnecessary pain to families or precipitating a direct break?

How to function socially—and in their jobs—without provoking suspicion?

What to do about whatever yearnings they might have for children—and how to bring them up?

How to handle the men who insist on insinuating themselves into their lives?

In pursuit of the answers to at least some of these questions, I joined in on a unique forum of lesbians one Sunday afternoon in a cozy house atop one of San Francisco's storied hills. With the fog swirling against the windowpanes, I sat surrounded by twenty-four acknowledged lesbians, all good-naturedly confronting me in a special session arranged by the Daughters of Bilitis. There was only one stipulation: that all names be reasonably disguised.

Professionally, the girls were a cross-section of society. They were teachers, social workers, clerks, secretaries, shop owners, draftsmen, engineers. They came from every part of the country, and their ages ranged from twenty-two to fifty. Some had married and had children; virtually all had dated men at one time or another; only a few had had no heterosexual experience. For the most part, they looked as feminine as the average female group nowadays, though there wasn't a dress in sight.

With two exceptions, both in shorts, every woman present was wearing slacks. When I noted the lack of standard feminine attire, one of the girls said with a laugh, "Have you ever tried wearing a girdle five days a week?" She gave a mock sigh of relief, patting her hips. "It's just more comfortable. There's nothing psychologically significant about it."

Amid a chorus of good-natured amens, two or three girls slapped their thighs to emphasize the lack of restriction.

As the girls formed a wide semicircle around me, I began to explain that I was trying to find out how lesbians handled problems created by their lesbianism. Before I had gone very far, a pretty girl at my left interrupted me with a smile. "I find it no problem at all."

As other heads nodded in agreement, I studied her with interest. She had big brown eyes, a Peter Pan haircut, an elfish expression to match, and was clearly amused by my momentary discomfiture. She seemed the sort of girl young men would like.

"Do you go out often on dates?" I asked.

She giggled. "How you mean that?"

There were a few titters in the crowd.

"With men," I said. "I think you understand."

"Some," she said with a shrug. "When they ask me and I want to."

She must have been in her mid-twenties.

"Has anybody proposed to you?" I asked.

She thought for a moment. "I guess so, though I usually try to keep them from getting to the fatal words."

"But what do you do when somebody does ask you to marry him?"

She contemplated me with a puckered brow. "I generally head him off by mentioning casually that I'm not quite ready for marriage."

"Do they take no for an answer?"

"With one exception," she responded easily, "and I finally had to let him know I wasn't interested in him."

"But you never let him know the real reason?"

She smiled. "I didn't know the real reason myself at the time, though I was beginning to wonder."

She was in a theater group at the time. "I should have known"—she laughed—"because some of the prettiest girls in the show were breaking their necks doing little things for me, but I just thought they were trying to be nice."

However, she wasn't crying over lost opportunities. "In the theater, you're always meeting new attractive people."

Would she marry if the right man came along?

She smiled impishly. "That isn't quite what I'm looking for." However, she still dated occasionally. "I see no reason to exclude half the population from my life just because I prefer the other half."

Yet she had never been intimate with a man. "How," I asked, "can you rule out something before you've tried it?"

The rest of the girls appeared to be following the discussion raptly. And as Miss Peter Pan hesitated, one of the two girls in shorts chimed in with a laugh, "You can be pretty sure that if you don't think you'll like it, you won't."

"But if you haven't tried it?" I repeated.

She chuckled. "I've tried it fifteen or twenty times myself, and I still don't like it."

There were a few disapproving gasps, but the girl in shorts seemed unconcerned. "When you've heard all your life that you're a girl, and the girls respond to men," she said, "you keep trying to fill the role expected of you. I kept thinking that maybe it was just the wrong man before I finally decided it was the wrong breed."

As some of the girls laughed appreciatively, the girl with the Peter Pan look returned to the conversation. "You see," she said triumphantly, "I've saved myself all that wear and tear."

Though most of the group had experienced intimacies with males, experimentally if not seriously, it was obvious that Miss Peter Pan was not alone. A pretty blonde dressed in form-fitting slacks and a tight blouse that outlined each curve raised her hand. "Once you find out," she said in a clear, bell-like voice, "that you're not the only lesbian in the world, it makes all the difference."

The "difference," of course, was that she no longer felt alone—or left out.

It was evident from her educational background and the way she looked and spoke that Josie came from a good family, and could have made a good catch in male waters.

"Do you have much trouble with young men?" I asked.

She tossed her tousled blond head. "What trouble should I have?"

In western New York State, where she had been born and brought up, she had made an adolescent discovery that she liked girls. But in her bewilderment she didn't know what to do about it. "I tried to tell all the boys that I was a lesbian, but they only thought I was trying to put them off." She had fantasies about other girls but didn't dare express them. She began to feel that she was the only lesbian in Erie County, but as yet she had known neither a girl nor a boy. But in California she had finally found herself, and now for the first time she was "living."

"You are an unusually pretty girl," I said. "You must have many male admirers."

She nodded indifferently.

With a glance at Miss Peter Pan, I asked Josie, "Would you consider marrying any of them?"

"If the right man came along, I suppose I'd marry him." She was quite casual.

"But how would you know he was the right man?"

She looked puzzled. "If I married him, he would have to be the right man."

"But you might discover only too late that you didn't care for men, unless you had tested yourself."

"I don't understand." Her tilted brow reflected her perplexity. "Would you say that again?"

One of the older girls laughed. "You have to be very literal with Josie."

"You might discover after marriage," I repeated, "that you had made a mistake, unless you had some experience previously."

Josie sat up in her chair. "I wouldn't think of having anything to do with a man," she said stiffly, "unless I was married to him."

I wanted to make sure there was no misunderstanding. "Do you mean," I said, "that you wouldn't, under any circumstances, consider a premarital relationship with any man?"

She seemed aghast at the very idea. "Emphatically not," she said.

"Have you ever had a relationship with a young man?" I pursued more directly.

Her color heightened. "I should say not," she said. She was rather put out at the suggestion.

"Then you are a virgin?"

Josie moistened her lips and looked around the room in embarrassment. "Since we're all being so frank," she said, "in a word, yes."

The other girls appeared to be watching her with some amusement. She eyed me defiantly. "I wouldn't think of having anything to do with a man unless I was married to him." It was a flat statement.

"You would consider it immoral?"

She nodded doubtfully. "I suppose so, but essentially I would not want to throw myself away on somebody—on anybody. I'd want to make sure it would last."

"Do you apply the same standard of morality with girls?" I asked.

She frowned. "I don't understand."

"Have you ever had a relationship with a girl?"

She looked around the room uncertainly, and finally nodded. "Yes," she said in a low voice.

"Were you married to that girl?" I asked.

She grimaced. "How can you marry a girl? It's not the same thing."

"Isn't the idea the same—the lasting relationship?"

She suddenly perceived what I was getting at. "I felt very much in love," she said, blushing like a bride.

"And you are now happy together?" I asked.

She turned the color of a beet. "I don't see her any more," she said in embarrassment.

I pursued the point. "Well, how long did it last?"

"Not very long." Her voice was barely audible.

"Was it a week?" I asked.

Her lips tightened. "It was longer than that."

"How long?" I persisted.

She shook her head. "I'm ashamed to say." She looked around the room with misgivings, but nobody seemed shocked or concerned.

"Three weeks, then?" I asked.

She nodded shortly. "I guess so."

"Then how," I asked, "do you account for your double standards?"

"My what?" She obviously saw no inconsistency.

"If it was all right to have a fleeting relationship with a girl—certainly a greater taboo—why not with a male?"

She showed signs of impatience. "I told you I thought the relationship with the girl would last."

"And it lasted three weeks?"

She was flustered. "But there's no way of determining if it'll be permanent, as there is with a man. There's nothing keeping you together if you don't want it."

"Who broke off the relationship?" I asked.

She hesitated only a second. "She did. She said it wouldn't work out."

I still didn't follow her distinction between the sexes, and she seemed confused herself.

"I just think that if any man loved me enough, he would want to marry me," she insisted stubbornly. "That's all."

She looked around the room as though seeking help, and it came.

"What she's trying to say," interjected a girl with a glint in her eye, "is that her family pounded at her all her life not to have anything to do with boys, but"—she laughed—"they forgot to tell her about girls."

Confused by their own yearnings, many of the girls had consulted psychiatrists as teen-agers in order to better understand themselves. "At eighteen," one slim girl with a halting voice volunteered, "this headshrinker gave me a Rorschach test and told me I was a homosexual." It was the confirmation she had feared.

When had she first suspected it?

"It had passed through my mind from time to time," she said. "I discovered I couldn't stand dancing with men, for instance: male perspiration made me ill."

"You mean that male perspiration is distinctive?" It seemed incredible.

There was a ripple of agreement among the girls.

"I can tell it in the same room," said Nana with a trace of

contempt. Needless to say, she had never had a sexual experience with a male. She couldn't get that close, physically, to any man.

Her orientation to an unfriendly male world was not unique. Her father had been an alcoholic, and when she was a child, he had once tried drunkenly to rape her. "Every man I've ever known since made me think of him," she said. She shuddered.

I wondered whether the psychiatrist had helped.

She smiled wanly. "He told me to resist it, but I drank so much resisting it that I became an alcoholic." Another psychiatrist advised that her alcoholism resulted from her latent homosexuality. "And so to cure my alcoholism I became a lesbian. And now," she added dryly, "I'm both."

She had never known a happy relationship, male or female. "I don't think there is such a thing," she said, unheeding of the dissenting cries around her.

"Speak for yourself, Nana," somebody said good-naturedly.

"All right," she said, "I will speak for myself."

In a flat, metallic voice she proceeded to do so. Her first statement was a jolter.

She had been brought out at the rather advanced age of twenty-two, seduced, she said, by a non-lesbian.

This didn't seem to make any sense at all.

"It happens all the time," a serious-faced middle-aged woman with a Texas drawl volunteered. "They get power over you this way."

"But if they behave like lesbians," I said, "how can you say they're not lesbians?"

Texas rejoined seriously, "Oh, they take the aggressive end and all that, but they get no pleasure or satisfaction out of anything but making you their slave."

"But why?" I asked.

"For power," the Texan responded simply, "just for the power it gives them over another human being."

"But how do they get this power?"

Nana winked broadly. "You have to be a lesbian—a passive lesbian—to know that," she said with a smirk.

While some of the other girls stirred restlessly, Nana still seemed intent on analyzing her own lesbianism.

"I finally met a girl I liked," she said, "a college professor, and then we broke up." She looked around the room coldly. "Do you know why? Because she said that everybody knew that I was a lesbian, and that they would begin suspecting her at the university if she didn't move out." They had had a few months together.

"How much did it mean to you?" I asked, recalling her assertion that she had never had a good relationship.

"I don't know," she said dispiritedly. "I thought she was everything that was good, kind, and beautiful, and all that baloney. Then she turns out not to be so much after all."

"Then you're not sorry you don't see her any more?"

"Who said I'm not seeing her?" Nana's voice rose bitterly. "Now she calls me and wants to go swimming or bowling. On the way back, she's always suggesting coffee or tea, but at my place. After and hour or two she returns to her precious campus. She's a real lace-curtain lesbian." She sniffed contemptuously.

Many of the girls were squirming uneasily during much of Nana's recital. "She's half crocked most of the time," a girl near me whispered, "and you never know what she's going to say next, she's so beastly frank."

Without looking at Josie, who was still blushing in her corner, I wondered aloud how long the average courtship lasted between lesbian couples—those trying to establish some sort of life together—before consummation was sought. Nana snickered without amusement. "Twenty-four hours," she blurted out dryly.

She was promptly hooted down by the girls around her. "I thought," one girl said sardonically, "that you were speaking only for yourself."

"I am," Nana replied, with a wry smile.

Many of the girls present had gone months, some years, before they got on to a physical basis. "It's up to the butch to make the first move," a femme said gravely, "and the femme, like any woman, can only indicate that she is receptive."

Nearly everyone, except Nana and the still brooding Josie, nodded in agreement.

Mildred, an attractive femme with a relationship of ten years' standing, said with a fond glance across the room at her partner, "It was three years before Belle finally got around to it." She smiled roguishly. "I was beginning to think that I'd have to be unwomanlike and propose." All eyes turned to Belle, who half smiled in reminiscence.

The middle-aged, staid-looking Belle, looking very much like the head of a literary tea, had been firmly entrenched in convention. She had been married for years, mixing exclusively in heterosexual society, and bringing up a child, before she kicked over the traces. Her story was like so many others. She had married for expedience's sake, to please her family and because she could not accept the truth about herself at the time. "Even the lesbian," Belle pointed out ruefully, "reflects the prejudices of the majority."

For years Mildred and Belle had kept their relationship to themselves. But with time, as they began living together, they minded not being invited to social functions together. They began dropping hints to their friends, and when these didn't get across, they became more direct. "When I finally told some of the straight girls in the office," Mildred said, "they just kissed me and said, 'Let's go to lunch.'"

But this was an unusual reaction. Through having confessed their lesbianism or being found out, many girls had suffered estrangement from their friends and family, loss of jobs, and humiliation.

Hence, the group agreed that discretion, regardless of any compulsion to declare one's self openly, was the better part of valor. "As long as there's suspicion, without confirmation," a young secretary said, "people can overlook it in their relationship with you. But once you confront friends or family with your lesbianism, you force them to a decision as to how they are going to think about you. There's bound to be embarrassment, and some begin to avoid you because they don't know how to act toward you any more. You've given them a problem they didn't want."

In many offices, the gossip of non-lesbians had cost many girls their jobs.

"This friend of mine was out sick for a few days," a handsome blue-eyed girl of thirty reported, "and the boss fired her the day she got back. His only explanation was that she didn't fit into the organization, and she didn't, since the married men in the office and the unmarried girls met every day for cocktails, whereas she went straight home to her girl-friend." One of the cocktail crowd had sarcastically mentioned to the boss that she was probably home taking care of a sick friend, and the story had gone on from there.

While ordinary girls often sniped at lesbians around the office, many males found them attractive and blandly refused to accept the reports. "In my office," said a fat, pleasant-faced girl with a squeaky voice, "this one fellow, Walter, is forever going out of his way to do things for me. He brings in my lunch, waits to drive me home, and has even bought a wedding ring, insisting he wants to put it on my finger someday."

Tillie's recital took the room by surprise. Her partner, a pale, saturnine girl, seemed to be regarding her quizzically, but Tillie appeared oblivious. "When we moved"—Tillie genially nodded toward her partner—"Walter insisted on coming over and helping us. I couldn't have stopped him if I wanted to."

Tillie didn't look like the type to make men swoon. She had a rosy face and blue eyes, and seemed the classic country milkmaid. Her lean friend, now eying her reflectively, was obviously the butch in this relationship.

"Did this man have any idea that you were a lesbian?" I asked.

She shrugged. "I don't know what he thought or may have heard, but I tried to make it clear that I was only interested in my roommate and wouldn't do anything that she would not approve."

It certainly was not a direct rebuff.

"What did he say to that?"

She laughed. "He said that he would come over and ask her permission to pay court to me."

I detected a slight frown of annoyance in Tillie's partner's face, but she only stared grimly ahead.

"Did he really want to marry you?" I asked.

Tillie nodded vigorously, meanwhile eying her partner, Georgie, out of the corner of her eye. "That's why he bought the ring." She seemed rather pleased with herself.

"And how do you feel?" I asked. "Would you marry him?"

Tillie shot an uncertain glance at her partner. "Well, I wouldn't now," she said at last, "but if anything happened to our relationship, I would think about it."

"But why," I asked, "if you're a lesbian?"

She hesitated. "I'm very feminine," she said finally, "and I think I'd like children someday." She smiled. "Not right now, of course."

By now Georgie's lips were a tight, thin line. "Then, if you two should break up, you might marry Walter?"

Tillie's face suddenly turned crimson with embarrassment. "It would all depend," she began falteringly.

Georgie spoke for the first time. "If that's what she wants," she said coldly, "it's all right with me. I can always find somebody else."

Tillie was immediately contrite. "We were only supposing," she said half apologetically. But Georgie was not so easily placated. "I have no strings on anybody," she said stonily.

Tillie was almost in tears. "I didn't mean anything," she said rather helplessly. "I was just supposing."

"Georgie'll give her what-for when they get home tonight," one of the girl near me whispered slyly.

"What do you think got into her?" another asked.

"She got carried away by one of those heterosexual movies," the other said, grinning back.

In an atmosphere of electric tension, the forum got back to more general discussions of lesbian problems. Nearly all agreed that the hardest task for the average young lesbian was telling her parents of her lesbianism, and yet some seemed almost compulsively driven to confess to their mothers, while keeping their fathers in the dark. It was a distinction many had wondered about. "More often than not," one in the group observed, "it's another way of girls showing resentment against the mother, whom they so often blame for their lesbianism."

But more mature lesbians, while wishing to proclaim they had nothing to be ashamed of, often reconsidered on sober reflection. "We wanted to explain to our respective families our need to be together during the Christmas holidays," one member of a tandem said, "but finally decided they'd have more of a problem with our lesbianism than we'd have keeping it from them." Consequently, they still visit their respective families separately.

But one partner did take the chance of revealing her lesbianism to her teen-age daughter, and has never regretted it. "Suddenly," Diane recalled, "Rachel and I were able to talk freely for the first time in front of my daughter, and I no longer felt I was compromising with the truth. All at once I felt free, as though I had thrown off the shackles of furtiveness and deception."

Nevertheless, the disclosure had come about inadvertently. "Since my divorce, Rachel and I had virtually brought up my daughter," Diane related, "and she thought of Rachel as her aunt." This had been the situation for years while the daughter, Virginia, was growing up. And then one night, pulling her nose out of a book, Virginia had asked her mother why she and Rachel had been away from home so much recently. Unknown to Virginia, the two older women had been helping nights putting out the Daughters of Bilitis magazine, *The Ladder*. As Virginia asked her question, it seemed to her mother that providence had at last shown her the way.

"We've been getting out *The Ladder*," the mother said casually.

The girl frowned a moment. "But isn't that a lesbian publication?"

The mother nodded. "Yes, dear."

"Then what," the girl asked, "are you two doing with it?"

The mother met her daughter's gaze evenly. "Because," she said softly, "we are lesbians."

Virginia did not appear terribly startled. Instead, a new reflective look came into her eyes. "Do you know," she told her mother, "in my first year at college, I often wondered about myself and wanted to talk to you about it, but didn't know how to approach it." Her doubts had been awakened by her liking for another girl."

The mother assured her that her misgivings were quite normal. That feeling of liking another girl to the point of wanting to touch her, of developing a crush on a teacher, was quite commonplace in the adolescent stage and did not necessarily indicate lesbianism.

The mutual respect between mother and daughter was in fact strengthened by this incident, and with the mother's admission, they could now discuss things previously considered taboo. Both were the gainers.

The daughter, too, had apparently inherited her mother's streak of stubborn honesty. Preparing to marry a California classmate, she felt that she should tell him first about the lesbianism in her family. Her mother agreed wholeheartedly. The prospective bridegroom took the news sitting down and then managed a wan smile. "I'm fortunate," he said on recovering, "to have two mothers-in-law." He got up and warmly embraced Diane and Rachel; the crisis was over.

The marriage is a success, with no signs of the daughter following in her mother's footsteps. Grandchildren have now happily arrived, and visits back and forth are common. "Because of our candor," the mother pointed out, "we can now sit around and discuss all kinds of problems *en famille*, including those of the lesbians. Otherwise, Rachel and I might be living in constant fear of what Virginia and her husband would think if they found out, or if some helpful 'friend' told them."

It had been her experience that the lesbian could solve any personal problem she put her mind and heart to—as long as she acted in such a way as to retain her own self-esteem. "We've got to stop thinking less of what people think about us," she said, "and more about what we think about ourselves. In many ways, we are people apart, and only we can help ourselves."

However, lesbians with the self-assurance of Diane and Rachel were rare.

"It is all right for them to talk," a younger lesbian told me after the meeting: "they have it made."

She pointed to Nana, headed forlornly for a nearby bar, and the duet of Tillie and Georgie, who were hardly on speaking terms when they left the cozy little house that was a standing tribute to the commentary that lesbianism could be rewarding.

When I caught up to Nana later, she was pouring down one drink after another. I was curious about her faculty girl-friend.

"Oh, her," she said disdainfully. "I don't know what the hell goes with her." She surveyed me with a jaundiced eye. "Do you know," she said, almost as though to herself, "that even when she's with me, she won't take off all her clothes."

I could think of no suitable comment, and she went on.

"The way my psychiatrist has it figured," she said, "this dame doesn't even want to admit to herself what she is, and so she just winds up as a tease." She wiped a driblet of whisky from her lips. "I guess anything is better than being a lesbian, even a miserable scaredy-pants tease."

My curiosity about Tillie and Georgie was not to be satisfied for some time. Almost a year later, returning to California, I asked what had happened to this strangely incongruous pair.

Diane and Rachel shook their heads slowly. "That's almost a story in itself," Diane finally said.

"Are they still together?" I asked.

Again she shook her head. "Actually," she said, "they never had a chance. What you witnessed that night—Tillie talking about a boy-friend and marriage—was only symptomatic of their problem. They should never have been together in the first place: that was the problem."

The breakup was a foregone conclusion. And in Diane's estimation, the culprit was not Tillie or Georgie—or even the hapless boy-friend, Walter—but an inflexible puritanical social structure. "Tillie," she said, "was practically forced into lesbianism, and in the process she was forced on Georgie."

In its various facets, the relationship from the outset had been shaped by the inexorable pressures of a hostile society. "In a way,"

Diane explained, "I don't think that Tillie would have ever turned to lesbianism if another course had presented itself at the proper time—or if the people around her had been more understanding."

The two girls had met in the women's branch of the armed forces, where both had enlisted. Ironically, an overture by Georgie, then a practicing lesbian, had caused such a revulsion of feeling in Tillie that she had reported the incident to her superiors. There had been other complaints about Georgie, and after a court-martial, she was drummed out of the service. "What a traumatic experience it must have been," Diane recalled, "to have stood there before all those people and had the buttons stripped from her uniform."

In a fit of remorse, Tillie had then tried to atone for the harm she felt she had done Georgie. And in the course of making amends, she reached a point of familiarity with Georgie where she too was separated from the service, though without the stigma of a dishonorable discharge.

Both girls returned to their homes, Georgie to Indiana, Tillie to Tennessee, where her father was a distinguished jurist. "There was no real attachment between the two," Diane observed, "and they had nothing in common, really, except for the fact that they had gotten in trouble together."

I wondered whether anything had transpired between them at this point.

"I imagine so," Diane said: "otherwise Tillie would not have been asked to leave the service."

The same sense of guilt that had brought Tillie into Georgie's orbit seemed to impel her now to keep up the connection, unfortunate as it had been. She corresponded regularly with Georgie, and one day she left one of Georgie's letters lying around on the living-room piano; it was almost as though she were calling it to the attention of the family.

The letter was sufficiently incriminating for Tillie's jurist father to become suspicious. On his questioning, she acknowledged her relationship with the other girl. Both her father and mother were horrified. "And the father," Diane pointed out, "was chiefly concerned lest his political enemies get ahold of this windfall."

Instead of giving her the sympathy and understanding that might have brought her back to their way of life, Diane pointed out, the parents wanted her out of town as fast as she could go. They offered her a weekly stipend to stay away. "And so," Diane related dryly, "she turned to the only person in the world she could share her problem with—Georgie."

The two formed an uneasy alliance, and headed for California together to start a new life. "But actually," Diane said, "even when we first came to know them, they didn't have a chance. They had been drawn together, not out of mutual affection, but out of mutual resentment. Georgie resented Tillie because she had turned her in, and Tillie resented Georgie because she felt she had made a lesbian out of her. How could it last?"

They had broken up three or four months before.

"Did Tillie marry Walter, the young fellow from her office?" I asked.

Diane laughed mirthlessly. "Oh, nothing as simple as that. She moved in with another girl, and she's still seeing Walter."

She had been tempted by Walter's offer and the security it offered, but she felt that it would not be fair to marry him now. "Walter," Diane said, "is a Catholic, and Tillie realized that any marriage for him would be for always. Not knowing exactly where she stood, she didn't feel she could commit him for life."

And why couldn't she commit herself?

Diane shrugged. "Until she finds herself, there's no chance of her successfully handling responsibility. She's still not sure of herself as a person to know what she wants."

But there had been somebody else besides Walter, and Georgie. Another girl. It had been inconsequential. Tillie was still testing. "In time," Diane said, "she may discover she is not a lesbian after all, and that her relationship with Georgie was only the by-product of misunderstanding and intolerance, and anything after that purely exploratory."

And what then?

"Then she may be ready for this Walter or another Walter. For, essentially, I think that is what she wants. And she might never have been a lesbian if it hadn't been for society."

3

THE WOMANOLOGIST

"Nobody knows more about lesbians," Charlie said, speaking of a venerated friend.

Charlie himself was an authority on women. He had been meeting the buses, trains, and planes coming into the city for twenty years, guiding pretty girls from the "sticks" into the Broadway chorus lines, the Hollywood shuttle, and perhaps to more sinister activities fostered by a juvenile desire for easy living.

"You ought to talk to Victor," Charlie said. "He's been studying lesbians all his life."

Victor was a round little man with a surprisingly gentle manner. He lived in spacious bachelor quarters with a commanding view of the Hudson. He was a producer, publisher, raconteur, and had made a career of beautiful young women whose very beauty often marked them for tragedy. He had studied women as some men have studied the culture of ancient Rome. And as some were archeologists and psychologists, he was a womanologist.

Victor's interest in lesbians was twofold. "Beauty has always intrigued me," he said, "and some of the world's greatest beauties are lesbians." He reeled off the names of well-known personalities of the stage, the screen, and café society. "A true connoisseur of beauty," he observed, "cannot avoid lesbians."

He stared at me with his curiously limpid eyes. "I have always had a weakness for the underdog, and whatever they tell you, lesbians are unhappy people. When they seem most happy, they are so often on the brink of disaster."

He was not especially interested in the ultra-masculine lesbians with the short butch haircut. He thought them vastly unappealing. "They are like barracuda," he said with a slight shiver, revealing a typical male distaste for this obvious caricature of the male. "And they give all lesbians a bad name."

Many people, he felt, had the idea that all lesbians were like that, because only butches could be readily identified. But many were beyond average in looks and sensitivity—different from other women only because they did not prefer men.

Victor had known many types: the glamorous jet set, wintering in Switzerland or Mexico and summering in Spain or Italy, often marrying well but discreetly sampling their own kind; the lovely dancers, singers, models, and actresses who—Narcissus-like—had fallen for their own types; the mousey office and shop girls who had never known affection and were dangerously susceptible to any lively display of sympathy; the glandular freaks who shaved like men and actually thought of themselves as male, though they could not bring themselves to use the same bathroom a man had.

But it was the feminine type he dwelt on—the femme. "Often," he said, "they are the most feminine of women. And though they may be more slowly aroused than others, when they are aroused"—he kissed his finger tips eloquently—"they are magnifico."

I thought I understood. "Do you mean they are bisexual?"

He shrugged. "Something like that." But he felt that even among themselves they had brought back the art of seduction. "They get a thrill out of waiting, of just being patient, poised for the apple to drop," he said. "And, of course, it is easier for them to establish some sort of contact, even with a woman who isn't interested originally. The sisterly or maternal approach is nearly always effective in the beginning, and by the time the interest is correctly diagnosed, the rest is often academic." He chuckled, thinking about it.

I wondered whether even the femmes were genuinely interested in men, as he had suggested, or were merely playing a role for reasons of their own. But Victor was convinced that many enjoyed both relationships. "They are fifty-fifty," he said, "depending on their own make-up, who they happen to be with, and their mood of the moment."

He had known many bisexuals; some had experienced men first, others women; the distinction didn't seem terribly significant. He mentioned a celebrated blond beauty whose name had recently splashed into the divorce headlines.

"Every time she had an argument with her husband," he said, laughing, "she would cry on her girl-friend's shoulder."

This did not seem sinister in itself.

He grinned owlishly. "But when that shoulder is a lesbian's, something drastic may develop."

But couldn't the unhappy wife find a manly shoulder equally sympathetic?

Patiently Victor explained, "Cheating with a man would have made Sheena unfaithful. But being caressed comfortingly by a woman seemed harmless."

He seemed remarkably well informed.

"It takes two to play, and the girl with less status is generally talkative. But Sheena told me herself. She was grateful to the older woman for getting her over a difficult emotional hurdle. And"—he smiled slyly—"she didn't mind her husband knowing."

Sheena had eventually remarried. "She's a girl," he said dryly, "who requires social approval."

I had thought seduction a lost art, but Victor disagreed. "The lesbians," he said, "spout poetry and prose, serenade one another, and interminably ply their subtle campaign of conquest."

He looked up impishly. "Have you ever heard of thunderstorm parties?"

I shook my head.

"They're quite common in boarding schools. When the thunder shakes the skies, one girl douses the lights for fear of attracting lightning and huddles under the covers. And then, as she begins to sob in fright, the roommate comforts her. Soon they are pressed warmly together and boom, it's happening."

"And that," I said, "makes a lesbian?"

"Once they have left their impression," he said with a wag of his head, "the girl never again feels quite the same about men."

I was still skeptical.

He smiled complacently. "Nobody comprehends the female anatomy as well as another woman. Compared to the American male, who blunders through sex, the confirmed lesbian is an artist, for she understands precisely how the bumbler has failed."

I thought it unlikely that physical gratification alone should determine the sex object. "Even in their heterosexual relationships," the womanologist said, "lesbians favor the sex techniques of homosexual relationships."

While I was thinking this one over, he ticked off the primary lesbian sex functions on a pudgy finger. "*Cunnilingus*, a nice obscure Latin term for major consummation of the lesbian relationship; mutual masturbation, often equally exciting to the timid novice and the conventional male-female position, increasingly popular in experimental circles."

As I looked understandably baffled, he explained the latter enigma, in professorial style. "The so-called mound of Venus of the aggressive partner stimulates the principal erotic area of her submissive lover."

He smiled as I made a face. "If you don't get into the physical," he said, "you might as well write about the stars without mentioning their magnitude or luster."

His eyes gleamed wickedly. "Do you remember the exhibitions they used to feature in old Havana?"

I shook my head.

"What a pity," he said sardonically. "You would have had a detailed picture of women in action. It is remarkable how many nice middle-class Americans, men and women, turned out to watch these demonstrations."

Such proceedings, of course, were happily taboo in this country. Even the prospect of photographs of such exhibitions, at a vice trial in New York, had been enough to judicially exclude the press and the public.

Prostitution was quite common among lesbians, or was it that lesbianism was quite common among prostitutes?

Even Victor was not sure. "Many lesbians," he pointed out, "prostitute themselves to support lesbian relationships." He laughed. "I knew a couple of lesbians who financed a world trip visiting the most expensive resorts by living off the fat of the land, so to speak."

I wondered that they didn't get jealous, seeing as how they seemed inordinately jealous at other times.

"Like prostitutes," he pointed out, "they figure they give the male nothing of themselves."

Was there any way of definitely telling that a prostitute was also a lesbian?

Victor countered, "Is there any way of telling any lesbian when she doesn't want you to? She can wear her hair long, favor feminine dresses, use cosmetics, laugh and talk and move normally, and nobody will know the difference."

Lesbians had told me differently.

"How do they know?" he said sharply. "Think of the many times they overlook one another without realizing it, or confuse a straight girl for a lesbian."

Over the years, he had observed some uniformity among masculine-type lesbians besides the butch hair-do and slacks. "They're chain smokers, dangling their cigarettes in their mouths like men, they drink badly and too much, finding escape only in drinking, and they have a weakness for motor cars, tinkering like mechanics."

But masculinity in itself did not indicate lesbianism. "Droves of women exhibit more masculine traits today in the course of making a living than any lesbian, without being necessarily lesbian themselves," he conceded.

"But aren't they more susceptible because of these qualities?" I asked.

"They might be, but they still think of themselves as women and organize their lives at home that way, and so, while they might be latent homosexuals, they may never express it sexually except in their coolness toward men."

"Wouldn't a man's reactions to a woman be some indicator of her sexual personality?"

"Perhaps," he said, "but men frequently charge even feminine women with lesbianism, because they can't get anywhere." He smiled. "Or because they hope she'll prove she isn't."

Was frigidity a sign of lesbianism?

He snickered. "There's no such thing as frigidity with the right person."

He felt that only those lesbians who specifically acted like degenerates were degenerates. "It is just as possible," he said, "for men and women to be depraved together: it is the concept behind the relationship that determines its status." He frowned a moment. "It could still be sex for sex's sake without being depraved as long as it was honest passion." Victor was obviously broad-minded.

"What would you consider degeneracy?" I asked.

His eyebrow went up. "Have you ever heard of dildoes?"

I had vaguely.

"They're devices fastened around the waist of one lesbian to simulate the male sex act with another lesbian." He pursed his lips. "That's degeneracy, a mockery of a natural act."

Even counting only lesbians who organized their lives around lesbianism, Victor felt there were more lesbians around than anybody suspected—even Kinsey. "Why shouldn't there be a female homosexual for every male?" he said. "If the causes are similar, why shouldn't the effects be the same?"

The estimate varied. I had "several million" from the Daughters of Bilitis and "fifteen million" from male homosexual sources, who stubbornly insisted, "There's one of them for every one of us."

Victor's eyes gleamed. "You'll never get the stud male to agree with these figures, because the virile male likes to feel that any attractive woman is within his reach."

"Do you get the impression," I asked, "that there's more lesbianism today or just more talk about it?"

"It might be a little of both," he said. "Certainly with their so-called emancipation from *kirche, kuche,* and *kinder* ("church," "kitchen," and "children"), women were developing strong aggressive drives previously dormant. They're taking over men's jobs, competing with men, establishing men's standards."

Two wars, he felt, had helped promote homosexuality. "When the boys are away," he said with a broad wink, "the girls will play."

But Victor agreed that there must be some predisposition to homosexuality for it to emerge in adolescence or adulthood. "The emotionally stable," he said, "couldn't become confirmed homosexuals, no matter what the temptations in prisons or the service."

Victor had his own ideas of what ripened a girl for lesbianism. "They all have pretty much the same story. I remember one girl who was already a confirmed lesbian at nineteen. When she was eight, her stepfather had tried to rape her. At fourteen, she was gang-raped by hoodlums. At sixteen, she eloped with a sympathetic young man she met on a park bench. She followed him into the service, where he took to drinking and to abusing her. Vivian," Victor said, "was beginning to be tired of being black and blue." She fled to New York and met another sympathetic figure —an older woman. "She'll do well until her mentor tires of her," Victor predicted wryly. "And then she'll do as well as she can."

The ill-starred Marilyn Monroe, a classic symbol of femininity, I pointed out, had apparently undergone comparable hardships in childhood without becoming a lesbian or suffering a loss in femininity.

Victor was unimpressed. "The men she knew certainly brought her little happiness. She obviously didn't adjust well to conventional relationships."

Victor was no armchair authority. In the capitals of Europe, in New York, Los Angeles, and San Francisco, he had studied the lesbians in their private habitat. With his air of innocent inquiry, his neutralizing obesity, he had no difficulty getting on an easy footing with even the man-shy.

He had found his research exhilarating: it was so unpredictable. One night in a Greenwich Village drugstore, a sort of crossroads for deviates, he spotted a superb beauty of eighteen with a bleached-blond butch. The beauty, of course, fascinated him. She was in a white shirt, tails flapping charmingly over the blue jeans encasing her smooth, slim hips. Her hair, of newly burnished gold, fell carelessly in lustrous waves over her shoulders. The open shirt revealed a marble-like throat and the gentle swell of virginal breasts. She had a clean, wind-swept look that made her seem sultry and unattainable at the same time.

As Victor silently drank in her beauty, his friend, Charlie, an old hand at engaging strange beauties, managed to get her name and address, the butch being occupied at the cigarette counter. She seemed intrigued by Charlie's suggestion that she would "wow" them on Broadway. But when the butch rejoined them, the conversation abruptly changed. However, in that short time Charlie had learned quite a bit about Ellen. She had lived in New Jersey but had left home because of her family's strictness. She had moved in with a beautician from her home town, not knowing she was a lesbian. She had met the butch there.

"Ellen was not yet a lesbian," Victor concluded, "but the butch was patiently brain-washing her before launching her frontal attack."

The two men chatted amiably with the two girls, and when it was time to leave, Victor left his phone number with the butch. He never expected to hear from either of the girls again, but he saw no harm in sending an arrow into the air. Weeks later, however, the butch telephoned. She had persuaded Ellen to leave the beautician, but they had no place of their own for a few days. Could she bring Ellen to Victor's?

He agreed readily enough. "I was anxious to see all that beauty again."

His hospitality was considerable. "We all had two or three

drinks," he said, "and then they disappeared into their room." He smiled dreamily. "That Ellen had the most beautiful snow-white figure I have ever seen."

And how had he managed to see that?

"Through the open door," he explained with a wink, "as I was passing the pajamas."

They left after a few days. The thought of the butch and Ellen together had been more after a while than he could bear. Unable to get her off his mind, he called her home in New Jersey a few weeks later. Ellen's mother picked up the phone. "So you're the one who's corrupting my daughter!" she shouted. She had not seen her daughter for some time.

Victor hastily dropped the phone and tried to forget Ellen.

But a year or so later he was to hear from her again. She phoned to ask if he could help her get a foothold in the theater.

When he saw her, he hardly recognized her. "I have never seen such a change in a girl in so short a time," he said. She broke down and sobbed as she correctly read his expression of disbelief. She was more suited for an institution than the stage. For the first time, the womanologist found himself disliking lesbians. "The wonderful softness and freshness were gone. The features had changed. Her skin was coarse, her eyes dull, her hair unkempt. Even her nails were dirty."

On her slim, rounded arms he saw the telltale needle marks. Not yet twenty, she was already a drug addict and a prostitute. "She didn't need a job but a psychiatrist working around the clock seven days a week to put her together," Victor said.

Her story didn't have the saving grace of being unique. After a last break with her family, she had moved in with the butch and two other lesbians. She got on marijuana first, smoking those "harmless" brown cigarettes. One night she was introduced to horse (heroin). She balked instinctively, but they held her while she screamed, and shot the needle into her arm. The sensation had been pleasurable, and she did not rebel the next time. "And once she was hooked," Victor said solemnly, "she would do anything to get money for the drug."

I couldn't help wondering why this beauty hadn't walked out on her butch, while she still had her beauty.

Victor's smile creased his heavy jowls. "She was hung-up with her butch. Like the French say, she had her under the skin."

Afterwards, it was too late.

The drugs numbed Ellen's mind and broke her spirit. "She was earning about five hundred dollars a week in the beginning, and saw only a few dollars herself. The Johns and the women in the Betty Books paid the butch direct."

It seemed a routine chronicle of another unhappy girl's downfall. "She was obviously a sick girl, or it couldn't have happened," I said.

Victor laughed. "But of course," he said, "they are all sick."

Not long after, I encountered Victor quite by chance. He was with his friend Charlie. "If you haven't finished your book," he said, "you should meet Charlie's new friend."

Charlie shrugged indifferently. "Yeah," he said, "the barefoot girl from Sunset Strip."

He had met her in Hollywood, in a drugstore on Sunset Boulevard. She had been standing barefoot, in capris and shirt blouse, coolly scanning paperbacks on a book rack near the front of the store. He had struck up a conversation, and she had responded readily enough, and it soon developed that they knew many people in common. "Would you like to come to New York?" he had asked. She was a very pretty girl, just out of her teens, with a Hollywood starlet look that I found vaguely familiar.

Three days after Charlie had returned from his California tour, she had followed him to New York, and she was now installed in his bachelor apartment in midtown Manhattan. "She means nothing to me," he said defensively. "She's not good for anything, and I don't want anything of her. I'd just like her to get a job and move out."

"How do you know she's a lesbian?" I asked.

Victor laughed slyly. "What do you think the poor man is so

unhappy about?" He turned to me. "You should talk to her. It's an education, and she's"—his eyes rolled merrily—"so appealing."

"All right," Charlie growled. "So she's appealing. That's how little you know about it."

Victor laughed. "The poor man's frustrated."

"You can talk to her," Charlie said, still surly, "but I don't know what you can get out of her, she's so confused. She's running down to the Village to these lesbian joints all the time. She's an escapist, like the rest of them."

Victor's merriment increased. "You'll have to excuse Charlie," he said. "Wait till you see this girl." He kissed his finger tips. "Lovely, just lovely."

Victor had not exaggerated. Carol was a raving beauty.

Every head in the restaurant turned as she walked in and gracefully slumped into the seat next to mine. It was Thursday, and she had remarked facetiously over the phone that she would be wearing green. "Actually," she said, "I don't have much choice. I have only two dresses."

She offered a cigarette for me to light, and I noticed her slim hands, the long tapering fingers. She drew deeply on her cigarette. "I warn you," she said, "I'm very honest and you may not like some of my answers."

Her deep-set eyes held mine evenly; her lips, untouched by lipstick, curled ever so slightly; her upturned face rested lightly on one hand, and she looked very much the starlet waiting for the Hollywood reporter to ask his next question. She seemed vaguely familiar.

"How did you happen to wind up with Charlie?" I asked.

She replied coolly, "It's just a temporary arrangement until I find a place of my own." She paused. "He's been very nice, considering."

"Considering what?"

She frowned, stuffing her cigarette into the ash tray. "Considering that we are just friends."

"Charlie," I pointed out, "is old enough to be your grandfather."

She laughed. "That's why I thought it would be all right to stay with him." She hesitated a moment. "How well do you know Charlie?"

He was not one of my personal friends. "I have known him a good many years, and he's been helpful in certain stories."

She sighed. "He told me that I could stay with him as long as I liked, no strings attached, and now he's getting difficult. I don't quite understand."

I studied that wide-eyed countenance, with the ingenuous expression. "Are you quite sure?" I said.

She smiled. "What I meant was that I don't understand why he encouraged me to come here on one basis and now wants to change it all."

"Maybe," I said, "he doesn't believe you are a lesbian."

She sniffed into her tequila cocktail. "I'm not so sure what I am myself, but"—her nose wrinkled prettily—"I certainly wouldn't want him to know. He would never leave me alone."

Did she know that the beautiful lesbian was the supreme challenge to the virile male? "Oh, yes," Carol said lightly, "they all feel they have what it takes to convert you."

"Why did you take Charlie's offer in the first place?" I asked.

"I wanted to get away from my mother and my whole crowd. And I thought I could do well in New York." She smiled half apologetically. "I know I am more attractive than most girls."

"But weren't you afraid of getting into a sticky situation?"

"I've been in a lot of tight squeezes before," she said with a trace of bravado, "but I've come out all right."

She sat there looking amazingly pretty and independent. "What were you doing without shoes?" I asked.

She laughed, the light, tinkling laugh of a child. "I like to feel free." She flung out her hands expressively.

She seemed to enjoy talking about herself, though her face occasionally darkened as she dwelt on the more somber events in her checkered career. She had lived in Los Angeles most of her life. After her father was killed in the war, her mother had taken on a succession of husbands, all much younger than herself. Neglected by a mother who apparently thought of her as a rival, Carol had repeatedly run away from home, and at sixteen she was already pretty much on her own. For a brief period she had lived with her grandparents back East, but had bridled at their strictness; they frowned on dancing, dating, or any other teen-age activity involving boys.

"I can't stand any kind of restriction," Carol explained, her dark eyes flashing. "It's like being cooped up."

We had conversed amiably for an hour or so when suddenly she remarked, "I'll bet you're a Taurus."

I confirmed that I had been born the last week of April. "And so was I," she said. "That's why I find it so easy to talk to you." She was a bug on astrology and seemed delighted that I had done a book on psychic phenomena.

For one with such slight schooling, she seemed surprisingly well read. "I read everything," she said, "and nearly everything written about lesbians is bunk. What do the psychiatrists know sitting in their offices, or the sociologists looking down their long noses?" Her voice rang with defiance.

She had thought endlessly about her problem, and inevitably tracked it back to her mother. "My mother always married boys in their twenties, and I never did understand whether she was competing with my sister and myself or whether she was afraid we were competing with her."

The bridegrooms all had one thing in common: they were attracted to Carol, who had matured early, and her blond sister, equally mature though a year younger. "They were always after us," Carol recalled, "behind Mother's back, of course, and then when she finally married a young man who had proposed to me the night before, I knew it was time to take off."

She was only fifteen then. She and her sister ran away to a resort south of Los Angeles. There, in a bar, they met a young man who took them in for the night, and there they stayed several nights, unmolested, until the police came for them.

Even though their host had been the perfect gentleman—Carol felt he was homosexual—moral charges were brought against him.

"Nobody would believe he hadn't bothered us, because he had such a wonderful physique. He went in for body-building exercises, but that was all he was interested in."

When the case blew over, Carol found she had another new father. "Mother had taken a fancy to him," she said. He was only twenty-two.

Her first experience with a woman was almost inevitable, looking back. "I guess I was looking for the mother I never had—or at least the comfort and security that I had always missed." And, naturally, Shorty was an older woman—in fact, three or four years older than Carol's mother.

"I never had any illusions about my feeling for Shorty," Carol said, "and I was completely honest with her. When she told me she loved me and wanted to look out for me, I told her that I was fond of her because she had been nice to me. But I couldn't give her anything more. She said she understood."

Shorty ran a bar and grill near Los Angeles, and had frequently fed and sheltered Carol and her sister when the mother had been busy courting her next husband. "I was almost as grateful for what she did for my sister," Carol said, "as what she did for me."

I wondered whether she had slid into lesbianism as easily as she made it sound. "The physical aspects didn't seem terribly important at the time," Carol said. "I had never had anybody worry about me before, and it sounded attractive."

But hadn't the thought of an unnatural relationship with another woman bothered her at all?

"On the contrary," Carol said smoothly. "The thought of my mother and her meaningless marriages revolted me. When I thought of her falling madly in love every six months, it didn't seem to me that the relationship between men and women was anything to emulate in any way."

And so she had moved in with Shorty, to the apparent indifference of her mother, freed from a rival. Her sister had found an older man to harbor her. "He didn't mind her interest in girls," Carol explained.

She seemed surprised at my surprise that both were lesbians.

"We thought so much alike, and were exposed to so much of the same things," Carol said, "that it would have been more surprising if we both hadn't turned out the same way."

They were inseparable, Shorty and Carol. Shorty picked out her clothes, squired her to dinner, watched over her like a mother hen, and shooed away interested young men. She was a butch, of course, but not in any offensive sense. "She could look quite pretty when she wanted to," Carol said, "even with her short hair."

The first year had moved quite smoothly, and then Shorty found herself losing her bar through neglect from her devotion to Carol. "She didn't like the idea of my being away from her," Carol said, "and for a while it was fun to think you were that important to someone else."

With nothing to keep them in Los Angeles, they moved on to Las Vegas, where Shorty thought she might get backing to open another place. Instead, they wound up working in the gambling rooms, which was great fun until the places were closed. The girls found themselves out of work and out of money.

Shorty, however, had the remedy. The town was full of men with money. Shorty worked the hotel bars rather successfully. "She made five hundred dollars a week catering to the Johns," Carol said casually.

It had been a sort of Hobson's choice for Shorty. Carol laughed throatily. "I guess she was afraid that if she didn't cater to the Johns, I would. But there was no chance—at that time—that I would go near a man."

When the town quieted down, they drove on to Texas.

In Galveston, Shorty became ill, and Carol helped out by taking a job as a barmaid. For the first time she became conscious of the age difference between herself and Shorty, and the problems arising from the difference in their attitudes toward each other. "I had always been aboveboard with Shorty," she said, "and I thought it was a little tiresome of her to demand more than I could give."

I didn't quite understand.

"Emotionally," she explained, with a quick smile.

While she was recuperating from her ailment—a lingering virus infection—Shorty would sit around the bar and watch every move that Carol made. "She got me nervous looking at me," Carol said, "and then she would stare down the customers who kidded around with me, not meaning anything."

"Other girls?" I asked.

"Lord, no," Carol said, "the sailors and the longshoremen that used to come around."

She felt oppressed, as though she were being stifled. "I can't stand anything closing me in," she said, "particularly people."

The climax arrived one day when a young sailor, charmed by Carol's saucy beauty, asked her to dance to the strains of the tavern's juke box.

As he put his arms around Carol's waist, Shorty started to her feet, pushed the startled sailor aside, and then furiously began raining blows on her partner's head. She seemed to have the strength of a dozen men. Carol threw up her arms defensively, but she was no match for a tigress crazed with jealousy.

The impact forced her back, and then, as she lost her balance, Shorty pushed her with such force that she crashed into the bar's plate-glass front. She felt a searing pain in her leg and everything went black. She regained consciousness in the hospital; where seventy stitches were required to close the wound.

For my edification, Carol displayed a shapely bare-skinned calf, tanned by the California sun and marked by a long thin scar. "That finished me with Shorty," she said flatly.

She had no qualms about breaking up their relationship. "I was bitter because I suddenly realized there was no beauty in our relationship, only a jealous possessiveness. I couldn't get away fast enough."

She returned to California, taking a job as a receptionist and finding her own apartment.

A penitent Shorty kept trying to see her. She stood for hours in front of Carol's doorstep waiting for her; trailed after her in the evening when she went out; wrote her daily pleading for her to come back. "Every morning," Carol recalled, "I would find a new letter or poem in the mailbox. They all said the same thing—Shorty couldn't live without me."

Spotting her in a Hollywood restaurant one night, Shorty had got down on her knees and, with tears in her eyes, appealed in a quavering voice for Carol to forgive her. "I was so embarrassed in front of my friends," Carol said. "I told her I never wanted to see her again, and I ran out of the restaurant."

She was already forming a new friendship. This butch's name was Duke, and she was a green-eyed beauty in her late twenties. Carol admired her crisp coolness and the well-bred detachment with which she spoke. She was well educated, well dressed, had an excellent job, and moved in the best circles. "She could have had anybody in Hollywood," Carol observed proudly.

It was a new type of relationship for Carol: the mother obsession had ended.

She thought of Duke as a moderately older, more knowledgeable friend whom she could admire and respect. She sensed the relationship would be transient, but she didn't mind. She enjoyed every moment of it, and she felt herself developing as a person. "We read poetry together, danced, swam, went for long drives, discussed plays, movies, and books. It was an education."

Not wanting any strings herself, she readily sensed the same aloofness in Duke and was prepared when the relationship gradually petered out. "Even though she didn't look it," Carol recalled pleasantly, "she was a butch, and she liked moving around and making new friends. She got a kick out of straight girls, too." She laughed. "I guess they were a challenge, like lesbians are for some men."

Nobody could have looked more straight than the girl sipping the tequila cocktails. "I understand," I said, "that you did have a boy-friend on the Coast, a friend of Charlie's."

She nodded casually. "We worked in the same office, only"—she laughed, showing her gleaming white teeth—"he was the boss."

He was married, and the relationship never had a chance of getting anywhere, even if she had wanted it to.

She had hoped he might help her. She had taken dancing and

singing lessons, and thought she might do well in a night club he controlled. "But he told me that business and pleasure didn't mix." She sounded put out, even thinking about it. "I would have stuck with him if he had helped me," she said. "It was not a matter of morals."

I was surprised that she had been able to move from a woman to a man with such ease.

She smiled grimly. "It wasn't easy."

I hesitated over the next question. "Did you get any satisfaction —physically—out of the relationship?"

For the first time she showed a trace of embarrassment. "Sometimes," she said finally.

I asked her to clarify.

She pulled self-consciously on her cigarette. "Whenever he did what Shorty did," she said.

It was my turn to be faintly embarrassed.

In view of the two relationships, I wondered whether she considered herself a bisexual.

"Not really," she said, frowning. "I don't know quite what I am, but I'm hoping to find myself."

"Wasn't it a little odd," I said, "your having a sex relationship with a man after two lesbianic relationships that were apparently satisfactory?"

She looked at me questioningly. "Didn't Charlie tell you what happened to me?"

I shook my head.

"Well, some time after Duke and I separated, I was attacked by a man."

I remembered suddenly Charlie's telling me that Carol had become a lesbian after being raped by a Negro.

She laughed coolly. "That's just like Charlie," she said, "getting everything half right. Actually, it was quite different. It started me thinking that perhaps I could have an affair with a man after that."

This was pretty much the reverse of everything I had heard

from lesbians and savants alike, except, of course, that Carol was already a lesbian when she was raped.

But her explanation, given in strangely cool, impersonal tones, seemed plausible. "Being raped, I discovered, was not nearly as traumatic as half the things I had gone through with my mother and Shorty. It wasn't nearly as horrible as I had pictured—even being forced like that. It didn't leave me as empty and miserable inside as when Shorty pushed me through a window. It didn't spoil anything I had thought of as beautiful, since I had no idea of what it would be like, except that I realize now that I must have shrunk unconsciously from something my mother obviously considered so wonderful."

I wondered what beauty she had found with Shorty.

"I thought her original devotion to me beautiful and unselfish, even though I was never able to return it."

As I remarked that she seemed to have thought things out, Carol smiled faintly. "I had to," she said, "or take the gas. I had to know what made me the way I am."

The time had passed quickly. She glanced at her watch with a little start. "We'll have to finish up some other time," she said. "I have to find an apartment and a job."

Three days later she called to say she had taken a job in a night club as a hat-check girl and had found an apartment just outside the city where there were trees and grass. "I couldn't breathe among all those tall buildings," she said.

She had some secretarial training, and I had thought she might take a nice clean job in an office.

"You don't understand," she said crisply, "I intend to make something of myself."

"As a hat-check girl?" I asked.

"It's a start," she said. "Could I tell you about it?"

We met for coffee shortly before she was due at the club. Her face was clear and shiny, and her eyes held a dark glow. She was enthused about her new job. "It may not seem much to you," she said, "but Marilyn Monroe had to start somewhere too."

I suddenly realized who she reminded me of. "Has anybody ever told you," I asked, "that you look like Marilyn?"

Tears suddenly came to her eyes. "I loved her without ever knowing her," she said. "When she died, I couldn't eat or sleep for days. It was as though part of me was gone." Her lips trembled. "She was everything I ever wanted to be."

Every inch of the road that Marilyn had battled, she had battled with her, emotionally. "I am going to be rich and famous like her someday," she said jauntily.

"A lot of pretty girls have thought that," I said.

Suddenly, to my surprise, her coolness evaporated, and she dissolved in tears. "I have to be somebody," she said tensely. "I just have to be somebody."

In a moment she had recovered and was quite apologetic. "It's just that I can't afford to think of failure. I must matter to myself and to other people." Her smile was still wan. "You know, I come from a very good family—my father's people." Her grandfather had been a senator, she said.

"Don't you think you might find happiness in marriage?" I asked.

"I'm not ready for anything like that," she said earnestly.

"Are you still interested in women?"

She shrugged. "I'm not sure. I still like to drop around to the Village bars, but I'm not looking for anybody."

"Do you think you could stop being a lesbian completely?"

"Only by falling in love with a man," she said.

It appeared to me she was putting the cart before the horse. "Until your own attitudes change," I suggested, "you can hardly change your direction."

She smiled. "The right man could change my attitudes."

And what would the right man be like?

She smiled dreamily. "What he looked like wouldn't be terribly important as long as I felt a rapport. He would have to be strong and tender, patient and wise, and an older man, because a younger man would only compete and be jealous."

"Anything else?" I asked with a smile.

She smiled back. "He would have to help me with my career, so that by meaning something to myself, I could then mean something to him."

She gave me her hand; it was cool. Then, with a last smile, she said good-by. "Remember," she said, "I'll be in lights someday."

Charlie called a week later. "Did you get any kind of story out of that girl?" he asked.

"A little," I said.

He growled into the phone. "She was over to the apartment yesterday and left me a rose. What do you think of a girl like that?"

I thought it a touching gesture.

"She doesn't know what she wants," he said irritably. "I wish I had left her in the drugstore, reading books in her bare feet. I just can't figure her out."

4

WHY OH WHY?

In their time, scores of lesbians had shuffled through his chambers and occupied his couch. Many were prostitutes and call girls; some were actresses and models; others were secretaries, students, and housewives. But none had come to this brilliant doctor of psychology because of their lesbianism. Many did not even think of themselves as lesbians, nor did they think this was their problem.

But all of these women—young, matronly, or middle-aged—had one thing in common: they were unhappy. And so their steps took them, hesitantly, to be sure, to the unassuming suite of Dr. Harold Greenwald, counselor extraordinaire to the confused, and internationally famed author of *Call Girl*, a study of prostitution.

Greenwald did not think of lesbians as sick people. He saw no reason to pile one stigma on another. Lesbianism was often just a symptom of their illness. "They are no more sick," he observed, "than anybody else with an emotional problem."

Lesbians, of course, agreed. "We have no problems," one girl had told me, "that society's hostility doesn't create for us."

As I mentioned this, the psychologist observed dryly, "In how many instances were these lesbians known to the people around them?"

I did not quite get the point.

"What I'm trying to say is that society more often than not is not even aware they are lesbians. Consequently, there is no external problem except what they manufacture for themselves."

"They do have to be secretive," I pointed out.

He shrugged. "The world thinks nothing of two women living together, kissing each other, embracing, dancing with one another. Unless they advertise their lesbianism, society may never know what they are."

Like the homosexual male, the lesbian often blamed others for her problems, indulging in waves of self-pity in which she dismally saw herself as a despised minority. But many lesbians seemed happily free of complexes; there was no fixed pattern. Whereas I had never encountered a truly happy male homosexual, I knew many lesbians who seemed to have adjusted pleasantly to life.

Greenwald had an explanation for this apparent discrepancy. "It is easier for a lesbian to retain her concept of herself as a woman than for a male homosexual to keep the male image. Consequently, there is less inner conflict and the woman may not even think of herself as being different or homosexual."

Many lesbians had been helped, and Greenwald had seen many startling change-overs during therapy, patients sometimes ending lesbian practices long before the head-shrinking sessions had concluded. But he did not think of these transformations as cures.

"What difference does it make what you call it," he said with a smile, "so long as they feel better." He tugged at his pipe reflectively. "Many lesbians might be worse off if they weren't lesbians. In other words, they have an underlying emotional problem which festers when it doesn't express itself."

In lesbianism, he pointed out, girls often found comfort in somebody with a similar problem. "When they first realize they are lesbians," he said, "so many girls feel they are the only lesbians in the world. And this is a rather heavy burden for them to handle alone."

Usually, by the time they got to Greenwald, they were no longer chiefly concerned about being lesbians. Their major problem was other people—bosses, parents, friends, even husbands. Their lesbianism came to light only in passing, and there was no attempt to alter their sex drive. "I have no aims," Greenwald observed, "that are not my patients'."

How, then, had some stopped being lesbians?

"When they understand what they're doing and why, they are often able to change a course of behavior that has brought unhappiness, and normalization follows."

"Normalization" was rather vague. "I suppose," I said, "they identify with the analyst somehow, and he becomes the man in their lives—mentally—while they are undergoing this transformation?"

He smiled. "Normalcy actually is a matter of relating to society. The lesbian generally feels outside society, just as she has felt outside her family from almost the first day she can remember. Had she been able to relate with any one person, this estrangement might never have occurred."

In a way he had answered my question.

While the butch and the femme were often utterly different in appearance, many lesbians thought these apparently dissimilar roles readily interchangeable.

"Actually," the psychologist explained, "both roles mock the normal sexual relationship. The butch is more obvious because she ostentatiously imitates men, while the femme is playing a part more closely resembling herself."

Yet today's butch could be tomorrow's femme and vice versa. Through understanding their own motivations, many butches have gradually become feminine in manner and some have made the complete reversal—to apparently normal femininity.

One example was especially notable. "This particular girl was so much a butch," Greenwald said, "that you had to look twice to make sure she wasn't male—hair, dress, manner, aggressive attitude." In therapy for several months, she gradually grew less aggressive and then suddenly ended her analysis just as he thought she was beginning to normalize.

"I had not seen her for a year or so," the analyst recalled, "when she called one day for an appointment." He went out to the waiting room but saw nobody he knew. "A young lady was sitting there very demurely. I assumed she was waiting for the other doctor until she looked up and said, 'Don't you recognize me?'" It was the long-lost butch. She was wearing a pretty dress and her hair was long. She looked young, attractive, and quite feminine. It was the first time he had seen her without slacks and a man's haircut.

But, even more surprising, she was a mother. Her story was rather amazing. Her roommate had been through a hysterectomy and, through a sense of loss, had developed a morbid desire for a child. To satisfy her partner of several years, the butch, over-coming her personal antipathies, had gone out and become pregnant by the first man she could stomch. "After the child was born," Greenwald said, "her long dormant maternal instincts began asserting themselves and helped to awaken normal drives and reactions. She normalized."

I thought of the many lesbian mothers I had observed and it seemed doubtful that just having a baby would free a woman of her lesbianism and make her normal.

Greenwald nodded in agreement. "She herself thought she might never have become normal enough to care about a baby if not for the earlier therapy."

"What did the therapy do for her?"

He shrugged. "It goes back to what we were talking about be-fore—identification of the patient with some reassuring figure in society. That starts her back on the road to normalcy."

That figure could have been a new-found friend, a previously unappreciated relative, or the therapist, though he did not ac-knowledge as much in so many words.

Now the mother had a new problem—her roommate. "She did not want to hurt her," the analyst pointed out, "but because of the changes in her own outlook, she was thinking of a home for the child, and a husband who would give that home a happy note of normalcy." A split-up was inevitable, and the former butch saw that for herself before she left.

Lesbian behavior was as varied as heterosexual. While some lesbians clung to the basic maternal instinct, others became ill at the prospect of bearing children. "One lesbian," I recalled, "told me that she would rather be dead than have a child."

Greenwald showed no surprise. "That reaction is sick, not necessarily lesbian," he said. "The usual surface reaction is indifference."

Why had so many lesbians married, then?

"Because they were women and did what women were supposed to do."

The next question was a corollary. "Why do so many married women turn to lesbianism when they have been married awhile and had children?"

"Quite simple," Greenwald replied. "They were latent lesbians all along, and when married life proved unsatisfactory, these tendencies began to assert themselves."

"Does the lesbian," I asked, "handle marriage better than the male homosexual?"

He smiled. "First off, the lesbians don't have the problem of impotence that so many male homosexuals have, and, second, they're women at all times, whatever the façade."

"What do you mean by 'women?'" I asked, while mentally registering his judgment that many male homosexuals were physically incapable of a heterosexual relationship.

"What I mean," he said, "is that they are fundamentally homemakers. The male homosexual talks about seeking a lasting relationship, but the female gives it a serious try, for, woman-like, she is interested in security."

Another aspect of the married lesbian intrigued me. "Why is it," I asked, "that a wife whose husband has been unfaithful turns to other women instead of having an affair with a man?"

Greenwald smiled. "That's the greatest revenge of all—the wife's way of showing she has no need of any man. But, of course, the lesbianism had to be dormant."

One other point had puzzled me. "Why do lesbians, if they dislike men, so often imitate them, particularly in the early stages of deviation?"

Greenwald shrugged. "It's not uncommon to imitate what you hate, especially if you make a parody of it, and some of these butches are certainly no more than caricatures of men." In the first stages of lesbianism, the imitation clearly indicated a state of bravado and rebellion. "In their immaturity and confusion," he said, "they are defiantly telling the world, 'So what are you going to do about it!'"

But even while mocking men, consciously or otherwise, many lesbians had acknowledged gratifying sexual relationships with men.

The analyst looked at me with a faint grin. "Why not? Above all, they are women, and as women they react to men." It was apparently a matter of preference, not exclusivity.

Researching a book on prostitution, I had discovered, with surprise, that many of the girls, despite the nature of their calling, preferred women to men. It was no surprise to Greenwald. "Three quarters of the prostitutes seeking my help were lesbians, and the others were afraid they might be," he said.

But just being prostitutes didn't make them lesbians. "The same underlying cause, disdain of men, seems to influence both groups," he continued. "Any woman who shows the call girl a little love can win her over, she is that susceptible to tenderness and affection —qualities she has not found elsewhere."

Like myself, he had found that only a thin veneer of gay sophistication cloaked the prostitute's fundamental despair.

And yet to the wealthy Johns who paid fifty or a hundred dollars to indulge in their mockery of love, a lesbian prostitute was a coveted commodity. "Whatever the going rate," Greenwald said, "these girls get twenty-five dollars more just because they acknowledge their lesbianism." And other men were similarly interested. "To some men it is supremely stimulating," he explained, "to draw a response from a woman traditionally indifferent to men."

Was lesbianism part of an apparent homosexual revolution? Was it in any way connected with the recent sharp upsurge of male homosexuality, or did it stand by itself as a curious phenomenon?

Greenwald was, by temperament, inclined to underestimate rather than exaggerate, yet he felt the rise was clearly obvious and was part of the growing homosexual pattern since World War II.

"There's no question," he said, "that lesbianism is spreading, just as male homosexuality is spreading. Perhaps not as rapidly, but this is difficult to judge, because of the secret nature of lesbianism."

The so-called emancipation of women, with the fairer sex taking a more active role in outside affairs, had a lot to do with the rise of homosexuality in general. With the woman frequently absent from the home, there was no longer the emotional security and assurance that sensitive children required; no longer a strong parent image.

And the world outside the home was a place of shifting values, offering little to the youngster looking for stability. "The norms are changing so fast," psychologist Greenwald said, "that we often don't know what they are any more."

Two great wars and the threat of another holocaust had done much to unsettle the moral climate. The decline had also affected heterosexual relationships. "In a world where the atom bomb may change anything at any time, it is often difficult for adults and even children to follow tradition."

Sexual aberrations were inherent in the very nature of war, as an Old World proverb drolly pointed out: "When men are at war, women will find strange beds."

But was it all due to changing conditions? Was not some of it an accident of birth? I had seen many obese, unattractive lesbians, some with noticeable hair on their face and arms. I had seen others with coarse skins, lumpy faces, and deep voices who struck me as glandular cases. I had seen some whose mannerisms were so much like men's that it was difficult to believe they hadn't been born this way. Many lesbians shared this view. "It is my feeling," a scholarly lesbian told me, "that some female homosexuals, like the males, have homosexual tendencies from birth."

It had seemed to me that environmental factors plus an inherent disposition to homosexuality might, during the formative years, be an important factor in lesbianism.

With many lesbians, every sexual contact in the most malleable years had been such to turn them in revulsion from men: one girl raped at eight by an uncle, another ravaged at twelve by a gang of boys, still another forced to submit to degeneracy at sixteen. How could these girls do anything but abhor men? And yet, why turn to women?

"Bad things happen to all of us," Greenwald had observed, "and many girls have been raped without later becoming lesbians."

Were some constitutionally predisposed to lesbianism?

"Some of these butches," I had pointed out, "looked like real glandular cases." I recalled one middle-aged woman, a social worker, who shaved daily; others swaggered around in leather jackets like truck drivers and some knocked femmes about like Humphrey Bogart. "One of these girls had arms so big," I said, "that friends were grooming her for the Golden Gloves."

But Greenwald wouldn't agree. "Tests with sex hormones only served to accent the homosexual drive, not change its direction." And appearance could be more cause than result. "A woman's unfeminine looks, brought about by glandular imbalance," he said, "may have something to do with her becoming a lesbian. As she develops, she is made conscious of her masculine qualities— excess musculature, obesity, a mustache, a bass voice."

And how did this affect her sex life?

"Some people may be disdainful; others may accost her thinking she's a lesbian; even her family may have reservations, until she begins to doubt herself. And, finding no affection elsewhere, she may turn to the first woman who relieves her loneliness."

I mentioned the depressing histories of some girls.

Dr. Greenwald sniffed noncommittally. "It's never the rape but the reaction," he said, "and different girls react differently depending on their emotional balance." As usual, it all went back to childhood, hinging, as many analysts insist, on the infant's complex relationship with its parents. "Love is what the child needs most," Greenwald said, "and it may be the story of our times that love is the hardest thing to come by." So often the child sensed a lack in the father, the first male in her life. "Recognizing the mother as the stronger," the analyst said, "the child developed a subconscious fear of incurring her enmity. And so, as she grew older, she subconsciously turned away from the male image, represented by her father, toward the female, which appeared more important in her eyes."

Actually, she often had no positive feeling about either parent. But subconsiously she resented the failure of the father to become a respected prototype around which her feelings for the opposite sex could take shape.

There were, evidently, many secondary causes triggering the actual lesbianism. For, as Greenwald pointed out, "Those with only a slight predisposition might never have turned to lesbianism if some event in the impressionable years hadn't turned them against men. Others were so delicately balanced that almost anything souring them on men would tip the balance. And still others, with no real predisposition, might make an attempt out of curiosity and never try again."

Curious adolescents, exploring the mysteries of sex, were most vulnerable. Heroine worship often carried away a moon-struck girl. "It might be an older schoolmate, a teacher, an outsider," Greenwald said, "and it might come out of special situations—reform schools or boarding schools—where there was no way of developing normal relationships with young men."

For many girls, love between the sexes had been painted in fearful strokes. There were deliberately dire warnings of disease, pregnancy, and the devil, and the sorry example, in their own homes, of loveless marriages devoid of sexual pleasure.

"As long as we make sex evil, instead of accenting the positive force of a harmonious physical relationship," Greenwald observed, "normal intercourse appears shameful and dirty. Consequently, many girls, carrying the seeds of lesbianism from childhood, develop guilt feelings which keep them from enjoying the heterosexual relationship. They may fear pregnancy, childbirth, or disease, but, more fundamentally, they've built up a mental block against the normal sex act."

Virtually every woman with this fear was a potential lesbian. Yet, paradoxically, women most fearful of being lesbians, women with erotic fantasies about other women, had least to fear. "They are not latent lesbians, as they may think," the psychologist said, "for in passing through these love fantasies, the compulsion is removed. There is no necessity to perform or act out."

This didn't seem quite clear.

"But doesn't nearly everybody fantasize some aspect of a relationship with a person they love?"

He laughed. "That's more like imagination, between the sexes, and is more anticipation than anything else."

He had not found the lesbian a strange breed of cat.

"In considering the lesbian problem," he said, "you must always remember one thing."

I looked at him questioningly.

"In all things, and above all," he said, "the lesbian is a woman. And"—he smiled—"not too much different from other women."

I knew what Greenwald meant about the lesbian being a woman, or at least I thought I did, and then I met another psychologist and I was sure. For this psychologist was very much a woman in every respect, and she was very much a lesbian in every respect.

She would have stood out in any feminine group. She was attractive, not yet thirty, quite feminine in appearance. Her skin was pink and white, her eyes warm, and her figure curved everywhere it should. She had groomed herself for a career of research at an eastern university. Her original interest had been the psychological causes behind the development of the female deviate, though nobody but she knew the precise reasons for this interest.

In examining her own lesbianism, she had examined lesbianism generally. But hers was a special approach. "I have not been as concerned with why adult lesbians behave the way they do as with why they became lesbians in the first place," she told me.

She had read practically everything written about lesbians by the so-called experts. "They can't all be right," she said with a twinkling eye, "because they don't always agree—and I don't always agree with those who do agree."

I commented that the patient is not usually the best judge of his malady. She disagreed mildly. "Oh, I think it's possible for a professional to be objective about himself, just as a doctor can read his own pulse. I have no illusions about what I am."

When I again questioned this objectivity, she laughed. "Men have the idea that no lesbian can look at herself and like what she sees."

She looked as feminine as any woman, but this had not always been the case. Before getting caught up with psychology—and psychiatrists—she had been, incredibly, a butch type herself. "You should have seen me," she said, "with my short hair, storm-trooper jacket, and my cheroots. I was a regular whiz kid."

"What are you now?" I asked.

"I suppose you might call me a femme, but I see men now and enjoy them."

"And I am sure they enjoy you."

She laughed. "That's gallant, but we must really discuss what you're interested in."

"You are part of this interest," I assured her.

"I like to think," she said, "that my interest is rather less personal. I have tried to concentrate on family backgrounds and their effect on the child." She sighed. "So many parents propel their children into homosexuality, and yet they are the first to be horrified when a child develops these tendencies, and the first to upbraid her."

She had made a study of sex identification, dissecting a theory that homosexuality often results when the child identifies with the "wrong" parents. "One expert," she said, "suggested that the most striking cross-identification takes place in the passive male homosexual and the agressive female homosexual."

"In other words," I said, "the so-called fairy and the butch, the two extremes."

She nodded with a smile. "And then he proceeded to ridicule the homosexual assumption of a specific sex role, male or female, as with heterosexuals, claiming that the lesbian roles were quickly interchangeable and reversible."

Her smile broadened. "This is where first-hand information is so valuable. The experts don't realize the significance of individual erotic feelings during these 'reversed' homosexual roles." She laughed. "In fact, they don't even know there is such a feeling."

"Are you saying that the lesbian, already imitating a man, mentally retains this role while imitating a woman?"

Patiently she explained. "The girl who is a butch may make like a femme during the love act, but she's still thinking like a butch. While some degree of outward reversal takes place to please the partner, basic behavior patterns—the choice of words, styles, gestures, and other mannerisms—generally persist."

The act itself was thus not always indicative of the true role. "She doesn't interchange her role until she herself has changed within." She spoke as though she were very sure of herself. "How do I know all this?" She paused. "These are not my observations alone but those of women I have known as no male could have known them." Her smile was faintly mocking.

"But how about lesbians who had proudly proclaimed an easy ambivalence with their own and the male sex?"

"Oh, bisexuals are different," she answered, "from girls who are exclusively lesbian."

"Then there are bisexual lesbians?"

"Of course. The femme, with some degree of femininity, often expresses her lingering desire for the opposite sex. And sometimes she may just want to prove to herself that she is a woman. Still other lesbians like both, as their moods change."

She was in a testing stage herself. "Yes, there's a man in my life—my first." She frowned. "It's all so recent, I don't know how to classify myself."

She did not consider herself a bisexual. She was only an explorer. She thought the bisexual as distinct a type as the femme or the butch. "There's nothing very mysterious about the bisexual," she said. "He—or she—has always been with us." She quoted from Krafft-Ebing, the distinguished German clinician, who explored sexual aberration as it had never been explored before. "'The primary stage [of evolution] undoubtedly was bisexuality, such as still exists in the lowest classes of animal life and also during the first months of fetal existence in man.'"

Looking to see if I was following, she then continued: "'If the original bisexual predisposition had not yet received a definite sexual direction, and possessed strength, sexual characteristics of the opposite sex and under [special] circumstances even of an inverted [homosexual] nature may unfold. In most cases there is but a partial development of the characteristics of the opposite sex.'"

This special circumstance could have been present either in infancy, when the child was psychically aware of its parents' feelings for it, or during puberty, when it was most susceptible to sexual direction if it had predispositions to homosexuality. But obviating lesbianism exclusively, the inversion had been subject to modifying influences. "The bisexual may have had more parental cross-identification than the average lesbian, some older male figure she felt close to," the lesbian psychologist pointed out, "or in therapy she may have established some father-figure identification with her analyst."

It was not easy for the psychologist to judge his material. "You must understand the lesbian background to know how much to discount," she observed. "Some lesbians have blocked off parental problems out of remaining love for the parents and the desire not to blame them. Or, they may use the parents as an excuse and completely exaggerate home conditions."

She had no high regard for the experts. "Too many put down whatever the girls tell them."

But some studies were sound. In one, a research team had found no basic physical femininity in homosexual boys and no basic masculinity in homosexual girls. However, they did find a dominating like-sex parent (with whom the child could not identify) together with an inadequate opposite-sex parent.

Still another psychologist, James Coleman, had reported: "Where the child closely identifies with the interests and emotional attitudes of the opposite parent and strives in every way to emulate him or her, he may show many homosexual tendencies which may be crystallized by overt homosexual experiences."

It all seemed to add up to a girl needing a mother from whom she could learn to gaze evenly on the strange new world of sex. It appeared to me that if the mother respected her husband, the daughter would be inclined to absorb this respect as she matured.

The psychologist nodded. "That may be one way of looking at it." But Freud and Adler had introduced still another concept: more girls wanted to be boys than boys wanted to be girls. As usual, Freud had the answer. It all went back to the original penis envy of the girl. Once aware of this male "advantage," girls had a hard time accepting what nature had given them.

Adler agreed that the embryo lesbian felt short-changed, but suggested another reason. "Adler felt that the girl's greater difficulty in sex identification lay in the socio-cultural advantages of the male."

One point seemed rather obvious. "If girls have more difficulty identifying," I said, "shouldn't they then have a greater homosexual problem?"

She nodded serenely.

"Then," I pursued, "shouldn't there logically be more female homosexuals than male?"

She gave me a quizzical smile. "Do you find that surprising?"

"Certainly unexpected."

"Well, there's no way of establishing it except by an accurate head count," she said, "and I don't think society is quite ready for that—yet."

It had occurred to me, as we talked, that many of the authorities she was quoting with such assurance would have been only too glad to quote her.

Her own formative years had not been happy. "I spent most of my childhood feeling sorry for my father and resenting my mother for downgrading him. Later I resented him, too, for allowing her to push me around."

She had wound up, she thought, with a resulting distaste for men, not as individuals—she liked to sit and chat with them well enough—but as an emotional outlet. "Sexually, I was not drawn to women so much as repelled by men."

Lesbianism had brought little happiness. At times there had been a fleeting feeling of belonging, a sensation of excitement, and then a gnawing emptiness. She had consulted psychiatrists, deliberately choosing women, but found it difficult to relate to them. She was referred to a male psychiatrist and began, gradually, to establish a rapport. As the therapy proceeded, she showed increasing signs of femininity.

She let her hair grow, began to use make-up, only lipstick at first, and gradually discarded her men's shirts, sweaters, and flats. Her slacks were the last symbol of rebellion to go. But she was still a lesbian, even though she now became embarrassingly aware at times of admiring male stares.

Lesbianism had become so much a part of her that she felt her defection would be a mark of disloyalty to friends who thought themselves an aggrieved minority. But she was beginning to realize that her happiness lay in her own hands. She was indeed "mine own executioner."

All this she discussed calmly, as though conducting a lecture.

From experience, she knew the importance of the home in molding its human clay. Even the tiniest infant could sense parental disappointment in her gender, and this too might influence homosexuality if the child sought to repair the "wrong" it had done its parents; or, if the parent treated the child as though she were of the opposite sex.

While not a Freudian, the psychologist applauded Freud's analysis of an eighteen-year-old lesbian: "At five, comparison of her brother's genital organ and her own had left a strong impression on her. Her mother favored the child's brother and saw her daughter as an inconvenient competitor for the father's affections and kept an especially strict watch against any close relationship between the girl and her father."

It reminded her a bit of herself. She had had no brother. "But," she said wryly, "my mother wished that I was my own brother."

If the home was so influential in determining homosexuality, how important, then, were factors outside the home?

"It is commonly supposed," she said, "that a homosexual experience at an impressionable age will corrupt the ordinary child. Yet a majority of children with such experiences have shown no further interest in a homosexual relationship." They were not susceptible, and susceptibility was a home responsibility. The well-integrated child might never become lastingly homosexual, no matter what developed in later life. "I knew of a case," the psychologist pointed out, "where two girls hid out from the Nazis in a cellar for four years. In their loneliness and fear, they formed a lesbianic attachment, but with the end of the war, one girl married and raised a family. The other is still a lesbian. Their backgrounds had to be different."

As well as compiling data from the experts, she had independently researched children raised in lesbian homes. "It is not uncommon in middle-class lesbian groups for children to be on the premises," she pointed out. "These children were often born of an earlier marriage by one of the partners and remain with the mother. Others were the result of a deliberate desire by a lesbian couple to have a child."

In one notable instance of child-bearing, one lesbian, a Caucasian, had gone out and secured a Negro as the father, paying him for his contribution to her posterity.

It seemed a rather drastic step. "Why couldn't she have tried artificial insemination?" I asked. "At least it would have been impersonal."

"It's a sick case," she said. "They probably never heard of artificial insemination, and neither woman had ever known a man before."

With every good intent apparently, they had made as much of a caricature out of child-bearing as they had of the normal marriage relationship.

"What chance can children like that have?" I asked. "They can't help but grow up homosexual."

She shrugged. "Some parents don't think it's bad for their children to be what they themselves are."

"And do you agree?"

"The children of homosexual parents don't have to be homosexual."

In one lesbian home, the mother was aggressively masculine, ostentatious in male clothing, and promiscuous. Prior to announcing her lesbianism, she had been married for six years and had a girl thirteen and a boy seven. They seemed healthy enough, though nervous and thin.

Psychologically, though, the girl had no feminine identification with a mother who mistreated her and was anything but feminine herself. There was no masculine identification. And the fruits of a home life in which lesbians were constantly on the move were already apparent. "The girl," the psychologist reported, "showed definite homosexual tendencies, but was drawn curiously to masculine girls." Even in homosexual resentment, she desired a role contrary to her mother's.

Some lesbian mothers were more considerate. "In another lesbian home," the psychologist observed, "there seemed no prospect of the children becoming homosexual." The mother had carefully shielded her children. "Even though she had serious relationships, averaging three to four years, she had never allowed the children to be present at lesbian parties or other group sessions," the psychologist noted, "and was never more than normally affectionate with her partner when the children were about."

There were two children, a boy twelve and a girl eleven. "They were healthy and quite normal. The girl identified with the mother, whom both children respected. She realized the importance of masculine identification, and tried to teach them to respect the divorced father, even though he wasn't interested and they rarely saw him. The boy identified with an uncle whom the mother took pains to invite to dinner. "That made up, in a way, for not having a father around."

An expression almost of admiration stole over the psychologist's face. "You see," she said with a smile, "by compensating for a lack of masculine identification, she reduced the risks that a non-lesbian mother might not even know about. And, while homosexuality is rooted in infancy almost, children can still be helped in the impressionable later years if parents would recognize such telltale signs as tomboyishness for what they really are."

But the problem lay considerably deeper.

"Often," she said, "lesbianism occurs when the girl's psycho-sexual development is arrested in adolescence. This appears more likely if a predisposed teen-ager has had a relationship with another girl—or adult—and finds satisfaction in it. Her choice of a sex object may then become fixed. That is always the possibility, of course, in a same-sex relationship in this period, in what some of us call the clitoral stage, as opposed to the vaginal stage, when a girl's sexual attitude has matured to where she is thinking strictly in terms of the male approach."

Many lesbian virgins, she felt, had been arrested emotionally in the clitoral stage. "Professional virgins," she suggested, "may easily make lesbians of themselves, but only, of course, if the predisposition is there." With Krafft-Ebing her authority, she pointed out that the whole anatomical emphasis of sex changes after the first normal sexual experience. " 'These hyperesthetic [ultra-sensitive] zones in women,' " she quoted, " 'are, while she is a virgin, the clitoris, and, after defloration, the vagina and cervix uteri.' "

I had asked her many of the questions I put to Greenwald. "Why is it," I asked, "that so many men appear interested in lesbians?"

She laughed. "I'm one of the world's greatest living authorities on that." She paused to arrange her thoughts. "It's the excitement, the stimulation, all based on a male conception that the lesbian is amoral, thinking only of sex, and that they can convert this amorality to their own purposes. It's the male ego at work."

She frowned. "And I suppose there are other things, too. Some of the lesbians, particularly the butches, are openly looking for men to finance their lesbian relationships. They think they're putting one over by taking money for an affection they're not really giving."

I had observed that after a good many years of lesbianism, it became rather simple to identify an older lesbian from the severity of her features and from mannerisms that seemed distinctly part of her nature. She nodded with quick comprehension. "I have often thought," she said, "that lesbians, just by the way they think, can affect their own hormone balance and bring about physiological changes altering their appearance, just as other people age differently as they think and act differently." She smiled. "There's little question that we all get to look like what we are after a while."

True, there were glandular sexual freaks, as Krafft-Ebing had so graphically pointed out—bearded women, breasted men—but these anomalies were asexual by nature, not homosexual or heterosexual. They were neuters, subject to transforming winds. "In other words," she pointed out, "even if the sex organs are different, it is still necessary for a psychological change to determine the sex direction. And this depends on the individual herself. She does not have to become a lesbian. She does not have to be anything, because she has no strong physical desires one way or the other. She's a true glandular case."

She picked up a cigarette and, as I casually watched, tapped it nervously with her thumb. She regarded me gravely. "In determining their sex-role preference," she said, "many girls try to emulate the male. In other words, they have to make an effort. These behavior characteristics do not materialize by themselves. By meticulous observation, the homosexual acquires the traits of the opposite sex." For a boy, this was the gait of a woman as she swung her legs from the hips, the tilt of a woman's head, the posture of her lips as she spoke. For a girl, it was the way a man smoked, held a glass, or stood.

It was not a very substantial posture. "In their hearts," she said, "they know they are not what they are pretending to be, and yet they don't know what they are. And that's when they're completely lost."

A hint of sadness lurked in her eyes. "A woman," she said, "can never forget that she is capable of bearing children, and this helps keep her constantly aware of her womanhood." She paused. "Men fancy themselves more as lovers, and so a male homosexual keeps fulfilling this role while realizing he really isn't acting like a man."

"Have you ever thought of having children?" I asked.

She nodded. "I suppose the thought crosses every woman's mind, even when she doesn't want them."

"Do you think children contribute to a normal outlook?"

"Not any more"—she smiled wryly—"than having children would help with measles."

"Do you feel lesbianism may be a sickness?"

Suddenly her face clouded over. "I think of it as a way of life, but many lesbians are sick, so sick that being a lesbian is something for them to hold on to—and belong to. They have little else."

What was this sickness people talked about so glibly?

"Loneliness," she said, "abject perpetual loneliness, relieved occasionally by the excitement of a new romance, a new thrill. Everything is transitory, fleeting, unreal, fading before you really know what it is."

Her whole mood had suddenly changed. She snuffed out her cigarette, raised her eyes, and spoke softly, from memory:

> Awful cursing in the night
> Self-cursing no one ever hears
> And there are dreams and longings
> For that peace of death.
> We are thrown out, condemned, given only hate. . . .
> One's self is such a lonely place to be
> Let us have one night when someone understands.

The lines had been written years before in the bitter silence of the night, the author a woman who could never forget what she was, no matter how much of a psychologist she was.

5

THE TRANSGRESSOR

The way of the transgressor is wondrously hard.

Women of culture and refinement intimately rub elbows in dirty bars with girls they wouldn't hire as maids. Others marry in bars and in alleyways, and a week later aren't even speaking. Some break up homes and forsake children for another woman. In big cities, teen-age baby butches rove in predatory packs, armed with lead pipe, ready to rob and assault whoever comes down the street. Seeming to do more of everything while enjoying it less, many lose themselves in a mirage of prostitution, addiction, and alcoholism. In their jobs, in the armed forces, in schools, they risk constant expulsion. And more vulnerable sometimes than the male homosexual, they are frequent targets of blackmail, shaken down not only for money but for homes, children, and even themselves.

Many have no real family ties and yet, ironically, they often sentimentally carry snapshots of the very parents they blame for their lot. In an alien world, they are nearly always on the defensive, regardless of their intelligence, culture, background, or beauty. Anonymity is often their only hope and refuge, but this, too, they must sacrifice to share loneliness that is intolerable alone. And though suicide, violence, and indignities are often their portion, they often seem curiously exhilarated over the very anguish they have heaped on themselves.

They pay a dear price for the life they have chosen. Some think of it as freedom, but more often it seems imprisonment. The days of splendor—in the bars and at clandestine gay parties—are as brief and illusory as the glow of youth. After that stretch years of loneliness marked by intermittent romance, disillusionment, and defeat.

Some have found happiness with one another, but these idyllic instances, over which Sappho once rhapsodized, are sadly rare. It is an uneasy road that the lesbian trods, and the path of transgression is often made easy for her.

In prostituting herself to finance a lesbianic relationship, she feels that she is getting the better of the male by feigning affection when she feels only contempt. And she finds it sweetly ironic that it is his money that should pay for her pleasure with a woman. Beyond the pale of society, she is often more amoral than immoral, and has no scruples about being used as a procurer by husband or boy-friend, recruiting pretty girls for them after first sampling them herself. In a moral climate that produces wife-swapping in suburbia, the wives themselves may often turn to each other in their common degradation and find ironic revenge in each other's arms.

Fearing exposure, the lesbian is often at the mercy of the unscrupulous who have divined her secret. If she works, plays, or even breathes, it seems that she is susceptible to blackmail. It can happen on any level, and at any time. And it may mean instant ruin.

A trusted cashier was grilled by government authorities for stealing five hundred dollars of her firm's money. She disclosed reluctantly that she had turned over the money to another girl in her office and that girl's boy-friend.

"But why?" investigators asked. "What was she doing for you?"

She was loathe to answer, but finally stammered out, "She threatened to tell my family what I was doing. She had a note I wrote."

"And what have you been doing?" they asked.

She shrugged in embarrassment. "Going out with a girl."

They were still perplexed. And she haltingly explained, "She was my girl-friend—you know, like she might be yours."

And the cynical pair, who had been systematically shaking her down, threatening to tell both her family and her boss, had been financing their own romance at her expense. The lesbian, pleading guilty to a larceny charge, was held as a material witness against the blackmailers, with some hope of a suspended sentence. There was no publicity. "But I lost my job," she said ruefully, "and picked up a record."

Occasionally a lesbian has the courage to confront her blackmailer when the price is too high. In the East Bay area of San Francisco, a pretty teacher lived innocuously, keeping to herself and corresponding regularly with a friend in Los Angeles. That friend happened to be a girl. And the letters happened to be love letters.

Living in the same building as the pretty girl, who saw nobody, was a young married man who found himself attracted to the aloof-looking schoolmarm. He had smiled tentatively a number of times, but she had only nodded politely. One day, however, he thought he had the answer to her coolness.

He called on her in the evening, his hands behind his back. And when he drew them out, they were holding an envelope—an envelope addressed to her. "How did you get that letter?" she demanded, immediately recognizing the handwriting.

"It was mistakenly left in my mailbox." He lied brazenly and openly.

"Give that to me," she cried, and wrenched the envelope from his hand.

There was nothing in it. "Don't worry," he taunted, "I made several facsimile copies."

She was a young woman of some character and resolve. "What do you want?" she demanded.

His eyes took in her flaxen-haired loveliness and her slim yet voluptuous figure. "That's easy," he said. "I want you."

She was not one to waste time on histrionics. "Don't be absurd," she said. "What else do you want?"

He shook his head.

She tried hard to conceal her disdain. "Well, what do you intend to do?"

He held up the envelope. "I think the principal at your school will be interested in the contents of this envelope." His voice became a sneer. "Maybe if I could write like that, you'd feel differently about me."

Two angry patches of red stood out in her cheeks. She fought down a desire to shove him out into the hall. "You realize, of course," she said, "that you have violated the postal laws by opening a letter that didn't belong to you."

He seemed to have some knowledge of the postal laws. "After the letter is delivered in your box," he said, "it becomes your letter and not the government's." He realized his slip immediately.

"So you did take it out of my mailbox," she said. "You insect."

He retreated a step, but still held tight to the envelope.

She took another tack. "You say you like me?"

He nodded sullenly.

"Then if you like me, why do you want to hurt me?"

"I just want to be with you," he said stubbornly. And then his mood changed. He laughed. "It might be just what you need."

She told herself to count to ten. "All right," she said, "if you don't care that much for me, how about your wife and children? Don't you love them, either?"

He was puzzled.

She explained. "So you go to my principal with my letter . . ." She paused. "Believe me, I will do nothing to stop you. And so I lose my job, and then you have to explain to your wife what you were doing in my apartment." The anger in her suddenly blazed. "Because, mister, as sure as you are standing here, I will charge that you attacked me, physically, violently, and shamefully."

With strength born of fury, she thrust him out the door. "Now get out, and do whatever you want—but just get out."

The following night there was a tap on her door. It was her

neighbor. This time his face wore a sheepish grin. He held out the envelope; the letter was inside. "I got to thinking it over," he said, "and decided that if I really liked you, I wouldn't do anything to hurt you."

She cut off his move to enter. "Thank you," she said grimly. "I knew you would see it that way." And she slammed the door.

That week she sent in her resignation and at the end of the school semester moved to the Los Angeles area. She and her Los Angeles girl-friend took an apartment together, joined a church together. But the teacher had had her lesson. There would be no more running and hiding for her. She bearded the pastor in his rectory one day and explained that she would like to teach in his Sunday school. But a smile of gratitude froze on his face as she added with quiet simplicity, "I think you should know that I am a lesbian."

The pastor, a sincerely kindly man, felt it would be necessary to discuss her offer with his elders, if she had no objections, as he did not feel it was a decision he could make himself. "But if it were up to me alone," he said, "the answer would be yes." He shook her hand. "You are a brave young woman."

That same week he gave her the answer. The elders had listened to him, and his church had taken on a dedicated new teacher. "But," as a friend observed, "she had still paid a price, emotionally, for the right to live in dignity."

The way of the transgressor is wondrous indeed. At a theater benefit in Baltimore, a prominent matron whose husband was quite active politically had met a younger woman, about twenty-five, over cocktails. They got to talking casually about the theater group, as the stranger was a graduate of the group and the matron's fifteen-year-old daughter was currently studying with it.

After the party, the husband picked up his wife and daughter, bowing courteously to the plain, rather plump young woman who had walked with them out to the car. As his family piled into the car, the politician mentioned that he had to pick up some campaign circulars from the printers on the way home. "I'll go along and help you," the young woman volunteered brightly. She cheerfully hopped into the car, rode to the printer's with them, and, taking a large stack of campaign folders, promised to distribute them in his election district.

The politician was touched by her generosity. "It was nice of your friend to be so kind," he told his wife.

She looked up startled. "My friend? I thought she was your friend. I never saw her before in my life."

"That's curious," he said, dismissing the incident with a laugh.

During the campaign, the young woman kept passing out political folders. Meanwhile, she had been inviting the candidate's wife to have dinner with her or take in a play or a concert. "I don't know what there was about her," the wife recalled, "but I felt uneasy." She mentioned her misgivings to her husband. "You're exaggerating the whole thing," he said.

The wife snorted. "She keeps calling me every day. She wants something, I know that, but I don't know what it is." She turned to her husband appealingly. "Tell me," she said, "what can it be— my jewels, my furs, my money? What is it?"

Her husband kissed her fondly. "You're just a little nervous," he said. "We've been through a difficult campaign."

But the calls continued for weeks. "I got so that I hated to pick up the phone," the wife recalled. One day she finally mustered her courage. "I'm tired of your calling, and I'm not going to meet you now or ever—that's final."

The young woman's voice rose angrily. "You tell me you never go out," she said, "and I've seen you at the theater with your daughter. Why do you lie to me?"

The calls continued, and the troubled matron consulted her sister. "Tell me," she pleaded, "what does she want?"

The sister laughed. "You know, Ruth, you are still a very attractive woman—and your husband is a much older man."

"What does that mean?" the matron demanded.

Her sister smiled. "Stop worrying about your jewels," she said, "she's after you."

The matron rose in annoyance. "That's nothing to joke about."

Her sister shook her head. "Tell her to stop bothering you or you'll call the police. It's no joke."

The matron was sufficiently impressed to call on the head of her daughter's theater group the next day. He listened impassively to her story and then said discreetly, "All I can tell you, madam, is that when the young lady was here, we had to ask her mother to withdraw her from the group class." He smiled thinly. "We do find it expedient at times to put some young ladies in our solo classes." Her sister's appraisal had been subtly confirmed.

When the next call came from her husband's volunteer worker, the matron declared sharply that she was too busy to see her then or ever.

The voice grew impatient on the other end of the line. "Then why not let your daughter go out with me?" she said. "She's quite grown up."

The air hissed through the long-suffering matron's lips. "If I so much as hear from you again," she said, "I am going to the police." She paused dramatically. "I had a little talk about you at the theater school the other day, and they told me all I had to know."

There was a sharp click; she never had another phone call. "Anyway," she recalled with a sigh, "it was nice to know she wasn't interested in my husband."

In a jaded suburbia, where wife-swapping is considered fashionable privately and juvenile delinquency deplored publicly, the lesbian is becoming, some lesbians say, the sobering conscience of America.

One young lady, formerly an *aficionado* of the Westchester and Connecticut country-club set, balking at find-the-key parties, which dictate the selection of a neighborly partner, had finally refused to turn up for any more of the Saturday-night wife-swapping festivities. "You can't indulge yourself like this," she told one host, "without having to pay for it somewhere along the line."

She received no more invitations to the suburban swap parties. But several weeks later, her doorbell rang and she found her one-time host at the door. He was wearing a long face.

"Trouble with somebody's husband?" she said dryly.

He shook his head. "Wish it were."

For a while he just sat and stared out at the East River; but finally he said, "It's Ada."

"Your wife?" she said. "Don't tell me she's finally getting fed up?"

He sighed. "Nothing quite that simple."

"Then what is it? Has she run off with another man?"

He chewed at his pipe disconsolately. "I almost wish she had."

By now Lisa was bursting with curiosity. "My God," she said, "tell me."

He sighed and closed his eyes. "She's seeing one of the women in the crowd—one of the girls I used to take out after those parties we had."

The excitement drained out of Lisa. "Is that all?" she said.

"You don't seem to understand," he said helplessly.

Lisa shrugged. "So she's seeing an old girl-friend of yours—so what? Wives do that sometimes to get the lowdown. Embarrassing, perhaps, but certainly not horrible."

"You just don't understand," he repeated desperately.

"Well, tell me," she said sharply, "so that I do understand."

His voice broke suddenly. "They're girl-friends," he said. "They're having an affair."

Lisa drew in her breath. "I can't believe that," she said. "How do you know?"

"Because they want me to know," he said, "that's how I know." The words ripped out of him savagely. "Do you want me to draw you pictures?"

"That won't be necessary," Lisa said quickly.

Suddenly he buried his face in his hands. "What can I do about it?" he cried.

Lisa could find no sympathy for him. "It's your own fault," she said. "You start indulging in all kinds of promiscuity, and nobody knows where it ends."

"Sermons won't help," he said. "I've got to get her back." She was now living with the other woman and her husband. The latter had been satisfied with the explanation of a domestic breakup, and thought his wife was being the good neighbor.

"You'll never get her back," Lisa said, "not the way you want her. She'll never be the same." She cupped her chin in her hand. "And I wouldn't be too concerned about scandal."

He looked up with revived interest. "Why not?" he asked.

She smiled sweetly. "Some of the other wives may be too involved themselves to gossip," she philosophized. "When women get to disliking men enough, there's no telling where they'll stop."

While the contemporary lesbian is hardly a full-blown threat to the ordinary marriage, her rivalry with the male is often provocative. Arriving home from the office one day, an advertising man found an unexpected guest at dinner—an attractive college classmate of his wife's. He was pleasantly surprised. She was bright, witty, personable, well informed. And he joined his wife in urging her to stay with them overnight. "We see you so seldom," he said. But a week later, when the guest was still there, he was reminded of the old French proverb, that guests—like fish—begin to smell bad after three days. His wife treated his protest coldly. "I enjoy Emma tremendously," she said, "and I don't see why you should care about her staying one way or the other. You're out of the house most of the time, anyway."

He shrugged, thinking glumly to himself how their marriage had deteriorated from a warm, mutually helpful relationship to a cool design for living, shaped by the necessity of raising their children, making payments on the house, and putting on a front for the community. Certainly there was no longer anything resembling love. "Oh, let her have Emma," he thought. "What difference does it make?"

And so, six weeks later, Emma was still very much around, and his wife had become even more indifferent than before, while somehow appearing in unusually high spirits. For no apparent reason she had taken a new lease on life around the house. She was up earlier, gay and smiling, more careful about her dress and appearance. At times he surprised a strange gleam in her eyes, reminding him of the time they were courting together. It was all rather baffling. But one day, stepping unannounced into the kitchen, he surprised his wife and her classmate kissing before the open refrigerator. It was not the affectionate peck of female friends but a long, clinging kiss. Suddenly the mysterious glances, the smiles he had found so baffling, the accidental grazing of hands all came together. In a towering rage, he ordered his wife to his room. "Either Emma goes, or I go!" he shouted.

She faced him coolly, even mockingly. "Is that an ultimatum?"

"Consider it whatever you like."

She shrugged indifferently. "As you wish," she said. "Your luggage will be ready any time you want it."

Though many lesbians marry and have children, others who never marry feel a strong maternal void, as one of the penalties the lesbian transgressor must often suffer. To many lesbians, particularly as they pass through the years of normal child-bearing, the stifling of the maternal instinct is one of the dearest concessions to their homosexuality. Even in harmonious lesbian relationships, there are often regrets that there is no patter of little feet. In one idyllic relationship, constant over the years, the feminine counterpart was getting bored with household chores and the unvarying monotony of each day at home. As a carry-over from the time when she had a fulltime job as a secretary and her own apartment, she still dated occasionally with the approval of her partner, as this helped disguise their relationship from the butch's friends in the business world and, the butch thought, kept her femme from getting too restless. However, as the femme began dating new men who were obviously straight, the butch began to show concern. One evening she decided it was time for a showdown. "Whatever the problem," she told her roommate as they sat together on the couch, "I think we should talk it over." She looked at her tenderly. "Isn't that what we always said we would do?"

The other girl seemed embarrassed and disinclined to talk, but the butch persisted. "You owe it to our relationship to be frank," she said. "After all, we have been together for five years."

The other girl came to a decision. "All right," she said finally,

"I'd like to have a baby. What can you do about it?" Her voice was slightly mocking.

In the silence that followed, the ticking of the grandfather clock beat like a trip hammer on the butch's brain. She put her arms comfortingly around the younger girl, and then said soothingly, "Well, have your baby, then."

The femme turned her head wonderingly. "How?" she asked.

The butch, older and more capable, was a resourceful businesswoman. She laughed easily. "You know as well as I," she said, "that you'd never be happy married to a man. Pick out the one you want for a father, the best of the lot that you are dating, and then we'll bring up the baby, you and I." She eyed the other girl fondly. "After all," she said, "children feed on love, and we have plenty of love in this family." Her eyes were moist with tenderness.

The other girl's surprise gave way to contemplation, and then suddenly her serious mood passed, and she laughed heartily. "You know," she said, "that's a perfectly splendid idea."

A year or so later, a little girl was born into the household amid great jubilation. She is now being carefully reared in a male-less home, casually passed off as the daughter of a sister of the actual mother. Intimates who know the secret have great hopes for the child's development. "It isn't every child," one said, "that has two mothers—or two fathers, depending on how you look at it."

It is often difficult to chart the road of the transgressor. With comfort, security, and apparent happiness stretching ahead, many girls have still taken the path to certain heartbreak. Even in the best homes sent to the best schools, they seemed to absorb only that which was bad for them, as though drawn on, masochistically, to their own destruction.

In studying the transgressor from school days, some have been struck by a rebellious complex that seemed part of a broader personality problem. And there was no way of telling when or how lesbianism would crop up as a symptom of that problem. "The students involved were often the last you would suspect," reported a teacher in an exclusive eastern girls' school. In the entire school, the most outstanding potential, she thought, was offered by a slim, lovely creature of seventeen who had a keen mind and a fresh-faced beauty, and came from a family of great social prestige and wealth.

Surprisingly, though, the girl had not been doing well in class, and the concerned parents had invited the teacher to their New Jersey home for the holidays to talk things over. She did not think it unusual. "I was used to such invitations from parents of failing girls."

The teacher was unmarried, though passing thirty, had no strong family ties, and was happy to spend the holiday there. She was soon grateful that she had; she had never seen a more exquisite home—rolling lawns, guest houses, stables, pools, tennis courts, servants. And her hosts could not have been kinder. She was impressed, and she envied the girl.

"She had every advantage that money could buy, and parents who obviously doted on her," she recalled. "She was superbly beautiful, with a figure equally pleasing in bathing suit or evening gown, and she was on the verge of rich, rewarding womanhood." Here, she thought, was the girl with everything.

She had promised the family she would do everything she could to help their daughter. "The problem certainly isn't boys," she had assured them. "She never shows any interest in our gang dates with the young men of the neighboring schools."

On the drive back to school, the teacher took the opportunity to stress to the girl the success that lay ahead if she could only learn to apply herself. "You need self-discipline to get anywhere," she said.

The girl nodded brightly and the teacher thought she was making headway. However, back in school, Jean's work continued to suffer. Since she had once been a good student, Miss Jones realized that something must be wrong. She called her in. "I asked about her classmates. I thought she might be frittering away time playing records or shooting the breeze. But she didn't seem to have any girl-friends, and when I thought about it, I had never even seen her walking arm in arm like so many other girls." She sent for her school record, and noticed that her class cuts were down to the limit. "But, oddly, she was cutting everything but gym, which most girls would cut if they cut nothing else, since they loathed dressing and undressing in the middle of the day."

Miss Jones decided to consult the gym instructor. "I thought if anybody had any influence over Jean, it might be the teacher whose classes she evidently liked." So one afternoon she unexpectedly dropped by the teacher's quarters. "It was in the middle of the afternoon, so I knocked and walked in, as was the custom among the faculty." As she entered the darkened studio room, she sensed a flurry of activity and heard a rustling noise. In the dim light she could make out two shadowy figures on the couch. "Their clothes were half off," she recalled, "and they were scrambling about in their confusion, trying to cover the upper parts of their bodies."

It was the gym teacher and Miss Jones's protégé, Jean.

Without a word Miss Jones stalked out. She was still debating her course of action that evening when the gym teacher strode in. "She didn't apologize or make excuses," Miss Jones observed, "she just sat there glaring at me as though I were a prowler who had invaded her private preserve."

Miss Jones was a solid New Englander reared in the Puritan tradition. "If you leave in two weeks," she said uncompromisingly, "I won't report you." She hoped to avoid a school scandal and protect the girl.

The gym teacher left a week later.

While she was too embarrassed to refer to the incident itself, Miss Jones let the girl know she would stand for no more nonsense. The girl only regarded her sullenly, and marched off without a word. Observing her wayward charge closely, the teacher soon discovered her in the constant company of another student. "I could never make sure," she said, "but when I considered Jean never had a friend her own age before, it wasn't too hard to figure that something was going on."

She gave Jean a failing grade. The family again invited her to their estate. They were having their daughter tutored during the summer to make up the failure, and wanted her advice on a tutorial service. As tactfully as possible, she took this opportunity to suggest that another school might be more suitable. "I would have suggested a psychiatrist," she recalled, "but at that time they would only have thought I was out of my mind."

After the girl entered another school, the family continued to see the teacher for a while. "Whenever I was in New York," she recalled, "they would invite me over, thinking, I suppose, that I could still be helpful with Jean." On the few occasions that she saw Jean, she was startled by her transformation. "Her beauty seemed to be leaving her. She was no longer feminine in movement or conversation. She had taken to drinking and using foul language around her parents, as though trying to make them uncomfortable. They were obviously distressed and embarrassed." The contrast with earlier visits had a depressing effect on the teacher. She saw no more of the family.

Two or three years later, however, having moved permanently to New York, she was surprised by a note from Jean, who was also apparently living in the city.

"I called her more out of curiosity than anything else," the teacher recalled, "and invited her to tea." She was struck by the girl's odd little laugh on the phone, but thought no more of it at the time.

The date was set up for the next day. But, though only five years had elapsed since their first meeting, when Jean was a teenager, the teacher hardly recognized her former pupil when she turned up that afternoon.

Her hair was short and unkempt, her face had lost its fresh complexion, was even coarse-grained, and she was dirty. She looked as though she hadn't washed in a week. She was dressed in slacks, a man's shirt, and a baggy sweater. She wore sneakers, and they were nearly worn through. But the greatest change was not in dress or appearance but in her attitude.

She walked around the room, her lips curled down in a sneer, examining the few heirlooms and *objets d'art* that the teacher had scattered around her comfortable living room. She even opened one of the doors and scanned the wardrobe closet and the hanging clothes. Miss Jones found herself becoming exasperated. "I felt like asking her if she wanted to buy something."

The girl had not even taken her hand in greeting, but had stood off and looked at her appraisingly. "Still not married?" she said with a mocking inflection. "Well, you're not getting any younger."

The teacher tried to put as good a face on it as was possible. "I would have liked to have thrown her the hell out there and then, but the thought of her parents, and my own manners, kept me from doing the right thing."

She poured the tea and assembled a few little cookies, which her guest regarded disapprovingly.

"How about a drink?" she asked.

"Help yourself," the teacher said, and immediately realized it was a mistake. For while she was sipping her tea slowly, Jean quickly downed three or four jiggers of her best Scotch, and stood wiping her lips with relish.

"How come you never married?" she asked the teacher suddenly.

The teacher felt like telling her it was none of her business but instead said crisply that she guessed she had never met the right man.

"There is no such animal," the girl said.

She slouched into a chair, thrust her legs over the arms as the teacher tried to control her temper, and said, "Men are a big waste."

She puffed coolly on a cigarette. "If I were you," she said, "I'd forget them all."

Miss Jones was wondering what her former protégé wanted and hoping that whatever it was, she would get it off her mind and get out. But, politely, she asked the girl about her parents.

"I don't see them any more," she said roughly.

"But why?" the teacher asked.

"They want to run my life," she said harshly.

"They only want what is best for you, I am sure," the teacher said propitiatingly, almost out of habit.

Jean downed another drink in a single gulp. "I know what's best for myself," she said.

The teacher shrugged. She was not borrowing any new problems. "Anyway," she said rather lamely, "it's nice to see you again."

"I thought you might help me," the girl said abruptly, eying the older woman squarely.

The girl's searching look, rather than her actual words, struck the teacher. "If I can," she said.

"I need money," the other said.

"Money? I don't understand. Your family certainly has all the money they need."

Jean shrugged coolly. "They threw me out."

"But why?" the teacher said. "I can hardly believe it."

Again the girl gave the teacher the same searching look. "You know why," she said. "Nobody knows why better."

"I don't know what you mean by that," she said. "I haven't heard from your family in some time."

"You know," the girl repeated. She fingered a cigarette idly, taking it out of a long silver box. "You don't have any of the brown ones?" she said.

"I don't follow you."

"Oh, I was only kidding," she said lightly. "Don't mind me. I get this way sometimes, moody and all that. But we did have a falling out, and I'm not living at home, and I find it hard to work regularly."

"But you can get a job somewhere."

"Just as a receptionist. I really can't do anything, not even typewrite very well."

"Well, I'll do all I can to help you find a job, though I'm new here myself and know comparatively few people."

The girl waved a disdainful hand. "Oh, not that kind of help," she said. "I need some money right away." She looked up. "I'll pay you back someday: my family won't live forever."

The teacher caught herself wincing. "How much do you need?" she asked shortly.

"Oh, a thousand dollars or so."

The teacher gasped. "You must be out of your mind," she said.

The girl was calmly dragging at her cigarette. "That's what I need," she said.

"Well, you're not going to get it out of me," the teacher said indignantly. She frowned. "What would you be needing a thousand dollars for?"

"I have a very expensive habit."

"What kind of a habit?" The teacher found her annoyance growing. "Will you please stop being so mysterious and tell me what you're driving at?"

"Like I said, I have an expensive habit." She looked up and casually picked the lint off the sleeve of her sweater. "As long as you have to know—the drug habit."

The teacher slumped back into her chair. "That's why," the girl continued, "I had to laugh when you invited me over for tea. That's what we call tea, marijuana, the brown ones."

The teacher found her voice growing hard. "You came to the wrong person with your shock treatment," she said. "I haven't got a thousand dollars and if I had, I wouldn't give it to you."

The girl didn't seem at all discomposed. She crossed and uncrossed her trousered legs, and casually slipped off her sweater. "Really," she said in a sarcastic voice, "I thought you would be more sympathetic."

"Sympathetic," the teacher said incredulously, "to somebody who has tossed away just about the best opportunity any girl ever had? Not on your life."

Jean sat there looking at the older woman brazenly. "You're putting on a pretty good show," she said, "but I think you'll still give me the thousand."

"You're out of your mind," the teacher said, "and you can't get out of here too soon to please me." Her patience was exhausted.

For the first time the girl's confidence appeared to waver; her eyes blinked uncertainly and the cigarette trembled in her hand. The teacher, watching her narrowly, was afraid she might cry.

Seeing her distress, her mood quickly changed and she threw her arms around the girl's shoulders.

"You need help," she said. "Why don't you let me call your family and see what I can do about bringing you all together?"

Sympathy was not what the girl wanted. She got to her feet and stood tensely, teeth bared. "Don't you dare," she said. "I'm through with them, and you too." She gave her a poisonous look. "If you weren't such a pill," she said, "I could have been nice to you."

"Nice to me," the teacher said. "In what way?"

The bold look was back. "Don't give me that," she said in a bantering voice. "You know in what way." With a nonchalant air, she flicked an imaginary speck off the front of her shirt. "You know," she said, "I'm not that hard to take." She looked around the room carelessly and then boldly looked the older woman up and down. "Who knows," she said: "I might have been worth the thousand dollars."

And, with a last contemptuous glance, as the teacher stood transfixed, she sauntered out of the room.

"I never saw her again, thank God," the teacher said later. However, not until five years later, when she eventually married, did the effect of that meeting finally wear off. "I hate to admit it," the teacher recalled with a grim smile, "but she had me wondering for a while whether she might be right."

6

LACE-CURTAIN LESBIAN

Many lesbians would cheerfully die before admitting their lesbianism even to their closest friends. Even with lesbians they can trust, some never reveal openly what they are, the very word "lesbian" causing them to flinch, stammer, or flounder in a backwash of psychological trauma. "Even in the act of sex," one lesbian told me, "some won't comment on what they are doing, as though in not mentioning it they are not doing it. These are the lace-curtain lesbians."

Some even assume expressions of distaste—not always simulated—when they speak of lesbians, and noticeably use the pronoun "they" instead of the obvious "we." Others pretend innocence, even when they know you know they are lesbians.

In this rather curious game of deception, there is one principal target—themselves. They obviously do not want to think of themselves as lesbians.

In one case, for instance, I knew with reasonable certainty that a particular young woman was a lesbian. She did not look it or sound it except when denying charges that had not been made. She was a prominent cosmetician, and had many lesbian friends in this field whom she referred to as "they." She lived with another beautician, admittedly a lesbian, and quietly took her vacations in a lesbian paradise in the West Indies.

I had no reason to believe that she was maintaining top-security measures. Yet, when I asked impersonally if she could introduce me to lesbian life in the big city, she gave me a blank look.

"Why me?" she said with a shrug of annoyance.

"I just thought you knew many through your work," I said.

"Not any more than you would," she said testily.

When I mentioned casually that I had been to a lesbian convention, she snorted. "They must be out of their cotton-picking minds."

It was a precarious course she trod. Without thinking twice, she had recommended a vacation resort to straight friends and then recalled with a rush of embarrassment, "Oh, my god, it's crawling with lesbians."

In her own relations, she was careful never to risk a rebuff. One week she made plans with an actress she had met only a short time before to spend a weekend on Long Island. She made all the hotel arrangements. "When we stepped into the room," the actress confided later, "all I could see was that big double bed sitting there in solitary splendor."

She insisted on twin beds, claiming that she was an uneasy sleeper. The cosmetician shrugged, as though it were all a matter of great indifference. "I think this is the last room they had."

The actress picked up the telephone and asked for the manager. "You don't expect me to sleep in the same bed with a woman?" she demanded.

The bewildered manager agreed to put another bed in the room. And the actress, somewhat mollified, adjusted herself to a watchful weekend. "There was no hint of disappointment, not the slightest intimation of anything wrong after that," she said, "but that fluttery feeling of butterflies in my stomach told me all I needed to know."

Long before I dreamed of doing a book on lesbianism, I had casually known many lesbians in the modeling and theatrical fields, and had listened politely at cocktail parties as they earnestly discussed the usual difficulties of maidens with men in Manhattan. This was apparently a greater difficulty than they let on, for they usually left with another girl or alone. Like the men, they were cruising, and their objective was similar—girls.

It was not easy for the lace-curtain lesbian to communicate with another lesbian, her very nature often working against her taking the first step. Many silently admired girls for weeks, months, even years, before committing their admiration to words or print. And often, because of their hesitancy, an attraction would wither and die before it could be brought to flower.

Many people had thought that Terry and Hester were enjoying a lesbianic relationship. They were in their early twenties, opposites in type: Terry, blond and beautiful with soft curves; Hester, square-jawed, with short-cropped hair, not particularly attractive, and perennially clad in male shirts and slacks. Both were living away for the first time, and they were inseparable.

Terry was a neighbor, and I don't think I had ever been to her apartment that Hester wasn't there, either alone or with other girls. Terry eventually married, but long before, there had been ugly whispers. "That beast," a friend of Terry's, speaking of Hester, had said one night. "Do you know what she dared suggest to me?"

I had asked Terry about this later, and she had shrugged her shapely shoulders. "I'm sure it was a misunderstanding," she said earnestly. "Hester doesn't even like Suzy, and I know that for a fact."

All this was ten years ago. In the intervening years, Terry had casually mentioned Hester from time to time and once surprised me with the remark, "I think she is better off now that she is no longer forcing herself to be what she isn't."

"Are you trying to tell me, finally," I said, "that Hester is a lesbian?"

"I don't know for sure," she said, "but I'm reasonably certain, and it seems to have done wonders for her. She looks like an entirely different person, and"—her voice took on a tinge of pride —"she has a very important job."

"Did you ever suspect then that she was a lesbian?"

"Not for a moment, and I really don't know now, except that from what has happened, it seems likely."

Over the years, Hester had completely disappeared from my perimeter. "Can you put me in touch with her?" I asked Terry.

She hesitated. "I'll give you her telephone number," she said at last. "I'm sure she'll see you."

"Wouldn't it be better," I said, "if you told her about the book I am doing and asked if she would talk to me?"

"I don't think so," she said slowly. "You see, she knows I have these ideas about her, but we've never mentioned it, and once we did, it might make things so embarrassing we could never see each other again."

"But you two were so close."

She laughed. "I was just a dumb thing then, fresh from the country. We all were, all too young and unawares to realize what the problem was."

It had seemed very clear to some.

"But didn't you think it odd," I asked, "that she stayed over with you so many nights when she had a perfectly good room of her own just a few blocks away?"

"I thought nothing of it then," Terry said. "I was lonely, and I assumed she was lonely in the same way. I don't think there was anything in her mind, nothing that she understood at the time, or I would have known. There was not the slightest overture, not even as I think back."

"Then what happened to your friendship?" I asked.

"We just went our different ways. I married, of course, and she got busy with her friends."

"Girl-friends?"

Terry nodded. She seemed to be thinking hard. "In a way," she said, "Hester's estrangement was all our fault. We drove her away when we might have helped her."

Hester had lived with some of Terry's friends in a women's dormitory in the Village. They had thought her masculinity a mark of shyness and had set about to revamp her.

"One of the girls," Terry recalled, "bought Hester a pair of high-heeled shoes and dumped them on her bed. Another girl got her small vials of perfume. These were all by the way of hints. None of us had any idea she was queer, not for a moment. We just thought she was a little peculiar because she came from Wyoming, where we thought there was nothing but cowboys and Indians."

I still didn't know how Terry's suspicions had finally been aroused—without a word passing between them.

Not answering directly, Terry said reflectively, "As I look back on it, it was a little cruel." She frowned. "Along with everything else that made her different, she had begun to let her hair go without brushing it; she didn't wash or bathe regularly, and she was just generally dirty. We kidded her about this, without realizing, of course, that it was her way of unconsciously showing her rebellion."

One day the girls got together and decided they would give Hester a lesson. They pulled off her clothing, while she screamed and thrashed about with her arms and legs, and threw her into the shower. "We realized it was a mistake as soon as we had done it," Terry said, "because instead of getting mad when she came out, or laughing it off, she padded quietly out of the shower room without a look at any of us. I don't think to this day she has completely forgiven us."

Not long after, Hester moved out of the dorm. She shared an apartment for a while with a friend of Terry's, a pretty sculptor of some promise. But Evelyn refused to put up with Hester's friends, as I understood it.

"They were such obvious lesbians," Terry said. She looked at me as though this was all I needed to know. "And you know what a sweet, patient person Evelyn was." She shook her head. "They must have been something."

"Did you make any effort to see her after that?" I asked.

"I did at first," she said, "but she wouldn't come to the phone, or if she happened to answer herself, she was cool and distant.

And"—she shivered slightly—"I just couldn't stand talking to her friend."

"Where was she living then?" I asked.

"Oh, she had taken an apartment in the Village with this other girl."

"Did you know the other girl?"

"Not really."

"Who was she?"

"I didn't know too much about her, except there had been stories around that she had to get out of the dorm."

"And so you assumed . . . ?"

Terry smiled thinly. "One day I saw two girls walking toward me. They were holding hands and their arms were interlaced. When they got close, I saw it was Hester and her friend."

"Did you speak to them?"

"Oh, yes, they stopped and chatted a few moments."

"How did she look?"

"She was radiant. I had never seen anybody so happy. She was dressed in a dirty old sweater, slacks, and her hair was in a boyish bob. She was wearing flats, and she didn't have a speck of make-up, but her face gleamed."

"What was the other girl like?"

An expression of distaste flitted unawares over her face. "She was the most possessive thing I ever saw—as though she was afraid I was going to take Hester away from her. It positively made me ill to see them together."

"Did it continue to bother you?"

"Not really. I had met Frank and gotten married, and we've been happy. But I couldn't get Hester off my mind. As time passed, I began to realize that it had been our mistake, not hers. We were trying to make her something she wasn't."

"Is she still with the same girl?" I asked.

She shook her head. "No, for the last few years she's been sharing an apartment with somebody else."

"What happened to the other girl?"

"I guess Hester found her too possessive after a while. Besides" —she hesitated—"wait till you see Hester."

"What do you mean?"

"Well, it's a new Hester. She's all spiffed out these days, with beautiful clothes from Fifth Avenue, made up exquisitely, her hair long, and a real sweet figure."

"Don't tell me," I said, "that she has a man somewhere?"

"Oh, no," Terry said, "but she's found her niche."

"What makes you say that?"

"Oh, I hear from her every six months or so now. She just calls to let me know what she's doing."

"Have you ever met her roommate?"

She closed her eyes. "Just once." And then she shuddered a little. "Once was enough."

She thought a moment. "I hadn't seen or heard from Hester for a year when she phoned one night. She was relaxed and friendly, and I thought it might be nice to see her." So she invited her to a party at her home.

"Well, Hester stepped into the living room first, and I was pleased as Punch. She was well groomed, even to her nails. She wore a necklace, earrings, and a smooth knit dress that brought out the trim lines of her figure. She looked very attractive, and I looked over her shoulder half expecting to see a male escort. Well, I was partly right. Her escort was in a beige tailored jacket with matching trousers, and had short hair. The only trouble was that it was a woman. I thought she had a helluva nerve bringing anybody like that to a party of mine. Fortunately it was a theater crowd and they're used to almost anything."

"Did you let Hester know how you felt?"

She made an expressive gesture. "What was the use? I just made sure I never invited her again." She reached for a cigarette, tapping it nervously. "But as I got to thinking it over, I realized that she had fulfilled herself as a human being. There was enough femininity in her that had to express itself somehow, but she couldn't make the complete adjustment to the male. Instead she had settled for a woman who played the male."

The years had given Terry the wisdom to probe for the hidden causes underlying human behavior. "As I look back," she said, "I realize that when I first knew her she was fighting it, even though she didn't realize it herself. I was pretty, soft and blond, and she liked being with me, and staying overnight, without exactly knowing why."

"You knew," I said, "that there was some talk about you?"

She sighed. "There's talk about every girl who doesn't fall into the arms of every male with sex on his brain." She laughed lightly. "You had your misgivings, if I remember correctly."

"Not really," I said, "though I did think it obvious that Hester had a problem."

She smiled. "You thought she had designs on me and I was too dumb to know it."

"I don't recall ever suggesting anything."

"But your friend did." She mentioned the name of an older man, a onetime Broadway producer. "Do you recall the time you brought him up to my apartment?"

I shook my head.

"You were taking Hester and me to a movie," she prompted.

Suddenly I remembered. I could still see the expression of distaste on Richardson's face as he surveyed Hester, dirty and unkempt in her sweatshirt and slacks, sitting next to the beautiful blonde with the creamy skin and soft blue eyes . . . on a three-quarter couch that fit snugly into a corner of the one-room apartment.

With a nod at Hester, he had whispered savagely, "Get me out of here: that one over there is a dike."

It was not the first time I had heard the word. But as he said it, with an expression of fervid disgust, it was perhaps the ugliest of all ugly four-letter words.

He was already reaching for the door knob, and I had no alternative but to make some excuse and leave with him.

In the street he repeated what he had said upstairs, adding, "The other one must be queer to have that dike around." He swore. "Did you see her looking at the blonde?"

"I think you're wrong," I had said. "Hester is a little peculiar. She's from Wyoming, you know, and maybe she thinks she's a cowboy."

"Look," he said, "I've been on Broadway for thirty years. I know a dike when I see one."

It had been a most unpleasant experience, and for years Terry and I had never referred to it.

"After you left that night," Terry said now, "poor Hester sat there and cried. She had always liked you and wanted your respect so."

"But I hadn't said anything."

"No, but she couldn't help knowing what you must have been thinking."

"But why did it bother her so?"

"Because she was obviously still fighting it. As you remember, she came from a good family, and it was a terrible thing to face. Now that she's made the adjustment, she's reasonably happy, but she's still human enough to want the respect of people she likes."

"Does her family know?" I asked.

"Oh, I'm sure her mother does, just as I do, but it's never mentioned." She hesitated a moment. "You know, if she had never come to New York, all this might never have happened. She'd be the same person, of course, with the same yearnings and the same dissatisfaction with being a feminine-type woman, but she would have been hemmed in by such a tide of respectability that she would have had to conform. Without her problem seen in the mirror of another's lesbianism, she probably never would have even realized what she was. She would have grown up a tomboy and then become a masculine-type woman who handled horses well and ran a ranch while still being married and having children. She might not have enjoyed being married, but she wouldn't have known enough to know what was wrong."

Terry seemed to have the situation pretty well thought out.

"Well," I said, "I'd still like to sit down with her and see how she has managed over the last ten years."

Terry grimaced. "I'll call her," she said, "but I won't say what you want to talk to her about. You'll have to break that to her yourself."

Hester seemed moderately pleased when I called. "Did Terry tell you what I was up to?" I said, putting out a small feeler.

Her voice came back bright and cheery. "All she told me was that you had written a book called *The Sixth Man*, and were famous."

She could meet me that evening, in a little bar not far from the midtown radio station where she had a responsible production job. "I'm looking forward to it," she said.

I would not have recognized her. The years had been kind. She approached my table, hand outstretched, with a pleasant little smile. Her hair was tidy, and curled artfully down her neck. Her features were good, if not distinctive. Her eyes were warm and friendly. She was in a simple dress that came to her shapely, silken knees. She looked the young woman of style.

"You look great," I said, thinking of what she looked like the last time I saw her.

"Oh, I could lose a few pounds," she said with a deprecating smile.

We sipped our drinks and chatted, talking about Terry and her husband and our respective careers. Suddenly, she frowned. "This book of yours," she said, "*The Sixth Man*. What was it about?"

I realized suddenly that she had not the slightest idea what the interview was about.

"Homosexuality—male homosexuality," I said.

Her nose wrinkled. "Oh, those people," she said with a faint expression of distaste.

I came to the point rather obliquely. "I am doing a sequel, on lesbianism," I said. And then, as she regarded me noncommittally over her drink, I explained that I had recently attended a lesbian convention in California and had been struck by the unique lesbian problem.

She was visibly startled. "You mean they actually had a convention?"

"Oh, yes, they sat around and discussed their problems and what to do about them, just as any social group would."

She laughed so hard I thought she would choke. "I think that's the most hysterical thing I ever heard of." She gulped her drink down. "You're not pulling my leg?" The tears streamed down her face.

I suddenly felt defensive about the D.O.B. "On the contrary," I said, "they are quite an impressive group—many of them professional people like yourself."

She burst into new peals of laughter. "What are they trying to do, change society?" Her voice was tinged with scorn. "Why don't they forget it?"

I explained that it gave them a purpose, and that getting together privately as they did, they didn't have to frequent bars and run the risk of humiliation and exposure. "They can meet in surroundings of their own choice and talk things out," I said. "It seems to have some therapeutic value."

She snickered. "So they have a cause. Well, it's a lost cause."

A curious gleam suddenly came into her eyes, and she said with a biting edge to her voice, "I'll bet they make a lot of friends and influence a lot of people while pursuing their cause."

I wasn't quite sure what she meant.

"Aren't you a little naïve?" she said. "What do you think all those girls are really interested in?"

"They don't have to form a club for that," I said.

She now gave me a coolly appraising glance across the table, and her mood seemed to change. "Exactly what do you want from me?" she asked briskly.

I saw no reason to beat around the bush. "I thought you might help me with my book on lesbians."

"Why me?" she said, gulping down another drink.

"You lived in the Village for some time. I had an idea you knew many of the girls."

She ordered another drink, her face telling me nothing. "I don't know that much about them," she said finally.

I looked squarely across the table at Hester, and she returned my gaze evenly, her dark eyes twinkling.

"Do you remember Suzy?" I asked.

She shook her head doubtfully. "Help me a little."

I described her as best I could; she had been quite the rage on television at the time, though she did little more than walk off and on the viewer's screen.

She apparently remembered. The hint of a smile left her face. "How could I forget her?" she said harshly. "What about her?" There was the faintest challenge in her voice.

Without preliminary, I repeated the story Suzy had told years before. "She said that you accosted her in the shower room of the dormitory where you both lived."

Hester made no pretense of not knowing what was meant. "She said that?" she echoed in disbelief.

"In no uncertain terms," I said. "I remember mentioning it to Terry at the time."

She looked interested. "What did Terry say?"

"She didn't believe it."

Hester appeared suddenly relieved. She had been toying with her drink, rye and water, fiddling with a cigarette, apparently debating what course she should take. Abruptly, she seemed to come to a decision—but not before ordering another drink. "Suzy is a liar," she said, carefully enunciating each word. "I never cared much for her, and she knew it."

Often, she said, Suzy had gone out of her way to invite her to dinner or for a walk. Once she had telephoned and, in an urgent voice, asked Hester to please come to her room. "She kept insisting," Hester said, "and I finally went, to get rid of her."

Hester found herself in a darkened room. Suzy was on the bed, face down. The shades were drawn. The reclining girl lifted her head lazily. "I don't feel well," she said. "Will you please rub my back?" Her voice was a soft purr.

As her eyes grew accustomed to the darkness, Hester noticed with a start that Suzy was completely unclad. "Please rub my back," Suzy repeated.

As Hester stood transfixed with surprise, Suzy turned over and languidly held out her arms. "I took one look," Hester recalled for my benefit, "and I couldn't get out fast enough."

Contrasting Suzy's superb blond beauty with the modest charms of the girl across the table, I was mildly puzzled. Hester explained, "I just didn't like her."

"But why did she like you?" I said, and then quickly added, "Why should she approach somebody who didn't like her, when she had a whole dormitory?"

Hester grimaced. "I think she was one of those professional virgins who consider it immoral to do anything with a man but still want some sort of sexual outlet."

"But why you?" I insisted.

"With my short hair, the men's shirts, and all that, I guess she figured I was a cinch."

I was still puzzled. "But why did she tell me about your making advances?"

"She might have been trying to beat me to the punch." Her voice was a little bitter. "Who would believe who, if it came to a showdown?"

Hester eyed me speculatively. "We lived on different floors," she said, "and each floor had its own shower room. There was no possibility of my running into Suzy by chance, and I certainly wasn't hanging around waiting for her to pop out of her room." She sighed. "Anyway, if I had been in the mood in those days, which I wasn't, it wouldn't have been Suzy."

Inevitably, the conversation came back to Terry. "She had the highest regard for you," I said.

She nodded, as though this was expected. "Terry was great," she said, "but she always had to be the boss. She has that kind of marriage, too. She doesn't like Frank not being manly at times, but she married him only because she could dominate the situation. And yet, being a woman, she still wants to lean on a man occasionally."

She looked up with a curious smile. "I always thought Frank

was homosexual. You know, I introduced them. He was living with a homosexual at the time."

"He always struck me as being masculine enough," I said.

She snorted. "They always do."

"He seems to go well with Terry," I said.

She looked up abruptly. "You know, they almost broke up."

I vaguely recalled a little trouble. "This happens to married people all the time," I said.

"Yes," she partially agreed, "but it was what they had trouble about. She was angry about his claims of superiority in acting, painting, dressmaking, and cooking, whatever it was they did together or apart."

I recalled now that Terry had once complained bitterly about this rivalry, apparently without realizing that she was challenging the male role.

Hester's voice broke into my thoughts. "I told Terry," she said with a trace of satisfaction, "that it was a wife's duty to let her husband feel superior, even when he wasn't." She downed another drink. "Have you ever wondered why Terry doesn't want children?"

I shook my head.

"She has no real maternal instinct," Hester said, "and she gets all the fulfillment she needs out of her own drives."

"What makes you say that?" I asked.

She shrugged. "Obviously she didn't choose a masculine male but one she could control." She smiled. "And this isn't the kind she wants for a father for her children."

The conversation was taking a turn I had not anticipated. "Terry seems reasonably happy to me," I said.

"Oh, yes," she said, "but she could have had almost anybody she wanted." Her eyes gleamed for a moment. "She was unusual, and look what she picked."

I reminded her pointedly that Terry often expressed concern for her.

Hester guffawed. "What for? I did all right."

"Terry kept in touch with you through Evelyn," I said, "all the while you two lived together." I paused. "I guess Evelyn was afraid you were keeping bad company."

Hester appeared genuinely amused. "So you knew Evelyn?" she said with a laugh.

"As a matter of fact," I said, "she gave me one of her sculptures."

She snorted. "That was the bust she was going to give me."

It suddenly occurred to me that Hester was getting angry. She sat straight in her chair, eyes flashing, jaw jutting out. "It was like Evelyn to be so considerate," she began sarcastically. Her voice was a little thick with drink, but it was still discreetly lowered as she leaned across the table and said harshly, "Well, it was Evelyn who brought me out."

I didn't quite get it at first. "You mean, Evelyn . . . ?"

She nodded grimly. "She was no angel."

"She didn't strike me as remotely lesbian," I said.

Hester gestured impatiently. "How can anybody tell?"

I wondered whether Terry had known.

Hester shrugged. "She was too naïve then to see it, and she wouldn't have believed it if she'd been told."

I found the disclosure disconcerting. "How long did this relationship continue?" I asked.

"Maybe a year or so," Hester said. She was obviously enjoying my discomfiture.

I thought I knew why. "Did it break up when you started seeing other girls?"

Hester's face became grim. "It broke up," she stressed, "when Evelyn started keeping bad company, not me."

One night Evelyn had announced after the dishes had been cleared away, "I'm spending the weekend with a friend. And if it works out, I won't be back."

Hester was dumbstruck. She had noticed no signs of discontent. "Who is it?" she asked.

"Some man," Evelyn replied casually.

A cold anger took hold of Hester. "As you please," she said icily.

It seemed a rather abrupt way of ending things. "There must have been something else?" I said.

"Not that I knew of," Hester said. "She'd get picky at times, but that was the way she was."

I wondered where the man had come in.

Hester laughed mirthlessly. "I guess she decided to try one: she'd heard of them so often. It was a noble experiment."

Had Hester experimented similarly?

She grimaced. "Just one at the time, but it was nothing to get excited about."

Hester did not wait to see how Evelyn's weekend worked out. After Evelyn left with her overnight bag, Hester left too, taking a few belongings.

"You were lucky to find a place so fast," I commented.

"I moved in with a girl I used to see in this bar."

And what had happened to the noble experiment?

Hester smiled. "I could have told her it wouldn't work." Evelyn had returned Monday morning, discovered her roommate had checked out, and had toured the Village looking for her. She found her in a bar. Hester coldly spurned Evelyn's attempts at reconciliation. "Go back with him," she sneered, "if he'll have you."

When Evelyn persisted, humbly apologizing, Hester's new roommate emerged. She was a stompin' butch. She advanced with clenched fists and fury in her eye.

Hester laughed gaily as she recalled the scene. "Evelyn just turned and ran." They never saw each other again.

Hester thought her new roommate unusual. "She was the only real lesbian I ever knew," Hester recalled. "She would have nothing to do with any man." They called her Big Min. Her father had been an Army officer, and her mother, a much younger woman, had had one lover after another while he was away. When Min surprised her mother on one occasion, she was promptly packed off to school.

At first the relationship with Big Min had been exciting. But when she drank, Min became violent, and she used Hester as a punching bag. She was insanely jealous. "I finally walked out on her," Hester said, "and she took the gas."

The drink almost fell out of my hand. "You mean she killed herself?"

"Unfortunately, no," said Hester. "She made sure they found her in time." She had left a note blaming Hester, but Hester felt no pangs of remorse. "It didn't work," she said contemptuously, "and I didn't go back."

Min finally succeeded. "She shot herself this time," Hester said, "and staggered into the hospital, but she had waited too long." She laughed gratingly. "She surprised everybody, but herself most of all."

Hester's education continued. Months later, she met a much older woman, and they were still living together now, six years later. "We are just friends," she said, "and we have our own dates."

My memory stirred. "But didn't you go to Terry's party together?"

She flushed faintly. "Oh, yes, I almost forgot. I thought Terry would like to meet her."

We moved to less vulnerable areas. I wondered about her relationship with her parents.

"My mother stopped trying to marry me off years ago," she said, "and my father never asked questions." She had been one of the oldest of nine children, and was left pretty much to her own devices. Her childhood had been reasonably happy. "I was always a tomboy, and as long as I could remember, I wanted to be a boy." She had been traumatically embarrassed at the prospect of womanhood. "My mother never prepared me," she said. "I had never even known about menstruation. I woke up one night half frightened to death and went to my mother's room." She called out that she didn't feel well.

Her mother had called back sleepily, "Oh, take an aspirin and get back to bed."

Instead, she had taken a hot bath. "It was the worst thing I could have done," she recalled. In the morning, Hester was too pale and weak to come downstairs. Her mother finally grasped the problem and made the girl stay in bed all that day. She had only one visitor. "Today," her older brother jested, "you are a woman." And she was, in a way.

As she looked back, she held no grudge against her mother. "I'm enjoying myself," she said. "What more can I ask?" She swallowed the last of another drink. "And," she observed with a self-mocking leer, "there's no chance of getting pregnant."

Suddenly her thoughts turned again to Terry. "She's afraid of having a child, and yet she's married." She thought it absurd that she and Terry had never faced things squarely. "I think she got married so that she wouldn't be confronted with the truth."

I didn't quite understand.

"In those days," she said with a wry smile, "Terry bundled under the blankets and I slept on top of them: nothing was clear-cut." She sighed wistfully. "Things might be different now."

She was ready to leave. We said good-by amiably. She promised to read *The Sixth Man* through, and then said with a sly smile, "What are you calling your new book—*The Fifth Woman?*"

I shook her hand and watched for a while as she weaved down the street. I wondered how she would feel about the interview in the morning.

Terry phoned a few days later. "How did it go?" she asked.

"She didn't mention the word 'lesbian' once," I said.

Terry said understandingly, "I told you, it's better not mentioned."

"Don't be surprised," I said, "if you hear from Hester soon."

Terry seemed pleased. "Now that we've both grown up and know the facts of life, perhaps we can be friends again."

"If anything should develop," I said, "would you let me know?"

Over the phone her voice suddenly became testy. "What," she demanded, "could possibly develop?"

7

HOLLYWOOD SEX SYMBOL

Some of the most glamorous women in Hollywood—and on Broadway—whose femininity is a household word, are frankly lesbians in their private lives.

In Hollywood, where there are few secrets, lesbianism is as much taken for granted as male homosexuality. When two beautiful stars, a blonde and a brunette, dramatically recorded their friendship, Hollywood found noteworthy only the fact that the affair was flaunted in the face of an outraged husband, who reacted—manlike—by calling the police.

Like so many of their male counterparts in filmland, the glamorous lesbians are phony sex symbols. While they look languorous and seductive on the screen, in private life they are singularly crisp and businesslike, and can drive a bargain with any man. Thinking like men but looking like women, they have an advantage that has enabled them to flourish in the jungle that is Hollywood.

As lesbians—secret lesbians, to be sure—they have found themselves especially well equipped for Hollywood survival. By their standards, a Marilyn Monroe was too soft, too feminine to stand up to the pressures imposed on a great star. "Unlike the lesbian set," a Hollywood observer pointed out, "she couldn't stand up to men, in business or out of it."

In Hollywood, homosexuality—male or female—is regarded as a sign of the times. And a star's homosexuality is overlooked so long as that star is circumspect and successful. "Without the one thing," a producer observed with a shrug, "they might not have the other—the sensitivity they require for acting." Like so many others, he was convinced that emotional conflict made the homosexual more sensitive.

Paradoxically, lesbian stars appeared more stable than their male counterparts. "That may be," the producer pointed out, "because they have more of the male in them."

Unlike male homosexuals, they were seldom a problem on set and were known as good troupers. "Their lives are not constantly upset by breathless romances with men," an astute psychologist explained, "and they take charge with women. They are invariably the butches, though they don't dare look the part for fear of stirring suspicion."

They were part and parcel of the great lesbian grapevine, dramatically illustrating the pattern of artful secrecy that stretches across the country. But, even so, the lesbian seemed to be more privately concerned with her homosexuality than did the male homosexual, perhaps because with the exception of the stereotyped butch minority, lesbians seldom flaunt themselves. But even in a clandestine way, their public impact is considerable. "It is certainly no longer private," an observer pointed out, "when a false image of femininity is conveyed to millions of impressionable movie-goers who are being deceived by synthetic love scenes which are a mockery of the word 'love.'"

Because they traditionally make-believe, performers find it easy to simulate sex appeal and to dupe their audiences. In *The Caricature of Love*, Dr. Hervey Cleckley, professor of psychiatry at the University of Georgia and author of *Three Faces of Eve*, presents a revealing picture of a lesbian star who achieved fame and fortune through hoodwinking her public. On the surface, she appeared to have everything a red-blooded male could want in a mate. "Among other fine abilities and desirable human qualities," Cleckley observed, "she has the appearance of a pretty and sexually attractive woman. She is, in fact, remarkably endowed physically, having such glamour that she invariably arouses attention in men, and sometimes hopes that are never to be realized." He knew her well, for she was a patient.

Her rise was rapid. "After study and treatment by me and later by a psychoanalyst to whom she had been referred many years ago," Cleckley noted, "this woman established herself in one of the nation's large cities. She has become financially successful and prominent. Paradoxically, she has achieved this status through her charm and her appeal for men as an entertainer in a very high-class night club. As a talented dancer, a sultry singer, she is able to suggest subtly that she is as responsive to the male as most men are to her."

Admirers lined up at the stage door. "She has no difficulty at all in attracting suitors and enjoys this as a game and as a concomitant of her work," the psychiatrist reported. "She knows and uses, like a virtuoso, every gesture and tone in the vocabulary of flirtation, every catch of the voice, every erotic nuance of feminine motion or posture. Men often think they sense in her a smoldering passion of breathless intensity and often suspect it is particularly adapted for or directed toward them in person. It is thus not difficult to understand her success in her profession."

In bewildering succession, Hollywood sex symbols turned up with feet of crumbling clay. With millions of others, I had long regarded a celebrated star as the personification of romance. With her throaty voice and bold glance, she appeared to epitomize the new initiative of women in various fields, including lovemaking.

She had been married for years, though so quietly that few, even in her own circle, could have named her husband. He was trotted out occasionally as window dressing and then put back on the shelf.

As with so many of these lovely lesbians, her name was frequently linked with male stars and industrial giants. She had graced the Paris scene intermittently, and was a regular at a Parisian haunt for sophisticated lesbians the world over. She was friendly with Frede, the celebrated proprietor of the café and, some said, even its sponsor. Frede herself, formally attired, danced with the prettiest of her guests in a pleasant ritual cultivated over the years. But none was prettier—or more at home—than the visiting star.

Outwardly, the lesbian beauties of the films do not live any differently than the non-lesbians. With notable exceptions, they turn up for the usual parade of social functions for celebrities, attend film openings, submit to innocuous interviews with the press, and try not to retch over the fan magazines.

When they marry, as most do, it is invariably for convenience. But occasionally some are carried away by their own studio-contrived image, and may convince themselves they are marrying for love. But this conviction may not survive the honeymoon.

Nevertheless, Hollywood lesbians have married repeatedly, picking male partners whose femininity complements their own masculine streak. "When one of these marriages lasts," a Hollywood observer stressed, "the husband is usually homosexual, too, and they balance each other off." Or, as English actor Lawrence Harvey was recently quoted as saying, "Actresses really want men who will become wives."

Even in Hollywood, marriage often confers social approval and the semblance of conventionality, with all its comforts. It may even bring children, who are tolerated or welcomed depending on the whims of the mother. But, above all, with homosexuals, it provides a convenient shelter for a second, secret life. "These marriages are good cover-ups for an adoring public," this observer said, "and give these stars the freedom to do what comes naturally —for them."

A few lesbian stars have never married, to the chagrin of the fan magazines, eternally wallowing in their phony romances. But the ballyhoo never diminishes. One of the "bachelor girls" currently billed as a sex-bomb is strictly ersatz. Her publicists have loyally carried her to the altar, but have not yet been able to push her over the threshold, and it is little wonder.

One neighbor observing the antics of the star and her girl-friends for years thought it improbable that she would ever marry. From an upstairs window, looking down over the hedges into the star's private swimming pool, he had formed his impressions. "It was like a nudist colony," this staid middle-aged businessman reported appreciatively, "with five or six girls ducking into the water, with or without swim suits, as the mood came on them."

He rather enjoyed the display, and might have thought no more about it if it had not been for his Japanese handyman. One day this worthy, who also tended the star's house, approached the businessman, worrisomely shaking his head. "I don't understand," he said, "such a big house, so many bedrooms, and only one bed." He gestured expressively with his hands. "And such a very small one."

The businessman shrugged. "Many people prefer narrow beds." He laughed. "She probably wants to discourage overnight guests."

The handyman still frowned. "But the secretary, the pretty one, she stay every night. How do she sleep?"

Thereafter, the businessman noted the situation closely. "I observed," he said, "that the other girls turned up only when the star wasn't around. The day she left for a publicized trip to Europe, the group showed up. And the secretary took on such radiance that she looked like a star."

The grapevine had made this particular busty star a veritable queen in the lesbian set throughout the country. "She's the greatest," a teen-age beatnik told me dreamily. "You should have seen her at one of her parties: she looked like Aphrodite, the way she pranced around practically in the nude." And yet, despite her allure for the lesbian crowd, she still paid lesbian prostitutes to come to her home. "She could have anybody," the bobby-soxer said, "so I guess she gets a kick out of paying—like Johns do."

Other young lesbians worried lest this star marry and shatter the idyl they had built around her. "She'll never marry any of those jerks the columnists are pairing her off with," one said loyally. "She's just keeping up appearances. If she ever gets married, ten thousand lesbians will drown their sorrow in champagne."

The Hollywood caste system is notorious and it extends even to lesbians. At one time a small, select coterie of stars, together with some wives of film executives, had merged into a secret lesbian group limited to their own swank set. Each spoke several languages, was equally at home on the Riviera and in Rio de Janeiro, was exquisitely groomed and coiffed, and was fastidious about even a bridge partner. They were known to the cognoscenti as the Smart Ones, and one, a dazzling foreign-born brunette still of surpassing beauty in her middle years, was long hailed as one of the world's outstanding beauties. She was so supremely beautiful that she appeared unattainable on screen and off, but her chic friends knew better.

Beauty itself seemed a magnet. "We don't attract what we want but what we are," a beautiful lesbian had told me. Not only in Hollywood, but wherever beauty drew tribute, the shadow of Narcissus reared its beautiful head. Some stars, like the high-fashion models decorating the slick magazines, were infatuated with their own images.

However, as it was difficult to suitably gratify this self-love, they bestowed their affections on the images most closely resembling them, and kept true to this image by not marrying. Beauty was their goddess, and when they were not in love with some beauty, they were coolly unattainable. One great beauty, justly famed for her classic features, was particularly intriguing. She has become a living legend idolized by American women as the the epitome of feminine allure. Her male audiences have never been equally rapturous, unable, perhaps, to establish rapport with one who sought no rapport with them. But her beauty will never fade; her reflection on the silver screen will never change; screenwise, she will never grow old. Even Narcissus would envy her this triumph, for the image she has left as her legacy is timeless.

Where the emphasis is so much on symmetry of face and figure, strange fancies often develop in the intimacy of backstage dressing rooms. It can happen at any time. Captivated by a slim ballet star, a lovely dancer dashed off a few pages of verse smacking of Swinburne in ardor, and left them on the star's dressing table.

"What beautiful poetry!" the surprised recipient exclaimed, scanning the verse and handing it back.

The Edna St. Vincent Millay of the dance shook her head. "They're for you," she said.

The ballet dancer smiled uncertainly. "They're nice, but shouldn't you give them to a publisher?" She was trying to be casual.

The poetess stood next to the dancer. "I want you to have them," she said. Her eyes were suddenly tender. "You know, Julie," she said, "I love you very much."

"And I like you, too," Julie rejoined, taking a quick backward step.

The glow left the other girl's face; her eyes went blank and her figure drooped. Suddenly she seemed sad and forlorn. Listlessly she dropped the poems back on the dressing table. "Take these at least," she said dully, "if you want nothing else."

That week the poetic dancer returned to her home in the Midwest and married. She is now the apparently happy mother of two. But she has never written another line of poetry—no inspiration.

But, in Hollywood, inspiration is readily available. It is almost as though lesbians flourish in the Pacific air; the beaches up and down the rock-crested shores of California are alive with them, and they converge on Hollywood, the happy haven of stardom, beauty, and idiosyncrasy. Only a bare minority manage to get into the film industry, but many revel in just being on the fringes or, for that matter, going where the stars go.

Paradoxically, some observers have thought lesbianism an asset in attaining stardom. "Women need a sharp masculine drive to reach the top in Hollywood," a top film executive told me. "They are competing with men all the way—with the male producer, the male star, with agents, managers, press agents, and promoters. They would be eaten alive if they weren't just as tough, just as predatory, as the men." As a case in point, he mentioned a world-famous star whose name has been on every film-goer's lips for thirty years.

"But she has been married three or four times," I protested.

"Most Hollywood male homosexuals have been married," was the executive's tolerant answer.

But this woman, I pointed out, had made much of having children.

"Reflecting," he rejoined, "a proprietary, aggressive streak."

I remembered then that a writer friend, an attractive brunette, had first suggested that this particular star was a lesbian. "I saw her kissing this sweet young thing," she said, "and thought nothing of it. But as I looked up, they were still kissing five minutes later."

There had been a more recent incident. "Only a short time ago," the Hollywood observer related, "she brought this hairdresser from California to New York to do her hair. There had been nothing between them, but suddenly the star dropped her hand carelessly, and the hairdresser dropped her comb and brush."

The hairdresser was furious, and so was her husband. "He wanted to expose the star for bringing his wife across the country for something like that, when the wife had never given the slightest indication of being that way."

Our conversation turned to one of the brightest of the younger Hollywood beauties, whose life and amours have been dramatically flashed around the world from time to time. There was always a new admirer, always some new emotional upheaval. But she was always the pursuer, and she pursued both men and women equally.

She had little background or education, accounting, perhaps, for her limited interests. "Do you think," I asked, "that she turned to women because at thirty she is completely jaded and doesn't know what to do with herself?"

"That may be part of it," this Hollywood authority said, "but not all."

Everything she did, she seemed to do spectacularly, and lesbianism was no exception. Her husband had reportedly surprised her with another famous star, whose blond loveliness was a foil for his wife's brunette charms, and he was more surprised than she. They were divorced not long after, and the husband, questioned by a friend, commented rather sadly, "I know what to do about a guy, but how can you compete with a dame?" He didn't know what to make of it.

She was a novelty in a Hollywood notable for novelties. She made no secret of her liking for women. Many were prostitutes picked up for a day or a night and then tossed lightly aside, as she tired quickly of her latest kick. Often she seemed more sick than anything else.

"She's a disturbed girl," my Hollywood observer said, "and she gets no satisfaction out of men. She actually resents them, getting some perverse thrill out of giving herself to these little nymphs who are nobodies while the great men of the world are fawning at her feet."

On the other hand, many film queens were rightfully sex symbols, as they seemed to enjoy either sex. However, the male romances were generally attended with all the fanfare of a studio's high-powered publicity department, while the others were discreetly soft-pedaled in keeping with the desired image.

Although covertly acknowledged, lesbianism in the film colony is generally more underground than male homosexuality. However, through a sort of grapevine, the word spreads usually in a gossipy, offhand way. One of the major studios recently tried to develop a gangling blond model into a bright new sex-pot. But the girl, unhappily, wasn't up to her publicity. "When she walked on the lot for the first time," a veteran publicity man said, "all I could think of was a scarecrow."

As a model, she had projected well-bred detachment; but this quality was lost on the screen and her film career foundered. However, despite her Hollywood letdown, this synthetic sex-bomb still remained the ideal of gaunt, hollow-eyed sister models who regarded her as the epitome of femininity. But even this lingering image was impaired when she was seen everywhere with a New York fashion expert whose lesbianism was common knowledge. "I don't understand," a junior model wailed, "and she's married, yet."

"But aren't they all?" an observer said dryly.

Broadway gossip often lends itself to the lesbian burlesque of normal romance. With some interest, commentators had been following the romantic adventures of a bright new musical-comedy star whose captivating face and figure had inspired a procession of stage-door Johnnies. But the star herself, artfully avoiding her male admirers, would slip down nightly to Greenwich Village to her favorite lesbian haunt. There she met her most ardent suitor, a pretty heiress of Texas oil millions, who showered her with a barrage of candy, perfume, and flowers, and serenaded her with her own song of love.

The star didn't appear interested. But a month later she suddenly dropped out of her show and disappeared. And Broadway gossip had it that she had left the play because of a big romance with a Texas oil millionaire—male, naturally.

Lesbianism was frequently the hidden cause behind Hollywood breakups. There was the beautiful Hollywood actress whose marriage to a famous star ended with her getting all the sympathy and her husband being put down as the all-American cad. "At least," a friend said loyally, "he went off with another girl."

"And what about her?" a reporter asked.

He smiled. "She did the same, only much more discreetly."

If nothing else, I thought it rather revealing of the Hollywood climate that such stories could be carried by intimates—and accepted by other intimates without too much question.

While stars usually wander far afield to express the lesbian aspect of their natures, they sometimes seem unconcerned about their environment. "When my show folded," a shapely ingénue told me, "the English star was more solicitous about my career than my agent. She kept inviting me to her apartment, made telephone calls, and even cooked for me." The friendship was flowering when the ingénue suddenly decided to get married. The star did not attend her protégé's wedding. "She did not even send a present," the bride sighed, "or a note."

Many lesbians, ironically, masquerade as "professional" bachelor girls. While they may fool the public, they are not always as successful with associates. Writing a series on bachelor girls, a newspaperman called a television agency to arrange interviews with two of their luminaries—one an actress and the other a singer on a variety show. Both were attractive, young, and talented.

The agency man was wryly amused. "Bachelor girls," he said. "I should think they would be."

The reporter was mildly puzzled. "All I want to know," he said, "is how these girls regulate their social lives, why they're not married, how they handle the boy-friend situation, and so forth."

"And that," the publicity man said patiently, "is what I'm trying to tell you." He laughed. "Believe me, they have no problem staying single."

Unconvinced, the reporter interviewed the television actress, who has since won distinction in Hollywood and on Broadway. He liked her immediately. She was the soul of candor. Actually, she pointed out, she was not a real bachelor girl; she had been married and divorced. "He was a mamma's boy," she said, "and was looking for a mother."

"What were you looking for?" the reporter asked.

She shrugged. "I was too young to know."

Did she plan to marry again?

"Maybe," she said after some hesitation, "but it will have to be one helluva man—like nobody I have known before."

As the interview rocked along, the reporter looked for mannish indications in his subject. Her voice was husky, but no more so than that of a dozen other stars.

"Why do you always ask about men?" she rasped once. "There are many more important things in life."

"Like what?" he asked.

"Books, beauty, art—living each day for itself."

She considered herself a champion of the underdog. "I'm for the cat with a tin can tied to its tail, the rabbit chased by the dog, and for every minority group that ever was." She did not like the reporter's newspaper. "It's too fat and rich."

How did she feel about homosexuals in the theater? She shrugged. "There would be no theater without them—they need no defense."

Her private life was not very exciting. "I don't go out much," she said. "I find most men unstimulating."

"How about girl-friends?"

She didn't bat an eye. "I have little in common with girls. I'm not the kind to sit around and yak about men, and that's what they do mostly. I've always been a sort of tomboy."

She lived in a suburban art colony; it suited her moods, her range of tolerance. "I'll cook for you sometime," she promised the reporter. "I like your eyes." The future star gave the reporter a firm hand clasp. "Just don't make me look like a silly woman," she pleaded.

"How did it go?" the network man asked later.

"She liked my eyes," the reporter said.

The other laughed. "You must have reminded her of her sister."

"What makes you so sure about her?" the reporter bridled.

The answer came pleasantly. "Simple," he said. "I know the girl-friend."

Perhaps because there are so few stridently lesbian performers, the female homosexuals in show business have a much easier time than their male counterparts. Yet, even on television, where lesbianism is not nearly as common as in other areas of entertainment, some obvious lesbians do turn up.

On one show particularly, a platform for late listeners, they frequently shared the spotlight with a variety of male homosexuals. Still, while the males were closely screened and the bent-wrist brigade often barred, the lesbians remained unscathed. "They didn't even bother one obvious old dame who passed herself off as a society queen," a TV man reported.

More so than other lesbians, film stars observe the social amenities, not only to safeguard their public image, but to minimize blackmail. However, discretion sometimes fades at Hollywood parties, when the flow of alcohol has blunted inhibitions and prudence. "Imagine my amazement," the wife of a prominent actor told me, "when a producer's wife staggered over to me one night, not even noticing my husband, who was standing near, and said, 'Look, honey, I dig you the most.'"

She drew back and surveyed the actor's wife with frank admiration from head to toe. And then, unsteadily, she lurched forward to embrace the startled object of her affections. The actor's wife deftly disengaged herself and took a step backward.

"You've been drinking," she said disgustedly.

"I certainly have," the producer's wife agreed equably. She nodded scornfully in the direction of the girl's actor husband. "I can make you happier than he ever did," she said, "and I can put you in pictures, too." She cocked an eye at the distant figure of her own husband. "Daddy'll do anything I say."

The actor's wife, a prim Southern girl, gave her admirer a sharp push, grabbed her husband by the arm, and stormed out of the party. "Who says that it can't happen in Beverly Hills?" she demanded.

The lesbian grapevine was often insidious. Through osmosis, almost, the word seeped out about any celebrity who might be lesbian. In one Broadway night club the chorus line immediately came to life when a lovely Hollywood star joined the show as a headliner. Many of the starry-eyed beauties seemed bent on outshining each other as they flitted across the stage, whirling with remarkable verve as the star beamed back approvingly over the rhythmic beat of her own dancing feet.

"They are certainly putting on a splendid show tonight," a reporter remarked to a Broadway agent as they watched from their ringside table.

The agent smiled enigmatically. "In more ways than one."

The reporter looked at him questioningly.

The agent shrugged. "The girls are all putting their best foot forward, trying to impress . . ." He nodded at the smiling star.

"What good can that do them?" the newsman asked.

He winked broadly. "More than meets the eye." The reporter still didn't understand.

"In straight English," the agent said, "half of those lovely things are competing for her favor."

This was a double jolt. "Those beautiful girls?" The reporter was incredulous.

The agent laughed sardonically. "They're so beautiful," he said, eying them appreciatively, "that they even attract each other." He mused for a moment. "They can have the pick of the town's wealthiest males, and yet they give everything of themselves to girls who have nothing." He did not, of course, mean the star.

In the delicious intimacy of the dressing room, a camaraderie was often born, developing into something deeper. As an example, the agent pointed to two long-stemmed beauties as they paraded sinuously on stage to the accompaniment of enthusiastic male whistling in the audience. "They liked each other until the star arrived," the agent said, ignoring the male applause. "Now they're rivals."

But what about the star? Millions of Americans had once enshrined her as a pin-up queen. She was apparently happily married, and though she was no longer in pictures, she could still put over a number. Although past the first flush of youth, she looked feminine even with the burning spotlights glaring down on her. There was nothing to indicate she was anything but what she looked. But, as the agent judiciously observed, she had "gone Hollywood"—completely.

In Hollywood, for every male homosexual, there appeared to be a feminine counterpart. Though homosexuality was rife throughout the country, it was commonplace in Lotus Land. Droves of pretty little girls flocked to filmland, willing to do virtually anything to bask in the reflected brilliance of the stars. But where they once swooned over Gable, Tracy, Tyrone Power, and Errol Flynn, they now mooned over other great stars—women. And they often dressed and made themselves up to look like them. Many roamed the beaches at Malibu, Venice, and Santa Monica in hopes of scraping up an acquaintance with the more youthful of their idols. Some scissored these beauties' pictures out of fan magazines and secretly treasured them. Others spent days, even weeks, trying to finagle introductions, not to producers, but to the gorgeous stars whom the grapevine had indicated to be lesbian. But the grapevine was not always required. "I can usually tell by just looking at their pictures," one pretty beatnik told me. "They look cool."

There were many built-in reasons for the prevalence of homosexuality in Hollywood, including the tendency of one homosexual—male or female—to help another. Boredom and satiety were factors—too much of everything for people who had known too little of everything before fame and fortune came their way.

"In Hollywood," an agent observed, "many stars have youth, fame, beauty, wealth, adulation, and a life of ease in a sunny, subtropical paradise. But they don't have the solid background to take success in stride. They can be stimulated only by the physical, since their success has been based on the physical. So they try everything and anything, looking for a happiness they're not prepared for. And that seems to be the Hollywood story—shallowness, ennui, and disaster, built on the fragile foundation of materialism and sensuousness."

Was the Hollywood moral climate vastly different than that of more obscure areas? Were there other Hollywoods in Capri, the Riviera, Rome, and parts of Switzerland—wherever too much money and leisure combined with too little discipline and purpose? Hollywood was perhaps more a state of mind than anything else, capable of shaping into its own mold the malleable human material that succumbs to its spell.

But Hollywood had its defenders. "People there are no different from people anywhere else," a pretty secretary told me flatly. "They just get more publicity."

She had worked closely with the film set in both California and New York and knew many of them personally. She was pretty enough herself to qualify for pictures, her features sullied only by a vague discontent that turned down the corners of her mouth.

We had met through mutual friends, who had advised me that she was intrigued by the prospects of making a tour of lesbian bars in the Los Angeles area. But she had another preoccupation right now, closer to home.

"You know," she said accusingly, "you were very wrong in

your *Sixth Man* about one Hollywood actor. I dated him and he is very much male."

I wondered then how she knew whom I was referring to, as no names had been mentioned.

"Oh, some references were fairly obvious, like the marriage to his secretary. You made it a matter of convenience, though, and he was actually in love with her." Babs was very sure of herself.

"How do you know that?" I asked.

She shrugged. "He told me."

Nearly all her well-known friends in Hollywood and New York, it developed, were male homosexuals. "I don't care what anybody is," she said, rather defensively, "it's the kind of person he is that counts."

Her interest in lesbians reflected a normal curiosity. She had heard stories about a particular bar, and, attractively clad in slacks, had prepared herself for a sight-seeing visit. It was no problem locating the place, and I found myself as much interested in Babs' reactions to the bar as in the bar itself. Once we were in the lounge, she looked on cheerfully as several young girls danced together on a patch of hardwood floor. Her eyes took in everybody in the place but passed quickly over the few men alone or with dates, and moved on to study the faces of the girls. Nearly all were quite young, in their teens and early twenties; nobody appeared over thirty.

"That one girl," she whispered, nodding at a dark teen-ager with long hair. "Hasn't she the most interesting face?"

She seemed enthralled by the activity in the dingy room. No gesture, no whispered caress seemed to elude her. Her eyes glistened. The discontent I noticed earlier had vanished. She seemed pleasurably excited. Her husky voice was now confiding as she leaned forward and discussed lesbianism. She appeared to have given the subject some thought.

"A homosexual, male or female, is not really so much different from anybody else," she said. She motioned at some of the girls dancing with each other. "They're like anybody else," she said, "except they may be better-looking than the average."

She had had quite a few drinks and they seemed to have made her talkative. Her appearance, too, was undergoing a remarkable change, like that of a chameleon reacting to its immediate surroundings. Her short hair and flat shoes, her clipped accents and square jaw, now seemed painfully apparent. She held a cigarette like a man, tapping it with her thumb.

She was evidently brooding over our earlier conversation. "In Hollywood," she said, "people are unusually attractive." She nodded toward the dance floor. "Like some of those people there."

The point eluded me.

"Attractive people," she said, "may be drawn to both sexes. They're so strongly sexed."

"They could be oversexed," I pointed out, "and still be interested in only the opposite sex."

"The appreciation of beauty is universal," she said. "That's what they understand so well in Hollywood." She regarded me challengingly. "Why should you cut yourself off from anybody that's beautiful—just because of their sex?"

As I looked at this apostle of Hollywood ambivalence, I thought of the broken marriages, the shattered lives, and the heartbreak so characteristic of Hollywood. There seemed no end to the trail of tragedy. Then, suddenly, my train of thought was interrupted by the insistence of her voice, strangely metallic over the clatter of the music. "Anyway," she was saying, "they certainly know how to enjoy themselves in Hollywood."

8

JUST MARRIED

Clad in her son's shirt and slacks, sociologist Suzanne Prosin conducted one of the most unusual surveys on record—a survey of the married (to each other) lesbian. True, she interviewed only twenty couples, but that was because she could find only twenty couples that had lived together for more than a year—her basis for determining a real "marriage."

The shirt and slacks facilitated her meeting many lesbians in gay bars in the Los Angeles area. She took a recording device with her at subsequent meetings, and duly recorded her pioneer work for posterity.

A small, birdlike woman with a flair for interrogation, she was admittedly hampered by the fact that many lesbians were determined to keep their relationship secret and were not anywhere near as overt as the male. "I personally knew four lesbians on one college campus," she pointed out, "but I knew it was useless to approach them. One of them wouldn't even say hello to me when she knew what I was doing."

On the other hand, some of her subjects were as inquisitive about the heterosexual, comfortably married Mrs. Prosin as she was about them. "They would ask me," she said with a smile, "if

I had ever had a relationship, and I would say, 'Let's talk about you first.' " She had no wish to alienate them before she could get them interested in her project.

After many, many months of painstaking, often discouraging research, the woman who was to make this unique study of the lesbian was convinced that it would be unfair to say that the couples she interviewed did not have a bona fide marriage.

They had the same passions, desires, and aspirations as conventional couples, she pointed out, and some even had children to raise, the products of previous marriages with men. Nearly all jointly owned property, maintained joint bank accounts, and thought of their debts as joint obligations. Some had even drawn up dissolution papers governing the dispersal of effects in the event of a split-up.

Their attitudes toward each other were often acquired from observing the heterosexual world, but many felt that these heterosexual roles had changed so drastically that they could no longer imitate them and hope to stay "married" themselves. Instead, they had gone back to emulating the male-female relationship of a by-gone era, when the man was gallant and lordly and the woman dependent and taking care of the home. "It was difficult," Mrs. Prosin noted, "for some of the couples to describe husband and wife roles except in terms of what they should be." The aggressive, rough-talking, swaggering butch, considered an exaggerated copy of today's male, was not regarded as a good marriage risk, though many who thought this had been through the stage themselves. "She was not grown up enough or interested in responsibility," some decided.

There was some humor in Mrs. Prosin's findings. The functions of the lesbian femme in many of these relationships were identical, the sociologist discovered, with a Department of Agriculture rundown of an average woman's daily doings. "The list," she noted, "included all the domestic chores, and excluded repairs, household maintenance, heavy cleaning, and the upkeep of the car."

In the beginning of a relationship, superficial differences were distinctive. Hair and dress had a lot to do with conveying a partner's conception of her own role, but as the partners grew sure of themselves and their status within the relationship, she observed, there was a tendency among some for hair and dress distinctions to merge and sometimes disappear. However, the majority expressed their respective roles "in degrees of hair length that ranged from definitely male haircut to very tailored but feminine short-hair styles for the masculine partner, and definitely longer and more feminine hair styles for the other." Even when two partners had the same-length masculine cuts, one still had a distinguishing wave in hers. But more distinguishing than these superficials were the differences in attitude. Without deliberate effort, partners would frequently apportion their diverse duties. "They might explain that one partner was preparing the meal because she was a better cook, without explaining why she was a better cook," Mrs. Prosin observed, adding dryly, "She was often the better cook by default."

In the presence of the interviewer, the girl with the less masculine haircut would often wait on her partner. And the one with the shorter haircut, with a similar naturalness, would assume the male prerogatives. "I could often tell the masculine partner," Mrs. Prosin related, "by observing who moved the heavy chair for me, or who leaned forward to light my cigarette."

Togetherness was the keynote of these unique relationships, one or two of which had lasted as long as twenty years. There were usually no P.T.A. meetings or church functions to keep the partners even briefly apart. Occasionally they visited families separately, but many had even broken the family barrier, and insisted on their Sunday and holiday visits together, like their heterosexually married brothers and sisters. "In the lesbian group," Mrs. Prosin noted, "the only time spent apart was the occasional professional event, a closed function to which the partner could not be taken, or the time spent in school."

Though short on depth, the Prosin survey was as broad as the world around it. The ages of its female subjects ranged from twenty-one to fifty-seven, and their individual incomes from $2500 to $25,000, reflecting within the group a widely different scale in living and social standards. Some couples owned fifty-thousand-dollar homes in swank neighborhoods; others lived in low-cost housing projects or in both high- and low-rental apartments. "Like the heterosexual," the sociologist observed, "they were everywhere."

In the richer upper-crust areas, where the couples had status to think about, Mrs. Prosin discovered they were more prone to conform to their neighbors in dress and hair styling. Even casual sportswear—sweaters, jackets, skirts—were specifically for some conventional recreation purpose: camping, skiing, or riding.

Because of her obvious sincerity and her academic credentials, Mrs. Prosin was welcomed by many lesbians themselves interested in knowing more about that obscure phenomenon, the American lesbian. Sometimes they asked questions, regarding her as a veritable walking encyclopedia of lesbiania. The discussions were most frank, ranging far into the distinguishing anatomical aspects of the lesbian relationship. "Some," Mrs. Prosin pointed out solemnly, "were surprised at the physical possibilities (described by others in their reports).

Like Mrs. Prosin, I had originally had some trouble meeting representative lesbian couples, as publicity was the last thing many of them wanted. However, one contact often led to another, and I was soon *persona grata* with quite an assortment of lesbian couples, dining with some in their own homes, sipping tea and coffee with others at shops and businesses they managed together, observing others as we ate out at either straight or lesbian places. I met numerous others at bars and parties, but did not consider them partners unless they lived together and, as Mrs. Prosin had stipulated for her couples, for some significant length of time. All too often an eternal romance, marked with the gravest vows of undying love, had erupted a few weeks later in a storm of petulance or violence. Jealousy rooted in insecurity doomed many relationships from the start, and even in relationships that did manage to rock along, this frenzied jealousy often reared its disruptive head and was behind much of the togetherness that Mrs. Prosin had mentioned. "She doesn't leave me alone for a minute," was the common complaint of many femmes—and a few butches.

The refugees from conventional marriages, ironically, seemed to have a better assurance of success in the unconventional, perhaps because through experience they knew what they wanted. "It took ten years of one bad marriage," a middle-aged butch told me, "to prepare me for ten years with the right woman."

Where the lesbian union appeared mutually rewarding, there appeared one constant: a passionate desire for serenity. Long dead was the wanderlust that drove lesbians to bars for the excitement of ever-new faces; there was only a wish to live quietly in the warming sun of another's smile after the first flush of youth had shown the folly of the "green-eyed monster." "Nothing kills a lesbian relationship quicker than jealousy," a veteran of a lesbian marriage told me, "for it reflects the inadequacy of a partner who will, sooner or later, drive the other away by her attempts to possess her."

By itself, joint stewardship of cars, homes, animals—mutually beneficial insurance policies and wills—could not keep lesbians together any more than they have other couples. But the desire for these joint ventures, springing out of mutual concern rather than fear, seemed to heighten the possibilities of a continuing partnership.

Like Mrs. Prosin, I too was aware that I might not be meeting the lesbian types who formed the strongest unions intellectually and philosophically, for the reason that these women had so much to lose through exposure that they were not confiding their secrets to anybody, not even their psychiatrist.

However, like Sue Prosin, I did meet a broad cross-section: couples rich and poor, intellectual and mechanical, interested in the lesbian problem and uninterested. While their experiences varied with their personalities and background, their lives were all molded by a common denominator: regardless of how they rationalized, they were still affected by their own knowledge of their own taboo. "Only on a desert island," one lesbian told me wryly, "can you be a lesbian and not have some complexes."

Yet I have seen lesbian couples after three or four years of marriage as devoted and happy as other couples, though, to be sure, it was uncertain what the next day, week, or month might bring.

Despite a tendency to revert to traditional roles within the so-called marital relationship, only a small minority went through the travesty of a mock "marriage." And though I had never witnessed such a ceremony myself, I did note with amusement the sardonic account of a Gay Wedding by observer Jody Shotwell in *The Ladder*. "Soon," she wrote, "the bride-to-be appeared, dressed in kelly-green chiffon with rhinestone shoulder straps. No virgin white nor veil alas, but then, she had been married before!

"The 'bridegroom' was a fresh-faced youngster with red hair, freckles, and braces on her teeth. She wore black trousers, a white shirt and a black knitted vest, and revealed the nervousness of bridegrooms standard the world over.

"Other guests arrived, all female except for two young men, one of whom we learned was to perform the marriage service. We were curious about his qualification for this job but felt that any direct questions would be a breach of good manners. Later, we were able to discover only that he had 'performed this ceremony several times before' and that he was currently the manager-bartender of a local gay bar. He told us (rather naïvely, we thought) that he himself had been married in this fashion once, and that the marriage had lasted a month."

After the ceremony, Jody kissed the bride and shook hands with the groom while the wedding cake was cut and refreshments served. She extended her good wishes to the "newlyweds," feeling they could use them. "Having no status in the law of the land," she observed, "the homosexual marriage must be maintained only through the mutual love and devotion of those involved, and this love and devotion must be dependent upon their feelings and their behavior, not upon any public exchange of vows."

Most lesbians ridicule such ceremonies, pointing out, as Jody does, that they can have a salutary effect only if the participants "desire to live according to the mores of the heterosexual society in which they exist." Otherwise, the ceremony is seen as a big camp, a homosexual mockery of a deep-rooted social tradition. The most lasting relationships between lesbians have generally begun informally, without even talk of such ceremonies, though wedding bands are not uncommon. Many of these couples, particularly if one of the partners has been involved in a normal marriage before, are inclined to compare the two relationships, to the detriment of the heterosexual variety.

"We've already lasted longer than a lot of married people we know," Lorna said as she looked fondly at her partner, who was busily grooming a dog. And then this gay divorcee added, as her partner beamed approvingly, "Longer than my first marriage."

They were the classic example of togetherness, not only living together but even working together in a kennel they operated outside Los Angeles. They shared a big house, with four dogs, two horses, and two cats, owned two cars, including a Cadillac (driven by the male partner), and appeared to have an easy sort of bantering relationship, free of jealousy. I had visited their kennel a number of times; they seemed to handle their customers easily, both on the phone and in person, and their demeanor seemed to change only when their assistant dog handler came near. Then their voices dropped to a whisper. "What he doesn't know won't hurt him," Lorna said, and Dickie, her male partner, echoed the sentiment with a mild cuss word. They had not stopped working when I came in, and Dickie had now deftly turned a dog on its side and was expertly shearing the submissive animal.

"This isn't a lesbian kennel," Dickie said firmly, "it's a dog kennel." She brandished her clippers airily. "We don't give a damn about the private lives of the customers, and we assume they couldn't care less about ours, so long as the dogs get back to them in decent shape."

I looked at Dickie curiously. She was of medium height, lean and saturnine, with short sandy hair that fell over one side of her face. She showed strain about the eyes and moved nervously, and her expression was dour. "As long as you don't admit it," she said, "they got nothing on you."

Both girls were wearing slacks, but Lorna's hair was longer, and her shirt was more of a blouse. Her manner and voice were also feminine. And she laughed lightly, indulgently looking over at her partner. "Dickie's had a pretty hard time," she said.

Dickie shrugged stoically. "When I was in the insurance business, I had a broker call me once and ask me if I was a lesbian. He was the kind of guy that would never believe you if you denied anything, so I told him, 'Of course, I am,' and he naturally thought just the opposite."

She regarded me with pale blue eyes. "I admitted it once. I'll never make that mistake again." Her voice was grim.

"Oh, don't get started on that," Lorna said, "it's all dead and gone."

Dickie's lips tightened. "It's never gone."

She began working on another dog. "Talk about Salem witchcraft," she said, "it was nothing to what they did to me." She looked at me darkly.

Lorna still maintained her good spirits. "Oh, tell him if you're going to, don't be so blasted secretive, but remember, if it hadn't been for what happened to you—and what happened to me—we'd never have gotten together."

Dickie grunted an acknowledgment. She ran the clippers over the dog's back; standing stiff-legged, he cocked his head at her with a sympathetic look. "Atta boy," she said, "you're the kind of male I like," and she patted him approvingly.

Lorna laughed. "Isn't she something?" she said, shaking her head.

Dickie had finished with the dog, and was sitting on a handler's bench smoking a cigarette and sipping her coffee. There was a hard glint in her eyes. "There were five in our group," she began, looking off into space. "All working in this hospital, nurses and nurses' aids." She had been a technician herself, only twenty-one, new to New England. "We used to sit around and talk, play records, maybe dance, or go to the movies. There was nothing to it. But the interns and residents started to make cracks about the girls not going out with them, and one guy particularly was griping about a pretty nurse who wouldn't look at him."

Dickie's voice was low and controlled. Lorna, however, was a little edgy. But Dickie didn't seem to notice. "So they decided they had a nest of degenerates on their hands, and they had the damn nerve to call us in and ask us to leave. But we hadn't done anything, and if we resigned, it would have looked as if we had. So they brought in the State's Attorney." She gritted her teeth. "Can you imagine," she said, "bringing in the State's Attorney like we were a bunch of common criminals?"

There had been an investigation, and one of the girls, under grilling, had admitted to a relationship with a girl in the past. That took the lid off.

"Then they came back to me," Dickie said somberly, "and told me they wanted a confession. I thought they were out of their minds. I hadn't done anything and I wasn't about to confess. They accused me of the damnedest things, none of which was true. Then they threw Ruth's name at me and I knew I was in for it. Ruth was a girl I knew back home, the only girl I had ever been intimate with, and I had left home because of it, it had bothered us both so much." She had confided in one of the nurses, and now she was being confronted with the past. "If there was one, there are others," an investigator said contemptuously.

Searching her room, they had found letters from Ruth. They threatened to produce them and spread the case across the front pages. "And if you don't plead guilty," they said, "we'll send you to jail." Otherwise there would be a suspended sentence and a small fine.

The other four girls had already pleaded to charges of lewd and lascivious practices; Dickie was the only hold-out. "I thought of the headlines in the papers, and I didn't know what do do."

Dickie pulled hard on her cigarette, while Lorna began to fret a little. "Now don't get yourself all worked up and sick over something that happened ten years ago."

Dickie laughed mirthlessly. "It's like it was yesterday." Savagely she butted her cigarette. "I was young and confused, and didn't know what the hell to do. I knew that they had Ruth so scared that she'd be willing to sign anything they put in front of her. And they had those letters. I'd gone without sleep for forty-eight hours, and I was beat. I finally gave in. So I pleaded guilty to lewd and lascivious practices and took the twenty-five-dollar fine, and then they told us to get out of the state or they'd enforce the rest of the sentence." Her lips were a thin edge. "I couldn't get out of that state fast enough."

As it was, their names appeared in the paper anyway, and she felt thoroughly ashamed and dirty. "And mind you," she said, jabbing the clippers at me, "I hadn't done a thing all the time I was in that damn state." She threw the clippers onto a small table.

Lorna looked up moist-eyed. "Now, now," she said, "don't get yourself all upset: it won't do anybody any good."

Dickie hadn't wanted to face her family and she wanted to get as far away from the hospital as she could. With just a few dollars in her blue jeans, she hitchhiked to California. "I wanted to get clear across the country and forget everything I'd ever known."

By the time she reached Los Angeles, she was a thorough-going rebel. "I discovered that the California law said that if you were convicted of any kind of sex offense, you had to say so." She applied for a job at an aircraft plant without making this acknowledgment just to find out if she could get the job. But she didn't take it when they hired her.

Meanwhile, she had gone completely butch, trimming her hair, wearing only men's trousers and shirts, even male underwear. It was a man's world and she was living in it. She started frequenting the "queer" bars in L.A. and had one girl-friend after another—just like a man. "Never after that day in court," she said, "did I ever wear a dress again." She was mad at the world.

She also began drinking heavily. "Every time I thought of those sanctimonious hypocritical bastards who framed me, I'd reach for the bottle," she said harshly. She was obviously suffering through her story, but seemed under some compulsion to tell it, despite Lorna's concern.

Lorna was still trying to swerve the conversation into less traumatic channels. "She doesn't drink any more," she said with a rather wan smile.

"Naw," said Dickie with a bleak look, "I joined AA—Alcoholics Anonymous." She smiled again without joy. "Now I'm with Lesbians Anonymous. I'm a regular joiner in my old age." She had taken one job after another—in factories, offices, collecting her State unemployment insurance at the first eligible moment. "I'd write in some qualification for some practically non-existent type of work, like the operator of a hand machine of which there were only three in the world." She laughed. "They'd have a helluva time finding the machine, not to mention the job."

Lorna made a little chiding noise, and explained maternally, trying to make light of it, "Oh, she was still trying to get even with the dirty little old world for what they'd done to her."

Dickie had made herself as masculine-looking as a woman could get and still look like a woman. "I wasn't always this way," she said, reading my glance correctly. "I had my boy-friends back home, and I tried once with one boy, but I just wasn't interested. My family were strict Methodists. They didn't permit smoking or dancing or even near-beer, and sex was sinful." She looked at me with a distant eye. "I don't know, maybe that did it, but they were brought up that way, and it didn't do it for them."

One point of her story had puzzled me. Without looking at Lorna, I asked, "Why were you five girls always together if there wasn't some sort of feeling among you?"

Dickie laughed bitterly. "That's what *they* said." She shrugged. "We just didn't enjoy going out with men, and we enjoyed our own company. What is wrong with that? Now, if we'd been out sleeping with everybody in the hospital, that would have been all right." Her dark face flushed angrily.

Lorna shook her head at me warningly. "Now, now," she clucked, "don't get yourself worked up."

Dickie lapsed into a brooding silence without appearing to notice Lorna's look of tender concern.

Lorna had been through quite a bit herself. She had married

young and had a son ten years old, who was with her mother in Westchester County, near New York City. "Mother insisted on adopting him," she told me, her eye still lingering fondly on Dickie, "but I do think he would have been better off with us."

Dickie, who had gone back to her shearing, looked up with a disgusted expression. "Of course," she said.

"Wouldn't you have been afraid, though," I asked Lorna, "that he might grow up homosexual?"

Dickie gave me a fierce look. "And what, may I ask, is so bad about that?"

Lorna laughed. "As a matter of fact, there would have been less chance of his being homosexual with us, since I could have seen the signs and forestalled it." She sighed at Dickie. "Anyway, all people need to grow up whole is love—and we certainly could have given him that."

Dickie grunted agreement.

"Then why didn't you take the child?" I asked.

Lorna hesitated, and then said, "Well, Mother was getting difficult. She knew about Dickie and me, and said she wouldn't stand for Bruce being brought up in that kind of atmosphere."

As Dickie growled, Lorna laughed disarmingly. "I was going to take him anyway, but she threatened to bring the case to court and said she wouldn't pull any stops." She frowned. "She would have charged that I was unfit to bring the boy up properly, and by the time the case was over, I'm sure I would have been unfit, with everybody, including Bruce, thinking his mother was some sort of a degenerate."

"You mean that she would have mentioned you were a lesbian?"

"Oh, yes, she was convinced that was the worst thing anybody could be, and I'm sure the judge would have agreed."

She had seen the child the year before, visiting him over the Christmas holidays with Dickie. "As a matter of fact, Mother likes Dickie, she just doesn't like the relationship." She laughed. "She's been married four times herself, and that may have something to do with my feelings about men. When I was growing up, she'd tell me that men were meant to be used, and she certainly used them. Not only that, she was an actress, and we were always on the go, not really having a permanent home or making friends. I was always lonely."

She had married to get away from her home and to get over a girl she had met in college. "I didn't want to be a lesbian. I don't think any young girl who's been brought up in the conventional way wants to be a lesbian, and so I married. And he turned out to be less of a man than the girl I knew in college."

It seemed odd that her college friend had left such little impression on Lorna's life.

"Aw, go ahead and tell him," Dickie said, "I'm not jealous."

Lorna smiled rather sheepishly. "Actually, she brought me out, but I don't think it does any good to discuss things like that before your partner." She smiled prettily at Dickie, who kept grooming her dog as though she hadn't noticed.

"But if you were already that way," I pointed out, "perhaps your marriage never had a chance, regardless of what kind of man you married."

"It could be," said Lorna doubtfully, "but he wasn't that much of a man, anyway."

The marriage lasted only a few months; they were already separated when the child was born. She was Catholic and he Jewish, but the religious difference had been unimportant. "He was a mamma's boy, and every time we had any trouble, he'd go running home to cry on her shoulder. He didn't want the child, because he was too much a child himself. He wanted a mother, and I wasn't it."

Dickie broke in with a derisive laugh. "They all want mothers, and they call themselves the stronger sex."

After the marriage failed, Lorna opened up a kennel, which was successful in a small way. She had always liked animals and had a way with them. After a while she took in a partner, whom she had fallen for as she had fallen for Dickie. She was very happy with the arrangement—even the long hours seemed fun together —and Gloria seemed pleased, too, though Lorna continued to live at home with her mother and son. And then one day Lorna found a note. Gloria had left with the car and all available cash, and had headed for California with another girl. "And in my car, too," she recalled with a rueful smile.

Lorna was shattered. "We had our scraps, but I thought it was a good, solid relationship. I didn't even know she was seeing anybody else." As she looked back, she couldn't understand what came over her. But she was frantic. She left a note for her mother telling her to sell the business for whatever she could get, and she too headed for California. "I was broke, so I had to hitchhike." She knew her mother would take care of the child.

Though Lorna and Dickie did not know each other at the time, ironically, both had hitched their way to the Golden State. "Fate," Dickie said sardonically, "brought us together."

But it was not as easy to understand Lorna's precipitate departure.

"My whole world seemed to have collapsed," she explained, "and I just felt I had to take off after Gloria. The bottom had dropped out of everything."

"But you had your son," I pointed out.

She shook her head. "When these things happen, you don't think of anything. You just fly off, one way or the other."

In California, she eventually encountered her defaulting partner, but by this time she had already met Dickie and didn't care any more. They had been together for three years now, though Dickie had only recently joined her in the kennel.

"Aren't you afraid of history repeating itself?" I asked.

Lorna looked fondly at Dickie, who kept on with her shearing. "We've both found the security we need, and we've had all the bouncing around we want."

Dickie looked up with a tight-lipped smile. "You can say that again."

"Don't you ever notice other girls?" I asked Dickie.

"Oh, sure, I always see a pretty face, but serenity is the most important thing in my life, and I don't have any trouble remaining faithful. I had all that stuff I could ever want."

Lorna rolled her eyes and feigned shock, but she was clearly proud of Dickie.

It was evident from their appearance that Lorna was the femme and Dickie the butch, and yet, somehow, Lorna seemed to be the more aggressive of the two, dominating the conversation, running the shop, and apparently managing the tandem's operations, personal and professional.

It was Lorna I found myself addressing most of my questions to, and Lorna who seemed to have the answers to everything.

I had thought it quite possible that, seeing so much of each other—at the kennel and then at home—they might get a little on each other's nerves. But Lorna said primly, "Perish the thought." She turned indulgently to Dickie. "We can't get too much of each other, can we, dear?" Dickie went on with her shearing.

Inasmuch as both worked with equal vigor all day, I wondered how the division of labor was arranged at home. Lorna clucked like a mother hen and then, with a faintly chiding glance in Dickie's direction, said affectionately, "After I get through here, I go home and do the cooking, the dishes, and the housework."

It appeared an old story to Dickie. She shrugged indifferently.

"When you're tired, do you go out for dinner?" I asked.

"I'd like to," Lorna said, "but—"

"It's too expensive eating out," Dickie said shortly.

Lorna laughed good-naturedly. "You see how things are, but I don't mind. Dickie stayed out with a headache the other day and I had to work for both of us, but do you think anything was done when I got home? Nothing. There she was with her feet up on a chair watching television and waiting for me to make dinner."

Dickie yawned. "That's show biz," she said dryly.

Lorna looked over at her affectionately. "Here," she said, taking a cup, "let me get you some more coffee."

They were still sipping their coffee when I left. I saw them several times thereafter and each time had the feeling that, with all their apparent solidarity, Dickie was strangely reserved. "Do you two ever have any real trouble?" I asked Lorna.

"Oh, we get mad and throw things once in a while, but it always blows over." A shadow crossed her pretty face. "I only wish I had my boy out here with us. Dickie would be good for Bruce, and I think Bruce would be good for us. It's nice to have kids around a house. It makes it a family." As usual, Dickie was noncommittal.

As lesbian relationships go, Dickie and Lorna appeared twin towers of strength. Other lesbians marveled at their togetherness and envied their financial stability. "They must be good for twenty thousand a year between them," one friend estimated. "Their food bill for their dogs and horses must be more than most people spend on their tables."

It was to be some time before I would hear of Lorna and Dickie again. But, meanwhile, I had no reason to believe they weren't blissfully happy together, and said as much to a lesbian friend of theirs. I was rather surprised when she shrugged and said dryly "Well, one of them is happy," and put it down to sour grapes on her part.

Other lesbian couples, not as well fixed financially as Lorna and Dickie, appeared to thrive even in adversity.

Bee and Mabel, for instance, could recall the time that they had lived on Mabel's meager pension—and dog food. "And then," said Bee, "I finally found a job."

Like Dickie and Lorna, they too had been together three years, but they had been uneasy years. They seemed to be roommates more than partners, perhaps because of the age difference, and with Bee some twenty years younger, Mabel had initially assumed a protective role, at times quite authoritarian.

Originally, Mabel was the butch, but she had become seriously ill and the relationship had changed. "Not much chance of her being the aggressor now," Bee had explained. And with the change in the physical, the psychological relationship had subtly changed too. Bee was now more assertive.

She was concerned about Mabel's drinking and frequently

hid the bottles. "Don't bring anything stronger than beer," she said when she invited me to dinner, "if you bring anything."

I had met them at the D.O.B. convention, which, Bee imp-ishly explained, they had been "cruising." She grinned. "I thought it would be a hot sketch if some of those high-minded types cruised us." But only a curious reporter had troubled to speak to them. Everything about them was unorthodox. They had met through Mabel's brother, who had been dating Bee. "He was a real slob," Bee said, while the older and wiser Mabel nodded impartially.

At the time, Bee had been running a bar with another lesbian. "It was good business to go out with these Johns once in a while, lesbian or no lesbian," she said.

Mabel dismissed Bee's statement with a wave of the hand. "She's not really a lesbian," she said: "she really likes men. And I'm not really a lesbian, either, but they finally wore me down." She smiled. "The men, I mean." She was a widow, about forty-five, while Bee had never married.

We were sitting around in their cozy little cottage on the crest of a hill overlooking Los Angeles, in a lower-middle-class sector cluttered with children and small cars. Mabel and Bee had won-dered at first about moving in among what they thought were so many squares. But they were in for a surprise. "Hell," said Bee, "every other girl in the neighborhood likes girls, and every other guy is a fag."

After a few drinks and much conversation, we finally sat down to a thick steak, with red wine, as Mabel announced, "Bee's a good cook. She'll make some man a good wife."

Bee frowned into her plate. "There she goes again marrying me off, and me once a stompin' butch."

Mabel got up from the table. She was a little unsteady. "I'll show you some pictures," she said, weaving across the room. She brought back some snapshots of a smiling young man. "That was Bee three years ago," she announced triumphantly. "Isn't it won-derful the way she's changed?"

There was no resemblance between the long-haired, feminine-looking Bee in her low-cut dress and the sullen face in the snaps. "I guess I was going through a rebellious phase then," Bee said, glancing at the pictures.

"The next thing I want is to see her going out with young men," Mabel said.

Bee was annoyed. "I have been seeing George," she said.

"Oh, that homosexual," Mabel said with a grimace. Mabel had obviously been drinking long before I got there. "You know," she said, "the trouble with Bee is that she's twenty-five and still a virgin."

Bee shook her head in renewed annoyance and vigorously signaled across the table to me, waving her hand like a semaphore. "It's not so," she whispered.

Mabel suddenly expressed interest in my writing project. "I'd like to know myself why so many women are lesbians. Wouldn't you, Bee?"

Bee laughed shortly. "Mabel's quite a comedian at times," she said. "Let's look to home first."

"Oh, we're not really lesbians," Mabel said, "we just had a few things happen to us and we've been helping each other. We're more friends than anything else."

"There's something in what Mabel says," Bee said seriously. "We certainly have helped each other." She looked over at her partner. "Mabel was going through hell when I met her. Her aunt was living with her—mooching off her, I should say—and getting her drunk every day."

It had taken months to get the aunt out. "She was a bad influence on Mabel," she said, "always criticizing her and then getting drunk with her when she had her feeling bad enough."

"Oh, she wasn't that bad," Mabel said in her vague, well-bred voice.

"There you go, always defending everybody." Bee turned to me. "Mabel doesn't see anything bad in anybody."

Mabel said lightly, "I wish I could feel that way about your mother."

Bee groaned. "There she goes with my mother again." She passed the butter. "Mabel thinks I have a mother complex."

Mabel only smiled and took another healthy sip of wine.

I wondered what had attracted them to each other in the first place.

"Mabel's brother would bring her to my bar with him occasionally," Bee said, "and we hit it off."

From what had been said before, I had understood that Pat, the pretty co-owner of the bar, had been Bee's girl-friend.

Bee frowned. "We were breaking up about the time Mabel came around. That's how I happened to be friendly with her brother, and then something happened to Pat." Bee's face had become curiously solemn.

"Did she leave town?" I asked.

"In a way," Mabel said with a smile.

"That's not something to joke about," Bee said irritably.

Bee turned to me. "Actually, Pat died rather suddenly."

"Was she in an accident?" I asked.

She hesitated. "You might call it that. She took some benzedrine, and it killed her. I don't think she meant to kill herself, even though she left a note, but the autopsy showed that she had been drinking so much that the combination had a fatal effect."

The police had called Bee to identify the body. "Her note mentioned me as next of kin," she explained casually. Pat was thirty-one, and had a nine-year-old son. "She left the bar to me, but I turned her share over to the kid," Bee added.

"Why," I asked, "had she taken the pills?"

"We had a fight and she was trying to scare me into coming back," Bee said. "I was just all fed up with having to jump every time she cracked the whip."

Mabel had not seemed to be following the conversation, but she observed casually, "That's the trouble with all those lesbians: they want to possess each other or else they have to be knocking each other around."

Bee nodded in hearty agreement.

"Now, take Mabel and me," she said. "She encourages me to enjoy my freedom."

Mabel laughed. "That's why," she insisted, "we're not lesbians. We don't act like them." She looked at me. "I wouldn't think of standing in Bee's way if she wanted to go out with a man."

Mabel had thought her brother was treating Bee badly, and had censured him for it one night. That had drawn them together, and soon the brother had to look elsewhere for a date. "Actually, he was married," Bee said, "and was just out for kicks."

Mabel, so far as I could gather, had sort of drifted into lesbianism. She had married young. Her husband had been killed in the war, and the adjustment to the shock had been difficult. She had gone for six years with a politician in her home state of New Jersey, and he had constantly humiliated her before her family and friends. "He had no respect for me, and he showed it," she said. "He was so different from my husband."

"Then why did you stay with him?" I asked.

She frowned. "Why do women love men who are bad for them? I guess they're masochists." She seemed to like the roll of the word. "Bee's a masochist. Until she met me, somebody was always beating her up."

Bee nodded. "I agree." She had read about everything there was to read about lesbianism, and had decided for herself that lesbians were driven to distraction by a secret need to punish themselves for their guilt.

Mabel smiled tolerantly. "But, my dear, we're not lesbians." She appealed to me. "Do you think we're like those other women?"

"By all means no," I could say truthfully enough.

I wondered why Mabel hadn't married her New Jersey suitor.

"I was too good for him when we started going together, but I wasn't good enough when we finished."

I didn't quite get it.

"What she means," Bee put in, "is that the son of a bitch forced her to do things sexually that she's still got guilt feelings about."

Mabel made a face. "I don't like to talk about things like that," she said, "it's, it's . . . disgusting."

Bee looked up seriously. "I quite agree with Mabel. I don't think she was a lesbian, but this experience drove her from men and prepared her for the lesbian sexual role."

Bee herself was from the Midwest. She was a bright, serious-minded girl who had won several college scholarships and was now working on her doctorate. After her partner's suicide, she had been unable to do anything for months, and Mabel's pension had kept them alive. "Many a day we had only beans, but"—she laughed—"there was always a fresh bottle in the larder."

She and Mabel appeared to have an easy relationship; they spoke frankly, discussing even the closest family ties. Unlike Lorna and Dickie, however, they were not as frank with their families. I had looked into their bedroom earlier and seen two narrow single beds pressed together. "When our families visit us," Bee said with a smile, "we separate the beds and put a night table between them."

Nevertheless, Mabel's cousin, on a recent visit from Connecticut, had soon guessed their secret, and had been properly indignant. "She tried to break us up," Bee said, "not even caring that Mabel would be lost without me, and I'm not thinking about sex"—she regarded me soberly—"because there hasn't been any since Mabel got banged up in an auto accident, smashed her hip and has had one illness after the other."

Mabel, quite tipsy now, gave a muffled laugh in her handkerchief. "You know what horrified my cousin? She was afraid that I might get posted at the country club back home if they heard about Bee and me." It struck her so funny that she almost choked with laughter.

Bee's mother had been more of a problem than the status-minded cousin. Her parents had moved to California from the Midwest and were living only fifty or sixty miles away—too close for comfort.

"She used to come over here every week," Mabel said. She smiled. "You should see how she still tries to hold Bee in her arms and even get her to sit on her lap—you know, like she's Mother's little girl again."

Bee grimaced. "Are you trying to ruin my dinner?"

"I'm only trying to get you to understand yourself," Mabel rejoined, "and I don't care if I have been drinking." She suddenly looked at me and said, changing the subject, "What do you think of Bee's figure?"

I passed the expected compliment.

"Don't you think," she persisted, "she should stand up straighter?"

Bee whistled in mock despair. "There she goes again," she said. She flung her arms up helplessly.

"Stand up, Bee," she said.

Reluctantly, Bee complied. "She'll keep it up until I do," she said. "I know her."

"There, you see," Mabel said triumphantly, "look how her shoulders stoop." She spoke to Bee. "Hold yourself up."

"I can't," said Bee helplessly. "I droop naturally."

Bee turned to me with a murmured apology. "When I was a kid my mother made me bust-conscious by buying me bras that were about three sizes too small, and as a result I never got the proper support."

Mabel's smooth features were ruffled by a sneer. "I think she was trying to keep you from realizing you were a grown girl." She turned to me. "You ought to see the letters she writes Bee— like you wouldn't write your best girl-friend."

Bee shrugged. "I've never been able to figure out my mother. Ever since I was a kid she was trying to get me to go out with boys, and she even called in a priest to talk to me." Her mannish attire and apparent lesbian tendencies had horrified the good father. "He told me," she recalled tartly, " 'I'd rather that you were a whore on Main Street than this other thing.' "

I wondered about the reason for all this family concern.

"Oh, when I was fifteen, Mother was already worrying about me," Bee said. "I had kissed a girl-friend of mine when I was fourteen, just as any chum would, and I liked it so much that I kept right on kissing her, and Mother happened to come in on us. But we didn't really know enough to do much more, except we'd fiddle with each other a little from time to time when we were alone."

She had been the classic tomboy, rarely out of jeans and a boy's shirt. "I guess Mabel was right. I was in revolt against my mother. I felt like I was a blob of flesh and she was trying to swallow me."

"How about your father?" I asked.

She snorted. "My poor father had all he could do to survive himself. My mother twisted him around her fingers until he had no mind of his own."

If Bee was imitating what she hated, as the psychologists were so sure, why didn't she then imitate her mother? It seemed a plausible question.

Bee laughed. "Subconsciously, I suppose, I actually resented my father more, because by relinquishing the dominant role in the family, he had put me at my mother's mercy."

"Yes," said Mabel thoughtfully, "a nice man but no backbone, like so many men these days."

Bee sighed. "So that's the story of my life—dull, isn't it?"

Mabel smiled. "Her mother just couldn't bear the thought of any other woman being closer to her than she was, and if she could have kept her to herself, she would have. But she figured that even if she did get married, she'd still be the only woman in her life. That's why she resents me. I'm a rival."

Bee looked at her ruefully. "Why don't you lie down," she said, "before you fall off that chair?"

Mabel smiled vaguely at the younger woman. "She's really quite talented," she said, adding peremptorily, "Bee, show him your paintings while I'm powdering my nose."

When Bee didn't make a move, Mabel rose uncertainly to her feet and brought out a few chalk pastels and a couple of oils. They were frightening in their stark reality. She then teetered toward a doorway, saying she would soon be back.

Bee arranged the paintings with a deprecating gesture. "You don't have to admire them," she said. "Mabel is always singing my praises."

She lowered her voice and then, turning to make sure Mabel was out of earshot, said confidentially, "Mabel likes to think of me as being pure: that's why she said I was a virgin." She regarded me evenly. "But I'm not. I just haven't bothered telling her. George—he's the boy we mentioned earlier—and I spent a weekend away a couple of months ago." She paused delicately.

Why had she cared whether I thought her a virgin?

"Because I feel myself becoming more and more a woman, and I wouldn't want you to think that I was a lesbian because I didn't dare be anything else." She seemed rather tense about it.

"Well, was the weekend satisfactory?" I asked.

"To be frank," she said, "I don't think he knew very much more about it than I did." She laughed. "I wouldn't want Mabel to know, but I think it was the first for him, too."

There had been no more weekends. "Actually, it didn't seem to make much difference in our relationship." But, in its hollowness, the incident had pointed up the "trueness" of her relation to Mabel and their importance to one another. There was no questioning Mabel's pre-eminence in her life. Through Mabel's influence, she had learned gradually to soft-pedal her lesbianism and to think of herself once more as a woman. "When I was working in the bar, I obviously didn't care who knew about me," Bee recalled, "judging from the pictures she showed you. But sometimes, as I've told Mabel, it catches up with you even when you're minding your own business."

With Mabel's approval, she had been working in a telephone-company office, holding down "a nice, straight job" and being eminently respectable, when one of the secretaries eloped with a female transvestite. Bee had been as amused as the next one at first. "It was a big howl," she said, "but then they searched the girl's desk and found a lot of love letters addressed to the girls around the office, but which she had never had the courage to mail. I don't think I had spoken two words to the girl—she was a real beast—but one of the letters was addressed to me, and I got fired along with the others."

"What was in the letter?" I asked.

"Oh, she kind of raved on, you know, the sort of thing sick people would do to get their jollies." It was a new expression to me, and she explained. "Kicks, thrills—I suppose she went home at night and had all sorts of exciting dreams. But she was so damn fat and unattractive that she had to settle for a transvestite."

Later, Bee had worked as a draftsman in an engineering office, but had finally quit when she got tired of being chased around the desk by her boss. "He was a real fink," she said. "He kept telling me he wanted to leave his wife to marry me, but I kept right on running."

She smiled. "It was a riot. I finally told him the day I quit that I could never marry him, not for a million dollars. He asked me why and I said, 'Because I prefer girls.'"

She laughed, just thinking about it.

"When Fran and Jane come over later, I'll have to ask about the old buzzard. Jane's still working for him."

This was the first I knew we were having company.

"I invited them for dinner," she explained, "but Fran had to wait for her mother to get there and baby-sit for the two kids."

By the time Mabel reappeared, the new guests had arrived. Jane was a comely young blonde, with a pair of shapely tanned legs set off by revealing shorts. Her partner, Fran, was a broad-hipped girl of thirty-five or so, with a dark, round face and impassive eyes. She looked like an Indian. They had driven over in Fran's car. "We can't stay long," Fran said, "my mother's only good for two hours with those bandits of mine."

After the usual pleasantries, Bee turned to Jane. "How's the old buzzard you work for?" she asked.

"Used to work for," Jane corrected with a smile.

"What happened," Bee said, "or can I guess?"

Jane shook her head. "You warned me, all right." She laughed. "This old fool had an office full of lesbians working for him, and he was the last to know it." She turned to Bee. "You must have told him about yourself."

Bee nodded. "Self-defense."

"Anyway," Jane said, "it was just too much for one dollar and seventy-three cents an hour."

She looked at me with a grin. "This guy was sixty if he was a day, but he had young ideas. He'd been married to the same woman for thirty-five years, but he was going to get rid of her right away for me—if I was reasonable." She laughed. "And his wife was working with him, too, in the outer office."

He had called Jane in one afternoon for a conference, and had reached out for her hand. "Come away with me to Mexico for a weekend," he whispered hoarsely. "I'll get a divorce there and we'll get married."

As Jane recalled how she had laughed in his face, Mabel appeared to suddenly come to life. "He was giving you the old Army game, honey," she said. "I got that for six years."

Jane smiled. "I was afraid that he meant it."

Jane seemed to enjoy discussing her experience. As she rose to her feet, she recalled how her importunate boss had tried to put his arm around her waist. "Don't tell me," he said, "that you're like that Bee."

This was an opportunity that Jane could not resist. "As a matter of fact," she said, leaving no doubt as to her meaning, "she's my special girl-friend." At that, she turned on her heel and stalked out, pushing her tongue out as she passed the wife in the outer office.

Laughing with the others, Bee consoled her. "Oh, you'll get another job soon."

"I'm not worried." Jane shrugged.

I had already started taking stock of the newcomers. Jane and Fran had likewise been living together three years, and they seemed as casual as any old married couple.

"Do you consider yourselves married?" I asked, noticing the wedding bands on their fingers.

"I've been married once," Fran replied, "and got two kids to show for it: that's enough. We're friends and roommates: that's good enough." Her voice was pleasantly husky.

"How about the kids?" I asked Jane. "Do you mind them?"

She smiled. "Mind them? I couldn't do without them. That's one of the reasons I felt drawn to Fran."

The children called her Aunt Jane, and she was inclined to spoil them. "I keep warning her," Fran said good-naturedly, "but she won't listen to me. I guess it's her maternal instinct."

Jane was obviously the femme, so femme, as a matter of fact, that she seemed femininity personified with her soft features, docile blue eyes, and trim curves. "Wouldn't it be more rewarding, perhaps," I asked, "to have children of your own?"

She admitted having toyed with the idea. Following a previous lesbianic relationship which had turned out badly, she had dated men for several months, and had even permitted a premarital intimacy as a sort of self-test. "The young man was nice enough," she said, "but after that, I knew it would be a mistake for me to marry anybody—any man, that is. I just wasn't interested, sexwise, and I didn't have to wonder about it any longer."

Her earlier lesbianic relationship, which had been her first, had lasted two years. She had taken a lot of punishment before she gave up. "I just couldn't take her beatings any more, but I felt sorry for her two kids, and so I stayed until I could make arrangements for the courts to find a home for them." She sighed. "But she got them back: a mother's rights are sacred in California no matter what she does to her kids."

They had met in the neighborhood, and it had been an exciting courtship while it lasted. "She was a stompin' butch, and she'd come right up to my front door in her leather jacket and boots to pick me up when she was first trying to get me to go out with her," Jane recalled. "She'd just look at me and I'd tremble all over. I tried to keep away from her, but then I found myself going to the bar where she hung out, and then she'd give me that look and I'd run all over again." She coughed dryly. "But as they say in the gay bars, she ran and ran until she got herself caught." Her voice was gently self-mocking.

Jane was nineteen at the time. Her parents had not liked Barbara but thought she was safer than most of the young men Jane knew—until, all too late, they discovered their daughter was moving out, and why.

I noticed that Fran had remained impassive during her friend's recital. "Don't you mind hearing about a former romance?" I asked.

She shrugged indifferently. "Why should I?" she said. "We're going home together." At that, she yawned and rose to her feet. I looked at my watch. It was getting late. "Time to go," she said sleepily. Jane took the hint, and so did I. As the two girls stepped outside, I thanked Mabel and Bee for an informative evening.

Mabel smiled. "As I keep telling Bee, it's nice to have a man around the place occasionally." She sniffed. "And I don't mean that George."

As Bee and I shook hands, I could not help commenting on how attractive and feminine she appeared. She thanked me casually, and let Mabel walk me to my car. "As I told you before," Mabel said, "we're not really lesbians. Bee thinks of me as she would her mother. I'm the gentle identifying mother she never had."

"And how about your feelings for Bee?" I asked.

She looked at me in surprise. "Why," she said, "I thought you understood. She's the daughter I never had."

It is often a mistake to look back on what one has written. Of the two relationships discussed here, I would have cheerfully put my money on the lasting qualities of Lorna-Dickie over the Mabel-Bee combination. And yet, a year later, when I looked up the couples, I discovered that Mabel and Bee were excitedly planning a move into the country, whereas Lorna and Dickie, the apparent lovebirds, were no longer in business, personally or professionally.

Their relationship had broken up with a crash that echoed through lesbian circles. My own first inkling of something wrong came when I phoned the kennel. "Nobody here by that name," a male voice had said crisply.

I later inquired after Dickie and Lorna of a lesbian who had known them well. She looked uncomfortable for a moment, and then said, "Oh, they broke up right after the Christmas holidays."

"But," I said, "they were the ideal couple."

"Not really," the girl said. "There was a lot of underlying friction."

"But how about all those interests they had together," I said: "their business and their home and their dogs and their horses?"

She snorted. "Possessions never keep anybody together. Besides, Dickie wasn't interested in the kennel: that was all Lorna's idea."

But what could have possibly happened to end this apparently idyllic friendship, in view of all the protestations of undying love?

History, oddly, had repeated itself. Lorna had suddenly discovered one day out of a clear sky that her faithful helpmate had, with all their togetherness, been seeing another girl. There had been a furious row, climaxed by a suicide attempt by a shattered Lorna.

Somehow I felt my sympathies going out to Lorna—the pretty femme. She had given so much of herself, and yet seemed doomed to ingratitude and infidelity.

My lesbian source considered it a waste of sympathy. "She brought it on herself," she said severely. "She wanted to be My Fair Lady and still rule the roost. You've got to be one or the other—butch or femme—if you're going to stay together as lesbians."

9

THE BACHELOR GIRL

While the "perfect partner" appears to be the major quest of lesbians, many manage to live alone and like it. They hole up like any other bachelor girl in a cozy bungalow or apartment, with a single bedroom—and bed—date casually, or even go steady, but in the end they wind up with their books, tv, radio—and cats. "It's so difficult," one lovely femme confided, "to find the one you love who loves you."

Disillusionment and disappointment in lesbianic romance have created many bachelor girls. "No matter what household arrangements you make," one girl told me ruefully, "you have no hold on anybody, and the ring you give them one week may be put on somebody else's finger the next."

Many lesbians have become bachelor girls because they couldn't live peaceably together under one roof; others actually prefer the single blessedness of being alone when they want to be—doing their own chores and living pretty much like any other bachelor, male or female.

Like other bachelor girls, the lesbian variety suffers from loneliness, but they also know a compensating peace of mind, unbroken by the jealous demands of an angry butch. "I can count the good relationships I've had on the fingers of one hand," a pretty femme told me, "and I'll continue to take care of my cats and putter around my garden until I find somebody who will take care of me."

Most of the bachelor girls I met were femmes—many of them so attractive that warding off the attentions of males was an additional problem. "These office wolves, particularly the married ones, become a headache after a while," a pretty femme reported ruefully, "and you can't turn them down too cold or they'll think something's wrong with you."

Some discouraged the blandishments of the rogue male by flatly refusing to go out with married men. Others expressed a sardonic interest in the Romeos' wives and children. "In this way," a femme told me, "they might never get to the point of being rebuffed."

The single male was a problem by himself. Many bachelor girls had dated for the sake of propriety and in a bizarre hope that it might lead to something better. "Your escort might always take you to some party," a femme said with a smile, "where you might meet some beautiful butchy girl."

But, by and large, lesbian bachelor girls invoked any excuse to avoid male dates, even resorting to the white lie that they were already engaged. "And"—a femme winked roguishly—"I actually was—to the best-looking butch you ever saw."

Butches, too, prided themselves on their singleness, particularly the slim, elegant, well-bred type active in the arts and sciences.

While this type was not at all "butchy" in appearance, it kept its hair short enough to clue the lesbian group but not short enough to give away its lesbianism to others. It was a modest trademark.

But the thing that struck me most about the lesbian bachelor girl—femme or butch—was her almost feline stress on independence.

When I met Marla, I thought her the typical bachelor girl—typical in a way of life that most lesbian bachelor girls strove to create. She was in her late thirties, unmarried, had a good job, her own home and car—and plenty of cats.

Her looks were deceptive. She had long black hair, down to her shoulders, a bright, natural complexion, deep-set eyes, and heavy black eyebrows. She looked ten years younger than her age.

She greeted me with a friendly smile. "You're surprised that I am a lesbian?" she said. She was amused. "Well, not many men are, because not many—or should I say 'not any'—know."

In view of all this secrecy, I wondered why she had agreed to see me. "Oh, I get tired of seeing all lesbians pictured as freaks," she said, "when the only difference between me and other women is the choice of the love object." She laughed. "I've been working in the same place now for ten years, and I spend half my time listening to men tell me about girls they think are lesbians, and I'm probably the only lesbian in the place."

We had met through a mutual friend, a lesbian, who regarded Marla as one of the great beauties of her time. She liked her, she said, because she was independent, spent her own money, and mixed easily with straights without ever becoming part of their society.

"She makes better than ten thousand a year," this friend told me, "has supported her parents for years, and supports herself."

She made it clear she had never been intimate with Marla. "She's not my type," she said with a shrug. "Or put it this way: I'm not her type. She's a bit of an intellectual snob."

I had asked Marla if she would have dinner with me, anticipating with some confidence that she would not have any prior engagements with other men.

She regarded the invitation impersonally. "Why not have dinner at my place? It's so expensive eating out."

"There's probably some place you'd like to go," I suggested.

She smiled like a little girl. "As a matter of fact, there's a pianist I enjoy at a certain restaurant." She hesitated. "If you're sure it's all right." And then she laughed gleefully. "You'll be the first man I've been out with in years." She became even more attractive when her face lit up.

I wondered how she could be so pretty and so abstaining

without the egotistical male getting suspicious. "Didn't anybody ever have an idea you were a lesbian?" I asked.

"Oh, when I was younger, some of the boys I would go out with thought I was frigid, and"—she laughed—"some of the married men I wouldn't go out with would say, 'What are you, a lesbian?' but that was only part of their line."

The restaurant was pleasant; the music was low, the lights soft, the service unobtrusive, and many couples, taking the cue, were whispering with their heads together. At Marla's suggestion, we had taken a corner booth near the piano and away from other diners. "With the music and everything," she said, "nobody will be able to overhear us."

"You certainly are cautious," I observed.

She stiffened slightly and pouted. "That's the fault of you men: you just can't bear the thought of a pretty girl preferring another girl."

With great care, Marla examined the menu. "I like being taken out: it makes me feel very feminine and protected," she said.

"But I thought you hadn't had a date in years."

"Not with a man," she smiled, "but I've known a good many butches."

Whenever the waiter approached, she abruptly shifted the conversation from herself and then quickly switched back. "I'm a real ham," she said enjoyably, "because I don't get a chance to talk to a reporter every day." She permitted herself a cocktail. "I usually don't drink," she said, "but this is a special occasion."

"If I weren't a reporter," I said, "if I were just myself—say, an actor, bookkeeper, or engineer but still me—would you be sitting here with me tonight enjoying yourself?"

She looked puzzled. "What for?" she said blankly. "I can always get dinner at home."

Our conversation traveled along routine lines. "Were there many in your family?" I asked.

She shook her head. "I was an only child." Her parents had been farmers in Oregon; they had helped her through college, and then she had worked at various things: teaching for a while, singing and acting a bit, and then settling down to a bookkeeping job. She had risen to assistant comptroller. "I always had a head for figures," she said, laughing, enjoying her own double entendre.

"Have you ever wondered how you became a lesbian?" I asked.

She laughed shortly. "Every lesbian wonders, but I know." Her face had suddenly become stern and her eyes flashed darkly. For a moment she even forgot to be careful. The words rushed out of her. "My mother was always warning me about boys, always telling me how evil they were, warning me never to give in to them before I married, and telling me boys would do anything to get the better of me. She warned me of pregnancy and disease so much that I was afraid that if a boy even kissed me, it would do something to me."

Her father apparently had been no help.

"Oh, he did whatever Mother wanted. Between them, they were so cold and discouraging that I never invited boys to the house."

"Did you like going out with boys?" I asked.

She shrugged her pretty shoulders. "Oh, I liked things like movies and boat rides, but my parents were so strict that I never learned how to dance. When most of the kids went to the high school dances, I stayed at home."

"Can you dance now?" I asked.

She smiled. "Oh, yes. I had a very good teacher, but it was years later."

"When did you first realize you were a lesbian?" I asked.

Her face became serious. "Usually, you only realize what happened by looking back. When I was fifteen I developed a crush on this girl in high school. She'd come to my house and sleep over and I'd go to her house. We'd snuggle in the covers like a couple of bugs, hug each other and kiss good night, falling asleep in each other's arms." They also walked about interminably with their arms around each other. The other girl's family, concerned by what they saw of the attachment, tried keeping them apart. "They thought we were getting overly friendly, I suppose," she said carelessly.

But her own family had approved what they saw. She smiled

ironically. "They were for anything that kept me from boys. They had evil minds."

As she grew older, her feeling for the other girl grew, too. "I couldn't get her out of my mind, even when we were separated at different schools. I waited seven years for her, hoping she would one day give me a look that would let me know she returned my love." Instead, the girl she had waited for developed normally, married, and had three children. "I don't think I'll ever forgive her," Marla said with a disdainful expression. "She knew how I felt and she felt the same way, but she was afraid."

It seemed incredible that a girl as good-looking as Marla could have discouraged all her male suitors so effectively down through the years.

"I did have one boy-friend," she conceded. "He was gentle and kind and I respected him. We petted a little, but nothing serious. I let him kiss me, but I couldn't return his kisses." She shrugged indifferently.

He was willing to wait, but after a year and a half she finally called it off. "Every time he touched me I would wish that it was this girl. What was the sense of getting married?" It seemed a good question.

"He didn't seem a very ardent suitor," I said.

She hesitated ever so slightly. "He was very understanding."

"Was he homosexual?" I asked, thinking him strangely tolerant.

She thought a moment. "He might have been. He didn't want any children and was willing to do whatever I wanted, but what I really wanted was someone to make the decisions."

Why had he mentioned not wanting children?

"Because he knew I didn't want any." Her voice was resolute.

"But weren't you bothered by the thought of what you might be missing?"

"Missing?" she exclaimed. Her dark eyes smoldered and her jaw hardened. "Missing?" Her whole face was harshly transformed. "I never asked to be born, and I wouldn't bring any child into this world." She glared at me fiercely.

"Fortunately," I said with an effort at lightness, "most people don't agree with you."

Her lips tightened. "My parents didn't do me any favor by having me, and for all I know, they didn't want me. Most children are just thrown into the world." She laughed mirthlessly. "Whenever my heterosexual guests leave at night, I tell them to drive carefully, 'Ninety-nine per cent of our accidents are people.'"

Just as maternity was repugnant, so too was the thought of sex with a man. She had never been able to bring herself to it.

"How," I asked, "can you tell you wouldn't like something without trying it?"

She smiled frostily. "After all, you don't have to try dope to know it isn't good for you."

She spoke in a low voice now, looking around to make sure no one was listening. The piano player had given up, but there was new entertainment as a succession of fashion models paraded before us in beachwear, lounge clothes, and cocktail dresses. They were attractive, shapely girls, with engaging smiles, but Marla only seemed annoyed. "That's California for you," she said, "always show biz." And when one of the pretty models showed off a beach jacket, she said shortly, "Does this continue all night?" The startled model drew back with a murmured apology. She made no more stops at our table.

"You would think," Marla said, "that they would try not to interrupt people's conversations."

"Don't you find any of these girls attractive?" I asked.

She gave me an indignant look. "You have an idea, like so many men, that lesbians are attracted to any skirt. Even if I were attracted—which I'm not—I would never show it." There was a note of pride in her voice. "I never call anybody for a date or make an overture. After all, I'm a woman."

We had dessert and Marla had a cordial. "You don't mind?" she said. "Not many butches like to spend their money on a girl." She assumed an injured air. "Why should I do all the housework and then have to share expenses with some butch?"

"That seems to be a universal problem these days," I said.

But with it all she was very happy to be a lesbian, and couldn't understand why anybody would want to be anything else.

Her eyes had sparkled at times when she spoke of being in love. And she cheerfully acknowledged many lighter adventures.

"It's a regular game," she said casually, "like it is with men and women. The touch succeeds the look, and then there's the actual advance. If you really are infatuated and it's somebody new, you unhook your own clothes slowly and dilly-dally a little, like any other girl would, drawing the whole thing out to its inevitable pleasant conclusion and enjoying each moment." Her whole face was aglow.

"And if you know the other person well?"

"Oh, then you just go ahead quickly and do whatever it is that is indicated."

"And the same thing is always indicated?"

"With me it is. My role never changes." She was quite steadfast on this point. "I am always the passive one—the woman."

"Have you ever permitted the use of a device?" I asked.

Her face was blank. "Do you mean a dildo?"

"Something like that."

She was horrified. "Why, that would be perversion," she said. "You might as well have a man."

She was still shaking her head in dismay when the check came, and we got up to leave.

As we left the restaurant, she said, "I would like you to see my house. I'm quite proud of it."

It was a pleasant drive up a winding Hollywood hill, and then we came to a little white doll's house with a small but lovely garden enclosed by a trim white picket fence.

Two or three shadowy figures rustled against our legs. "Don't mind them," Marla said lightly, "they're my little babies." They were her cats and all had been spayed. "They're too ornery the other way," she explained.

Marla took me for a brief tour of the house. There were only three or four rooms: a living room, a dinette, a kitchen, and a bedroom. "I keep a single bed deliberately so I don't have a lot of girls using my place for a hotel," Marla said. "I don't mind being alone. I have my music"—she pointed to a guitar—"my books, my radio and tv, and now I'm trying to get a record player."

She paused. "I'm saving green stamps—you know, from the supermarket." She pointed proudly to the radio. "That's how I got that."

She sat down and crossed her knees, displaying a shapely calf, and began stirring the tea she had made. "Now," she said with a bright smile, "what more can I tell you about myself?"

"You can tell me," I said, "about your coming-out."

Pertly she offered me the sugar. "One lump or two?"

Stirring her tea, she regarded me reflectively. "You know, at first I thought something must be wrong with me. I had got hold of *The Well of Loneliness* and decided that the author and I were probably the only two lesbians in the world." She brooded through four years of college, without doing anything about her lesbianism, and then headed south, away from family and friends, to try to carve a new sort of life. "My instinct drew me to Southern California. Maybe it's the sunshine and the warmer climate, but people seem easier and more understanding when they're not fighting the weather."

She took a room in a Los Angeles roominghouse, and one day met another girl on the way to the hall bath. They had rooms on the same floor. They smiled, stopped to talk, and struck up a casual acquaintance. Occasionally, when they had nothing better to do, they had dinner or went to the movies together.

Marla wondered about her new friend, but there were no false moves, either by glance or innuendo, and she had nothing to go on. Yet at times, as Elinor caught her eye, she felt strangely excited.

Marla noticed that Elinor seldom talked about boy-friends. "Most girls," she observed, "are forever gabbing about boys." Then one evening Elinor took Marla to a gay bar. "For the first time in my life," Marla said, "I felt at home." Elinor had asked her to dance, and she had been ashamed to say she didn't know how. "But Elinor was happy to show me, and it was great fun just being held." They sat at a table by themselves, and soon she was conscious of Elinor's hand grazing hers and then of a foot touching hers under the table. "It sent a delicious feeling through me. I felt that warm-all-over tingle for the first time in my life. And then"—she grimaced—"a couple of creeps came over and asked us to dance."

They were homosexuals, but as far as the girls were concerned, they were still outsiders.

"Dance with men? I should say not," Elinor had said to them contemptuously.

Marla laughed as she recalled the scene. "You should have seen them slink off with their tails drooping."

The encounter seemed to have cleared the air between them. With a surge of excitement, Marla understood now that the next step was up to her. All she had to do was indicate her willingness by a glance, a word, the pressure of a hand.

She smiled, squeezed the other girl's hand, and in ecstacy they took a cab back to their roominghouse. In a matter of hours its bleakness had disappeared and it had become an inviting hacienda full of promise.

She was not disappointed.

She was almost twenty-four then. The coming-out was sealed by an exchange of rings. But even as a novice she understood that it was not a serious relationship but had served the purpose of painlessly introducing her to gay society. "I never again felt as though I was all alone," she told me with a reminiscent glint in her eyes.

She had had only three serious romances—serious enough to involve her emotionally and to jar her. "I lived with one girl for three years in my first serious venture," she said, "but her mother finally broke it up and I moved out lock, stock, and barrel."

Marla laughed hollowly. "That's the last time," she said, "I'll ever put up with a mother-in-law." The relationship had been fine, she said, until her partner's indigent mother moved in with them. "She kept interfering in everything, complaining about everything

I did, until Jeanne had to take sides, and she took her mother's because she would have had to support her anyway."

With the breakup, Marla almost had a nervous breakdown. "If I hadn't had the cats to take care of, I don't know what I would have done." She had taken custody of the four cats they had collected together.

She decided then that she would try the life of a bachelor girl. "I had toyed with the idea that I would like to be taken care of—not that I wanted to be a kept woman or anything like that, but I thought now I might be better off in light housekeeping by myself."

Despite her resolve—and her cats—Marla was still very blue when she shortly thereafter met a well-known lady writer at a party on the Coast, and was immediately bowled over.

"I never in all my life met anybody I admired so much," she recalled enthusiastically. "She had a brilliant mind. She was strong and quite practical and successful, without appearing masculine." Marla was enraptured by this veritable paragon.

"Do you still see her?" I asked.

She shook her head ruefully. "No. I made a fool of myself, and that wound it up."

"What happened?" I asked encouragingly.

She shrugged with a show of stoicism. "It was all pretty one-sided from the beginning. She sensed right away how I felt, and she was quite frank with me. 'I'd like to be friendly,' she told me, 'but I'm deeply in love with somebody else.' She pointed to the woman she had been dancing with earlier in the evening. 'You may not know it,' she said tenderly, 'but Sara is my mistress.'"

Marla was so blinded with love that she didn't care if the older woman had a hundred mistresses. She kept thinking of her and hoping against hope that they would break up. She had nothing to go on, but she kept waiting for her to call. "And then one night late," she related, "I heard a car out front and she was at the door. I could hardly believe it. It seemed too good to be true."

The writer, some twenty years older than Marla, looked tired and disheveled. Her eyes were red from loss of sleep, but to the love-struck bachelor girl, she looked just like what the doctor had ordered.

There was no explanation of why she had dropped in. Queens do not deign explanations for their worshipful subjects.

She stayed for two hours. "But I was so awed," Marla said, "that I was petrified. She must have thought me a cold fish." She sighed. "It was the only time in my life I felt like that. I was just too much in love for my own good."

This puzzled me. "But why should she think you cold when you felt the way you did?"

Marla regarded me stonily. "Do I have to draw you a diagram?" she asked.

"But," I said, understanding dawning, "wasn't this short notice for an intimate relationship?"

Marla guffawed. "I would have done anything she asked, I wanted the relationship so much. But I was just paralyzed."

If the writer had been disappointed, she masked it well. She had been having trouble with her mistress, who had walked off. And now, apparently drinking down her sorrow in the neighborhood, she had dropped by for a momentary respite.

Marla, of course, devised another meeting. This time the writer came over for dinner. Marla had decided to play it cool. She advised the older woman that she had thought it over and decided she couldn't accept anybody she admired so much on a catch-as-you-can basis. She was angling for a permanent situation, but the strategy didn't work. "I have to be honest," the writer told her. "If I can get Sara back, I'll take her any way I can."

As Marla told her story, I wondered why she was so ready to toss away her hard-won independence.

She laughed and tossed her head like a balky mare. "I hadn't got used to the bachelor-girl life yet and was still on the rebound."

The writer hoped to bring about a reconciliation with her girlfriend over the Christmas holidays. But she, too, shrunk from the prospect of being alone. And so, on New Year's Eve, Marla received a conditional invitation to the writer's home on the crest of the Hollywood hills. She was to park her car and wait first to see if Sara arrived. "If I saw Sara's car pull up in the driveway, I was to drive off," she recalled, adding with a laugh, "I didn't wish her any hard luck, but I was praying that she'd get a flat."

When the car arrived, she was so disappointed that after she got home that night she turned to poetry for release. In her loneliness, she sat down and wrote with perhaps more fervor than artistry:

> I got myself burned, and I'll take my
> love where I find it.
> Tall, short, etc., I'll let them all find it,
> But my heart won't be at the scene of the
> crime.
> My heart's in the highlands—in a house
> in the hills.

As Marla recited her little poem to me, she laughed good-naturedly. "I have lots of fun," she said, "even when a romance doesn't work out." Her brow ruffled in a frown as she mused, "I always seem to be in love with somebody who doesn't love me—but isn't that true of everybody?"

Her mood changed quickly and she pointed to a guitar in the corner. "As long as I can sing a song, I know I'm all right." She picked up the guitar and started strumming. "Would you like to hear a little take-off I did?"

I nodded.

In a pleasant voice, she began her parody, which she called "I'm going to sit right down and write my butch a letter."

Breaking off suddenly, she looked up with an apologetic smile. "Can you stand any more? The girls love it, but they're an inside audience."

I smiled cheerful assent. Her voice, I must confess, had the engaging quality of a practiced folk singer.

Again she plunked expertly on her guitar, and resumed her little satire on lesbian life.

When she put the guitar away, I was surprised to notice the

suspicion of a tear. She smiled half sheepishly through misty eyes. "That guitar reminds me of Irene and all the fun we used to have."

Remembering her three romances, I asked, "Is she number three?"

Marla nodded slowly, reminiscing. "We had wonderful times just going for drives, horseback-riding, sitting in front of the fireplace, reciting poetry, and then she'd play the guitar while I sang. It was heavenly."

But it didn't last. Irene, a sales representative, was transferred to a new district in northern California. She had promised to send for Marla as soon as she got located, but her letters kept getting fewer and far between, and then one day came the letter that dashed Marla's hopes. Irene had completely disillusioned her. "She said that if I came to live with her, I'd have to get a job. She could not afford to keep a personal handmaiden or anyone else not worth her salt." Marla laughed bitterly. "I felt like sending her a bill for all the time she stayed with me—as long as she was the one putting our relationship on a business basis." They had been together for six months.

"Do you think she found somebody else?" I asked.

"She may have," Marla said. "You can never tell about these butches. Some are worse than men."

"Did you consider giving up your job and going to her?" I asked.

She shrugged. "How could I? For all I knew, she was just taking this way of discouraging me." She snorted. "What a fine fix I would have been in if I got up there and discovered she really didn't want me. Besides, why should I work all day and then come home and make the meals and do the dishes? That's not love: that's slavery."

But all this was behind Marla now. "I don't know if I'm getting old or weak," she said, "but I finally think I've worked out a way of life for myself. I like my own things. I don't mind getting myself dinner, and if I have a friend in, that can be very pleasant too, so long as she doesn't stay over." She thought a moment. "I've been doing well at the office, and the way things are going, I'll soon have the mortgage paid up. What more can a girl ask?"

Her serenity was unruffled by feelings of guilt, and she had little sympathy for the lesbian who became emotionally worked up over being a lesbian. "I think it's the only way to be," she said lightly.

My memory stirred. "Then why blame your parents?"

"Because I wasted all those years not knowing what I was when I could have been one thing or the other."

"But still," I said, "if you're happy now, you should be grateful to them for what they did."

Her lips tightened. "Whatever they did for me was certainly not planned that way. I was brought up to exclude men from my life and I did just that. They don't deserve any credit." She laughed harshly. "After I was first brought out, I was so quiet, thinking, that the girl in the roominghouse, misunderstanding, kept assuring me that everybody felt bad at first. And all I could think of was, 'Why should I feel bad? For the first time in my life I don't feel alone.'"

Though she resented her parents, she had never come out and told them about herself. "I think they suspected and that was enough for me."

"You mean you wanted them to know?"

Her voice was caustic. "I thought it would do them good to know, but still, I didn't want them to have anything on me." She looked unaccountably angry. "I don't like them," she said. "I never liked them." She almost spat out the words. "Whatever it is I am, they made me." At this point, lesbianism seemed a dubious attribute.

It was getting late, and she had to be up early in the morning for work. She saw me look at my watch. "Too bad it's so late," she said. "I have a few more parodies in the old kit bag, but they'll keep." With another lightning change of mood, she strummed an imaginary guitar and hummed with zest:

"Oh, to go on a hike
With a tall, athletic dike."

She broke off with a laugh, and her spirits seemed immediately restored. She looked like a young girl again.

She walked me to the edge of her garden, the four cats trailing behind, rustling against her legs. "Watch out going down those hills," she said, smiling. "Ninety-nine per cent of our accidents are people."

Two weeks later, still thinking of Marla, I was having cocktails with a lovely blonde. She too was a virgin and apparently proud of it. She was also a bachelor girl. Through her, I thought I had got to know Marla better. She seemed the same type of lesbian.

Ann was a few years younger than Marla, twenty-five at the most, and even slacks and a short hair-do could not minimize her fresh good looks. When the subject of lesbian virginity came up at a lesbian party, she had told me with a quizzical smile, "I think I can tell you how a girl can be a virgin and still enjoy life."

She had turned up for our appointment in Berkeley, California, with a girl-friend who was as unfeminine as Ann was feminine. In fact, I had to look twice to make sure the friend wasn't male. Her hair was trimmed to the contour of her head, her face was thin and sallow, her skin coarse, and her voice neutral. But her name was Kitty.

As we sat on a patio overlooking the San Francisco Bay area, she coolly discussed her reasons for talking to me. "I was afraid," she said, "that you might get the idea that lesbians didn't get a kick out of gay life. I for one find it very stimulating. I like all the byplay, the activity in the bars, the butches making their plays—it's exciting. Some of it is rough and dirty, of course, but there is even a ribald humor about this if you can view it all with detachment."

She spoke with the clipped accent of the well-educated. She had a master's degree and a doctorate in the arts. She had taught school for a while and then worked as a probation worker, but she had given it up because she couldn't maintain even the semblance of straight life and still express herself. "One wrong move," she said, "and it would have meant disgrace and jail."

Feeling that too many eyes were on her, she finally left the ticklish probation job, but she had no regrets about taking the big step out of the heterosexual world. "For the first time in my life," she said, "I know what it's like to be a woman and do as I damn please."

With promised backing, she was now considering opening a lesbian bar in one of San Francisco's broad-minded suburbs. "If I enjoy myself as much behind the bar as I have in front of it," she said with an easy smile, "it should be a lot of fun."

Thinking this hardly a ladylike pursuit, I pointed out, "The majority of people would say that you were living a mockery of a woman's life even if you are doing as you please."

She smiled equably, crossing her smartly trousered legs. "I'm quite aware of that, and of course that's what plagues so many of us before we take the crucial step. We're cursed with the majority view of ourselves."

Without actually living a lesbian life, she had been a secret lesbian for two or three years. Yet, though she got occasional satisfaction out of a clandestine relationship, she did not really begin to appreciate being a lesbian until her recent headlong plunge into the strange milieu of lesbian bars, homosexual parties, and the sporty resort areas around San Francisco.

Bar life particularly intrigued her. "There's a way of functioning in a bar if you're a femme or a butch," she said with a grin. "I generally sit on a bar stool, smoke a cigarette, but never look directly at anybody. The first thing you know, out of the corner of your eye you can see the interest beginning to form among the butches. And the more aloof and unattainable you seem, the more interested they get, without directly revealing it." She laughed. "It's like a spider waiting for the flies to buzz around, and finally the right fly tumbles over into the web and gets snagged."

Even the butches played the game. "Normally the interested butch will start talking to the person you're with—generally another femme—and slowly draw you into the conversation," Ann

related brightly, looking to her almost forgotten friend for confirmation.

There were other approaches, and Ann knew all about them.
"When the girls get up and dance, even when twisting they make
signs with their hands like dialing a phone, as though it were part
of the dance, or they wave their arms like they were throwing out
a lasso." Ann laughed. "If you wanted to, you could very easily
be caught."

She liked subtlety. Head-on approaches were enough to make
the woman in her recoil. "I don't like these butches coming on
full blast," she said, "sort of bumper-to-bumper. It takes all the
fun out of it." She turned to Kitty and mentioned an aggressive
red-haired girl they had just met. "She came up to me the other
night at a party and, without any preliminaries, started to tell me
what she was going to do to me." Ann laughed derisively. "I
just turned my back on her. There's no point to that kind of
language, and, besides, I can decide perfectly well for myself whom
I want."

Kitty nodded sympathetically, agreeing in placid tones that the
redhead had been out of order. "She was all over the place," she
said primly. "She even had her knee in my back once."

"Oh, kneesies," Ann said with a little laugh. "I wouldn't put
anything past that one."

I regarded the two friends curiously—Kitty as attentive as a beau
on his first date with a queen, and Ann, poised and relaxed, talking
about butches as serenely as she would about her beau back home
in Salt Lake City.

"How long have you two known each other?" I asked.

Kitty looked at Ann for confirmation. "Let me see," she said,
"it's been two months, hasn't it?"

Ann smiled. "I think so."

I wondered how far along they were. "Well, are you two living
together?" I asked.

Kitty looked flustered, while Ann only smiled pleasantly. "We're
still in the preliminary stages of our courtship," Ann said evenly.

She seemed to be evading the question. "Well, has anything happened?"

"It all depends on what you call 'happened.'" Ann was plainly amused. "Just a few preliminaries, as I said: nothing more. We're in the exploratory phase. We're trying to find out how we'll get on with each other. I don't want any traumatic partings with violent upheavals and all that sort of thing."

I turned to Kitty. "And how do you feel about it? Do you need more time to make sure how you stand?"

She shook her head quickly. "Oh, no," she said, "I'm satisfied, but," she added hastily, "whatever Ann wants, it's up to her. She knows exactly how I feel." Her voice was softly ingratiating.

Ann was still regarding me with amusement.

"You mentioned the other night that you were a virgin," I said. "That applies only with men, I assume."

"You assume correctly," she said.

"Then, how many lesbian relationships have you had?"

She hesitated. "Three or five, depending on how you look at it."

I waited for her to elaborate.

"Well, there were three that meant something and there were two brief episodes."

"But I thought you liked long, pleasant courtships."

"Oh, she does," Kitty said quickly.

"But how about those brief interludes?"

Ann appeared ruffled for the first time. "Well," she said reluctantly, "I had been drinking."

"Both times?" I said.

She nodded. "Both times."

"And you met these girls at bars?"

She nodded.

"But don't you always drink at bars?" I said. "What was so different in these cases?"

She laughed sheepishly. "I guess I drank more than I should." She had never seen either of the girls again. They were, in her own words, one-night stands.

I took a new tack. "Have you ever considered," I said, "that most men would find you very attractive?"

She seemed puzzled, and a little on guard. "I suppose so."

"And what makes you so sure you wouldn't respond to a man you found attractive?"

"I never have," she said.

"But suppose you were out with a man and drank too much?"

She grinned broadly. "I make sure I never drink with a man."

"What are you afraid of?" I asked.

She shrugged. "Why waste myself?"

I recalled Josie, the girl with the double standard on virginity, and asked Ann if she shared Josie's views.

She sneered. "Josie's a damn fool. I don't even think she's a lesbian. She's just in it for kicks." She turned to Kitty. "You don't know this one. She's one of those big, baby-blue-eyed femmes without a brain in her head. When she gets tired of the lesbian kick, she's going to wind up with a husband and three kids."

As I had with Marla and Josie, I asked how she could anticipate how she would react sexually to any men without actually putting her femininity to the test. It was purely a rhetorical question.

Ann smiled. "Whenever a man touches me," she said, "I feel as though he were crawling all over me." She shuddered slightly.

Kitty spoke up approvingly. "That's a very nice way of putting it, dear."

Ann's blue eyes regarded me patiently. "I'm afraid," she said, "I don't fit into your pattern of what the lesbian bachelor girl should be like, but I don't think there is any pattern."

"Most of the lesbian bachelor girls I've encountered," I pointed out, "just don't want anything to do with men."

"A lot of other lesbians feel the same way," she countered.

"But not as rigidly," I rejoined, "nor does their independence mean as much to them."

She was unimpressed.

I wondered how her family background compared with Marla's.

"I loved my parents," she said. "They were kind and generous to me."

And what could have been the possible genesis of her lesbianism? "Did you have any unpleasant experiences with men as a child?" I asked.

"Just the usual boys making nuisances of themselves—pressing against you and things like that."

"Which parent did you prefer?"

"I was closer to my mother. She was the stronger of my parents, but they were both wonderful to me. I hated to hurt them."

"Then why did you?" I asked rather shortly.

She shrugged. "I couldn't go on the way I was. I was being stifled."

At an age when other girls were beginning to think about boys, she first began to wonder about herself. She preferred the company of girls, and was very friendly with one girl at school until the girl's family sent her off to boarding school. But no realization of her true nature crystallized at this time, since she had no way of making comparisons. But as she grew older, entering college, her suspicions took tangible form. She walked around the campus with Havelock Ellis' scholarly study on homosexuality wrapped nondescriptly in oilcloth, and buried her nose in its edifying pages. She shunned physical education—the gym classes —because she felt like a peeping Tom. "I didn't dare acknowledge to myself what I was at this point," she recalled. "And I was afraid that the other girls would sense that I was watching them as though I were a boy."

With Havelock Ellis as a barometer, she studied herself, analyzing her own reactions, hoping that she was perhaps passing through a phase of ambisexual adolescence. She had been reared in a Mormon home, with its usual emphasis on marriage and children. "Lesbianism is particularly difficult for a Mormon," she explained, "because Mormons believe their children are sealed to them in heaven after death." And so she brooded through many sleepless hours, hating herself for what she now knew she was, and thinking darkly of suicide. "What I was," she told me, "society found despicable, and my religion damnable. There were only two courses open—suicide or adjustment."

She was young and healthy, and she adjusted. Thinking back on the girl who had first attracted her as a teen-ager, she telephoned her one night and said bluntly, "I think I'm a homosexual." She was then twenty-one, and felt she had to do something about herself.

The other girl, as Ann had intuitively surmised, had already taken the step. She was not surprised at the confidence, but cautioned Ann to be more careful on the phone. They met to talk things over, and her friend introduced Ann to a whole new world —girls she saw every day whom she had never dreamed as being anything but normal. The two, however, didn't pick up the threads of their adolescent friendship, since the mutual interest had not survived the years of separation. "We were two entirely different people," Ann explained.

As she moved in her new circles, Ann got an education in how lesbianism operated clandestinely behind the scenes. "There was no bar life for girls in our city," she said, "and I would have wanted to protect my family, anyway." But there were bowling parties and Saturday-night beer parties, skiing parties and golf parties—all available to the socially elite and well-to-do.

In due time she was brought out by a friend of her friend. The friendship endured for three years, with the two girls working for their doctorates together. But after they had finished up their college work in a large Midwestern city, they found themselves drifting apart. And the other girl, as was so often the case, had a new interest.

Ann decided to head alone for the tolerant climate of California, but felt an obligation to first see her mother. "I felt that I owed her the truth about myself." It had been a rough decision for her to make.

She told her story as delicately as possible, but her mother didn't believe it. "She kept telling me I was only going through a stage," Ann recalled. But Ann finally convinced her, showing her the correspondence she had exchanged with her friend over the years. The resulting shock was so great that her mother's hair turned completely white in three days.

"It was the most difficult thing I ever had to do," Ann said, "but I knew that once I cut those ties, I was on my own—with no family to fall back on."

I had not seen what was gained. "Did you realize," I said, "that the pain you inflicted could never be repaired? Why couldn't you have just gone off and left them in blissful ignorance?"

It seemed like the simplest solution. But Ann could not see it that way.

"I had to tell them: it was the least I could do." She was adamant.

"All you did was hurt them," I pointed out.

She did not agree. "I loved them. Think of all they did for me—a child not even their own."

I hadn't realized that Ann was not their own child. "Perhaps you resented the fact that they weren't your real parents," I said.

"Not any more so than any other adopted child."

I was about to pursue the point when Kitty, whom I had lost sight of, cut in. "What Ann says sounds reasonable," she said. "Having made her decision, she wanted to start off with a clean slate."

Her mother had asked only one favor of her—that she not tell her father. Ann had agreed. When she took a last lingering look at her mother, she almost relented. Her mother looked old and broken. But Ann resolutely turned her head and strode out of the house for the last time. "In the final analysis," she now told me solemnly, "our greatest obligation is to live a life of the greatest self-expression. And that, essentially, was the choice I made."

Ann was drawn to California by the climate—both sociologically and meteorologically. It was warm and receptive. She taught for a while and then applied for probation-department work in a small town near Los Angeles. She felt an impulse to work with the underdog.

She was not completely ready to compromise with society— not even for a job. For her job appointment she wore a dark, severe suit, combed her hair back short, and used only lipstick. Her eyebrows were so light that they blended with the golden tone of her skin, but she refused to apply an eyebrow pencil. She was bursting with principles and was half hoping that she would be accepted for what she knew herself to be. She told herself she hated deception.

The town fathers were favorably impressed by Ann's credentials and her obvious refinement. It was clear that she came from a good family. After the routine formal interrogation, which she handled with brisk efficiency, the head of the interviewing committee asked her to remain behind after the others left. With a sinking sensation, she stood poised for his first question. He gave her a penetrating look. "Young lady," he said, "I only want to ask one last question." His keen eyes probed her face. "Do you intend to live alone?"

She nodded slowly, comprehending the full implications of the question and the discerning yet tolerant mind that had framed it.

He seemed almost relieved.

"All right," he said, "that settles it. You will be notified of your appointment in a few days." He shook hands warmly. "I know," he said, "that you will do nothing to abuse my confidence." There was no doubt in her mind as to what he meant.

But he was not the only hurdle she had to get over. She had been on the job less than a week when she became aware that she was the center of controversy among her male colleagues. "They stopped whispering," she recalled, "and looked away whenever I happened to draw near."

Then one day they took the situation in hand. A young probation worker approached her in a visible embarrassment. "Some of us," he said awkwardly, "drew straws to see who'd brace you. I drew the short straw."

She waited stolidly as he mustered his courage. "What we wanted to know," he said at last with a lame smile, "was whether you use perfume or cologne?" His face had turned a beet red, and he looked as though he would like nothing better than to vanish on the spot.

She regarded him with a faintly ironic look. "Tell them," she said, "that I use both, but prefer cologne."

"Thank you," he said, "that's what we thought." And he hastily wheeled and fled down the hall.

She smiled now as she thought of it. "They were always polite and helpful from that point on," she said, "but they never bothered asking me out, not even the ones who weren't married."

While she was on the job, her attitude and deportment were impeccable. She knew, for instance, that lesbians in the Los Angeles area often wore green on Thursdays as a secret sign, but she deliberately avoided that color on that day; she knew, too, that many lesbians sometimes fingered their right eyebrow, but she neither used this signal nor reacted to it. She was determined to prove her capacity for the job—lesbian or not. And she was too proud to risk exposure.

Even so, she again felt suffocated. She dared not be seen at any of the better known Los Angeles queer bars, and the few on the outskirts were filled with diesel-type butches, whom she abhorred. "They were more weird than lesbian," she decided. And she still never knew who she might run into in one of these bars.

Occasionally she exchanged flickers of recognition with a teacher, and once surprised the delinquent girls in her care winking behind her back. Some of the wayward minors began closing the door after them as they came in for their interviews. She would deliberately reopen it and blandly regard them as though she was completely unaware of what was going on. "The delinquents would have just loved to get something on their probation worker," she said.

Her decision to leave, stirred by her feeling of confinement, was facilitated too by the attitude of the probation department's attorneys toward offending homosexuals. "They seemed to think," she said, "that they should all be drowned, and they virtually said so in court."

There were regrets when she left, because she had done a good job, but she would have been less than observing if she hadn't also noticed the sighs of relief.

She had been in San Francisco for six months now, long enough for a romance with a large, attractive butch from Seattle. "She swept me off my feet," Ann conceded, "literally." She laughed. "She weighs two hundred and twenty-five pounds and is stronger than any truck driver."

"She sounds monstrous," I said.

"Oh, no," said Ann defensively. "As Kitty will tell you, I can't stand stompin' butches. But Connie is only superficially a diesel. Actually, she's quite sensitive and comes from a top-drawer family. She has a very feminine face, but it's very difficult to be dainty when you're that large."

The romance was already fading, accounting for Kitty's being on the premises, but Ann still had a soft spot for her fat friend.

They had quarreled over money, and Connie, who was used to having her own way, had decided she would like to terminate the relationship.

"She was always gambling away our money," Ann said, "and I finally got fed up. So one night, as we were lying quite peacefully, she announced that she preferred single life. She accused me of putting her down in front of other people. I pointed out that I had to protest her gambling away our money or we'd be out on the street." She smiled grimly. "The money was all mine, anyway. I just let Connie hold it because it made her feel important."

They were still friendly, sharing the same quarters, and therefore Ann's relationship with Kitty was being held in abeyance, pending Connie's next move, literally.

"If she moved soon," Kitty said, looking protectively at Ann, "it might facilitate matters for us."

Ann regarded her prospective partner doubtfully. "I don't want to hurry Connie," she said gently.

"Of course not, dear," Kitty said. "I was only stating the problem. I only hope she finds a new roommate."

Meanwhile, Ann was full of her plans for her proposed lesbian bar.

"All you have to do is keep the bar sloppy and have a corner for the baby butches and motorcycle set, who come stompin' in with their leather jackets and buy a drink every now and then for the pretty femmes. They're the big attraction."

Kitty looked at her friend admiringly. "Doesn't she have a wonderful way of expressing herself?" she said.

"And what are your plans for Kitty?" I asked Ann.

As Kitty tried to look casual, Ann replied, "Oh, I think we might work together. I could handle the bar and Kitty the tables."

"Will that still leave you a bachelor girl?" I wondered.

Ann laughed. "I don't think there's much chance of my being anything but a bachelor girl." She patted her golden hair nonchalantly. "But I suppose I'll have to do something. Ever since Connie and I had our disagreement, every butch I meet wants to come home with me." She looked wryly at Kitty. "The next time I make a mistake, it's going to be one I can control."

Kitty purred complaisantly.

In a way, Ann reminded me of what Marla must have been like ten or fifteen years earlier. They were both independent, spirited women, totally immune to men. And yet, because she was older and had seen more of the world, Marla was more cautious and reserved. When I next saw her again, almost a year later, she had recently returned from visiting in the East. As she made us tea in her snug little kitchen, she mentioned casually that a friend, a wealthy woman her own age, had sent the plane ticket for the trip. "I made sure," she said, "that it was for both ways."

Though she had a good time, Marla was anxious to get back home. "In five years," she said, "I'll be eligible for a pension, so why should I give all that up to live at the beck and call of somebody else?"

"Did she want you to stay with her?" I asked.

"Oh, yes," she said, offering me the sugar, "she had it all planned. But I told her it wouldn't work. I didn't love her." She laughed mirthlessly. "And I don't think I ever will love anybody enough. It's a little late in the day for all that."

She fondly stroked a cat which had jumped into her lap. "He's a newcomer," she said. "I have three more babies." She now had seven cats in all, and several of them were walking stiff-legged around the house, watching me with their curiously unblinking eyes. Only one cat was a male, and he had been neutered.

"Is there any reason," I asked, "why you don't have a dog?"

"Oh, I like dogs too," she said, "but they're rather docile for pets." She laughed. "They do whatever you tell them." She reached over and fondled one of the purring animals. "Now, you take a cat: they're independent, and have minds of their own. They're still untamed."

As one of the cats jumped into my lap, I could feel its claws sink into my flesh. And, looking at Marla, I suddenly understood why cats appealed to so many lesbians. "Yes," I agreed, "they are very much untamed."

She smiled roguishly. "And I suppose," she said, "you would like to add just like me."

10

THE GENDARMES

"In all my thirty-five years in the force," the head of the vice squad told me, "we've never arrested a woman for being a lesbian." He shook his grizzled head. "They're not like the faggots. They could be living together and you wouldn't know any different." The corners of his mouth drooped. "What the hell would you do with them," he demanded, "if you did pull them in?"

"You certainly arrest plenty of male homosexuals," I said.

"Oh, that's because they're around cruising and generally flaunting themselves. But these girls don't bother anybody that don't want to be bothered. And"—his eyebrows lifted significantly— "they're not after children."

He seemed genuinely embarrassed talking about lesbians, yet he had arrested hundreds of women as common prostitutes without batting an eye.

"I was after the madams," he explained, "who live off these girls." A curious smile came into his eyes. "Come to think of it, some madams are friendlier with their girls than the girls are with the customers. Maybe that's how they keep them in line."

One well-known madam had won fame as the Virgin Madam after her arrest had resulted in a routine medical examination.

"Her girls used to be wild about her," the police official recalled, with an incredulous grin. "They all wanted to be the favorite."

As he saw it, it was all a social problem. "The police," he said, "are innocent bystanders."

"Then why keep closing so many of these lesbian bars?" I asked.

He shrugged wearily. "Because of newspapermen and do-gooders, who stick their noses into these places, enjoy them, and then run to City Hall or the cops."

Only that week he had raided a well-known mixed bar—male homosexuals and lesbians—not far from New York's Greenwich Village.

"And what does that solve?" I asked.

He grimaced. "It just gets the critics off our backs." It was a concession to a crusading columnist who had demanded the shuttering of the queer bars as an affront to society. "So we close them," he said, "and the queers go where we can't keep an eye on them, or flock to some other bar until we close that." He sighed. "Actually, I'm the first to admit I don't know what it's all about. And"—he wrinkled his nose—"I don't want to know."

He looked at me with a twinkle in his pale blue eyes. "Why don't you discuss it with the policewomen? They work with the girls." He waved an eloquent hand. "Maybe they understand it."

In other cities the lesbian problem, if it could be called that, was equally embarrassing to police who had no embarrassment about male homosexuals. While openly contemptuous of the males, whom they delighted in harassing, they had never formulated any clear-cut attitude about their female counterparts. In San Francisco some nine girls were picked up in a raid on a homosexual bar that netted seventy men. But virtually all charges were dismissed, and none of the girls was booked as a lesbian. And the California Supreme Court upheld the right of bars to serve lesbians.

Despite a roving "Homosexual Squad," it was so difficult for a lesbian to get arrested in San Francisco that lesbians laugh about the lesbian who vainly tried to get herself jailed. After a row with her girl-friend, a high-strung lesbian who considered herself jilted flung herself at a policeman in the street and shouted, "Arrest me, I'm a lesbian."

The officer looked at her indifferently. "Go home," he said, "and sleep it off." And he strolled off, leaving her to think of some other way of making her girl-friend "suffer."

One lesbian did manage to get arrested in this homosexual haven on a morals charge brought by parents of a teen-age girl. But this was unique. "Generally," another lesbian observed dryly, "parents are happy to forget such incidents, figuring that whatever happened, their daughter has lost none of her value where it counts—on the marriage mart."

In Los Angeles, police were equally indifferent to lesbians. Lesbian bars were numerous, and in one particularly, the antics of the participants left little to the imagination. "They do everything," a sensitive lesbian observed, "that darkness will permit." In this tolerant atmosphere, lesbianism flourished openly, and nobody was excited about it except a few male homosexuals who wanted equal rights.

The lesbian colony in sunny Southern California, favoring shorts rather than slacks, could recall but a single arrest over the years which was directly related to lesbianism, and even in this case police action was accidental. "Two girls were parked on a lonely road in the Hollywood hills," a lesbian recalled with relish, "when a policeman poked his searchlight into the car. He was so flabbergasted that he trundled them off to the station before he knew what he was doing."

In 1960, when the Daughters of Bilitis held their first national convention in San Francisco at a popular downtown hotel, the Homosexual Squad reconnoitered the convention curiously. But after scanning the list of lecturing clergy, sociologists, and psychologists, the gendarmes quietly disappeared. "We tried to get them to sit through the sessions," a D.O.B. officer reported dryly, "but they weren't interested."

As a relatively secure group, the lesbians in Southern California have frequently thrown in their support with the male homosexuals. In the legal crusade to outlaw peepholes in public rest rooms, they were in the forefront, defending the homosexual's constitutional right to privacy.

To lesbians, there was nothing mysterious about the easier lot of the female homosexual. "Regardless of what we do," one lesbian pointed out, "the police still regard us as women, while they look on the males as degenerates who have disgraced their own sex."

As an example, a lesbian who was pushed on the chest by a policeman breaking up a fight between her and her girl-friend turned on the cop furiously. "Don't you dare touch me," she cried. "I may be a lesbian, but I'm still a woman." The officer retreated hastily from the unequal fight.

Even among policewomen there was an uneasy tolerance for their sisters under the skin. Some were uncomfortable around them, but none felt that special disdain reserved for the male homosexual. Although they covered many lesbian bars and night clubs, the policewomen of the nation's largest city could not re-call—just as the veteran police official couldn't—a single lesbian arrest for homosexuality. Women had been picked up for dancing on illegal premises, for disorderly conduct, for breach of peace—but not for homosexuality. Significantly, officers could not even hazard a guess as to how a female homosexuality charge would go down in the court records, though all were familiar with the dreary list, ranging from sodomy to pederasty, arrayed against the male homosexual.

By the very secret nature of their relationships, lesbians offered less of a problem, being neither as promiscuous nor as open. "Most pick-ups for male homosexuality," a New York police-woman pointed out, "were made in parks, public rest rooms, bars, well-known 'cruise' areas—like Third Avenue or Times Square—but the lesbians don't go in for public cruising."

"Unlike the male homosexual," the policewoman explained, "they will not usually take up with just anybody at a moment's notice or leave themselves open to rebuffs. Their feelings are far more easily bruised, particularly those of the femme who will quickly crawl into her shell the moment she encounters indifference."

The policewomen, too, privately thought it absurd to keep closing and opening lesbian bars. "But," the chief policewoman told me, "we do have to make it difficult for them to congregate, or we might be inundated."

"Do you think there are that many?" I asked.

She shrugged. "Who can tell? They're not nearly as obvious as the boys."

"You can tell those butch haircuts—D.A., they call them—and the men's slacks, shirts, and boots."

She laughed. "I'm not thinking of the butch or dike type: they make a point of advertising what they are, but they're a small minority."

"Have you ever arrested any?"

"Oh, yes, but not for lesbianism. I've picked up a few butches for disorderly conduct, and they're real sassy, but I guess that's part of being rebellious, or whatever it is that they feel."

I wondered if she thought of lesbians as glandular cases.

"The butch type may be," she said, "but not the others. They may go either way, depending on the circumstances."

"What circumstances?"

"Individual pressures and things like that. In schools, youth shelters, and prisons, the pressure from the older girls is tremendous. In one junior high school the older girls waited outside the school and pounced on the prettier younger ones, practically carrying them off and indoctrinating them."

"What are the teachers and parents doing while this goes on?"

She smiled. "Doing what they usually do: keeping their heads safely in the sand."

"Does this make lesbians of the victimized kids?" I asked.

She frowned. "Oh, it gives them a certain ambivalence that permits them to swing either way, and it certainly breaks down moral barriers."

She looked up with a smile as a young, fresh-faced woman came in briskly and stood tentatively at her desk. With her well-scrubbed outdoor look, she could have passed for a pretty post-deb or a woman's golf champ. The older woman introduced her casually. "She's one of the brightest officers we have in the department," she said, "and has had recent experience in this field."

"What field is that?" the newcomer asked.

"Lesbians," her superior said succinctly.

The girl's nose wrinkled in faint distaste. "I'm no authority," she said. "I don't think there is one."

"But you've been around them quite a bit," her superior said. She nodded in my direction. "And it's all off the record—no names. He would just like to know what's going on in the police area."

She rang for another policewoman, a slightly older girl who had covered some of the institutions. "Maybe between these two you'll get what you're looking for," she said.

I permitted myself a smile. "I don't know what I'm looking for."

Another policewoman soon strode in. She looked like a suburban housewife. She was well turned out, down to smartly manicured nails, conservative make-up, neatly brushed-back hair, and a long-sleeved dress with a hemline just below the knees. Both girls were bright and articulate when we sat around later and discussed the problem.

"I didn't know what a lesbian was until three and a half years ago," the younger girl, May, said. "I had just come over from the Police Academy three or four weeks before when one of the inspectors called me in and said he wanted me to help them close up a lesbian joint. I guess I looked a little vague, because he started to explain, and before he got through with his explanation we were both blushing."

Even so, May was very much in the dark about what she was expected to do.

"Just sit at the bar, look pretty, and watch what's going on. If anybody makes a pass at you, all the better."

"And then what happens?" she asked.

"We'll send a couple of men around to make the pinch."

"Okay," May had said gamely, "and if I'm not back in a couple of hours, send them in anyway."

With mixed feelings she sauntered into a Village bar, sporting her best hat and coat, camped on a bar stool, and ordered a daiquiri while inspecting the dark recesses of the smoke-filled room out of the corner of her eye.

There were some twenty or twenty-five girls scattered around the room and one male, a homosexual bartender. Some were at the bar, others at small tables or dancing around the juke box in the back. Although nobody appeared to have noticed her, she felt every pair of eyes covertly appraising her.

They obviously figured her for anything but a policewoman. She might be a square who slipped in by mistake to sop up Village atmosphere, or, as seemed likely, a curiosity-seeker flirting with a problem of her own. Meanwhile, she was being left pretty much to herself.

In her survey of the dimly lit room, her sharp eye caught all shades of femininity. There were several butch types, clearly recognizable from the inspector's descriptions. She also spotted two of the most beautiful young women she had ever seen, in or out of the fashion magazines or the films. They were breathtaking. "One of the girls was a blonde with large blue eyes, a turned-up nose, and the fresh, sun-kissed look of a girl who had just stepped off the tennis court." The other was a cool-looking brunette who looked crisply aloof and unattainable.

As she watched, a butch in a stormtrooper's jacket stomped over, flung her arms around the blonde, and marched her off to the juke box. "Pretty soon they were fondling each other," the policewoman recalled with a blush. "You'd have to see it to believe it."

"What do you mean, 'fondling?'" I asked.

"Like a man would a woman."

"Could you be more explicit?" I asked.

She looked at the older policewoman. "Tell him," the latter drawled good-naturedly. "He's a growing boy."

"Well, both above and below, if you know what I mean."

"Were you disgusted?" I asked.

"Not really. I think I was too surprised. And while this blonde was carrying on in one corner, her brunette friend was enjoying the same in another corner."

The lack of circumspection in the presence of a stranger was somewhat puzzling. "Didn't anybody, not even the bartender, consider for a moment that you might not belong?"

"Apparently not," she said, "but that wouldn't be surprising, since I hadn't been a policewoman very long."

"Well, they obviously didn't think you were a lesbian, since nobody came near you."

"I almost forgot," May said. "One rather attractive woman about thirty-five came over to the bar, put her hand under my chin, looked me in the eye, and said, 'I don't know you.'"

"And then what?" I asked.

"And then she walked away without giving me another look."

"What was the reason for all that?"

May laughed. "I guess she was testing me, but she still didn't make a definite pitch. I thought she was just an odd-ball." But later, with more experience, she knew better. "I could have said 'I know you' or 'You know me now' or something like that, anything that would have picked up her remark. But I just sat still, waiting for her to come out and take the lead."

May had entered the bar a few minutes after eleven, an hour when lesbian spots are usually beginning to wake up. She had previously checked her service revolver and identification papers at headquarters, and carried only her shield, pinned inside her dress. "I was taking no chances on being taken for a cop," she said.

"But suppose you met with resistance?"

"There wasn't much chance of any trouble like that, since the plain-clothes men were scheduled to drop around in a couple of hours, entering on my signal."

She left the room only once, to visit the ladies' room, where she surprised a "couple" in a clandestine embrace. "Rather odd, this privacy," she observed, "since they were doing much more on the dance floor."

As the appointed hour approached, she was warily watching the door. Eventually she noticed two burly men on the walk peering into the bar. She nodded sharply twice, as prearranged, and the two came hurtling in. As they burst into the room, there was a flurry of activity and the bartender quickly began to usher the dancers toward a rear exit. "Here, you," he shouted at May in a high falsetto, "you better come out the back. Can't you see the police are raiding the place?"

"I am the police," May called out, "and you're under arrest."

Technically, the raid was a success. The proprietors were charged with permitting unlicensed dancing and were closed for a year.

"Did you have any trouble getting a conviction?" I asked May.

"A little," May said. "The owners had a smart lawyer, and he tried to trip me up."

In court, she had described how the butches had lounged around in men's clothing, with male haircuts, and had conducted themselves generally as men would with loose women. She was describing one butch in particular when the defense attorney suddenly cut in. "And how do you know this so-called woman wasn't a man, since you have certainly pictured him a man in mannerism and appearance?"

The judge showed his first interest. May thought fast. "If I had described the distinction in skin tone or the difference in voice, I knew the whole thing might deteriorate into a tiresome debate, with the judge getting bored and throwing the case out."

She laughed reminiscently as the courtroom scene flashed through her mind. "So I smiled sweetly, thinking of the judge but addressing the lawyer. 'Sir,' I said, 'there was no doubt in my mind because there was none in the minds of your clients.'"

The lawyer was patently annoyed. "Please clarify yourself," he said.

"Well, sir," May replied, "they all went into the ladies' room, even though the men's room was right next door, and if it was good enough for them, it's good enough for me." The judge nodded wisely, and the case was won.

The second policewoman had been following the discussion with interest. "Over the years," she said, "I've become convinced that among themselves, lesbians have as many variations as other women. The most beautiful and the ugliest girls are lesbians, the smartest and the silliest, the richest and the poorest, from good homes and from bad."

"Does their noticeable activity follow any pattern?" I asked.

She shrugged. "It's hard to tell, but among the younger ones it's often a matter of being antisocial." She looked up inquiringly. "Have you ever been to a youth house?"

I shook my head.

"What goes on in these detention centers for girls would make a book in itself. Packs of them, like hungry wolves, just sit and wait for the newcomers, and then they tear after them."

"Suppose the girls resist?"

She smiled thinly. "They overcome their resistance. Two or three will overpower their victim and get their way with them."

She turned to the younger policewoman. "Some of these social agencies discourage police visits, but you've been in there, haven't you?"

The younger nodded. "I've seen them nuzzling one another openly on their cots while the matrons are standing right there watching them."

"How can that happen?" I asked.

"They've got to be with it."

"You mean part of it?"

She shrugged. "Some of the matrons look more like men than men do. Have you seen their arms?"

The young inmates were institutionalized not as lesbians but as delinquents, narcotics users, prostitutes, rebels against nearly every convention. And yet many were already on the road to lesbianism when they finally checked out of the shelters.

Many girls had advised me that their first experience—and knowledge—of lesbianism had come in girls' corrective schools. "I was fourteen," one former inmate of a city shelter told me, "when this girl leaned over and kissed me." It was no more than a kiss, but she found the experience pleasant—at an age when it made a lasting impression.

In some adult institutions, women have charged that at least half the prison population were lesbians, while virtually all the remaining population participated somehow in lesbian relationships during these "school days."

One graduate drew a graphic picture of what happens when they leave it to the girls. "For some girls," noted a former schoolteacher doing time in Manhattan's House of Detention, for prostitution, "jail is the best place to enjoy themselves fully. They couldn't begin to have as much fun on the outside." Prison guards, she said, turned their heads indifferently as the inmates cavorted happily with each other. But the teacher turned prostitute was sympathetic. "Why stop it?" she agreed. "It kept the lid from blowing off the place."

Many inmates had husbands and boy-friends, whom they discussed fondly, but these weren't available. Meanwhile, the girls had built up a substitute life, designed for a no man's land. They even had a jargon of their own. The butches, dominating the femmes, were known as Jailhouse Daddies, and they liked their girls jailhouse sharp.

And what was "jailhouse sharp?" "Having a uniform so starched," the ex-teacher explained, "that it would stand up by itself." Also included were fancy cosmetics, or equivalents, that taxed the femmes' ingenuity. "For mascara," she said, "we used black tempera paint; for eye shadow, green tempera and cold cream." Lipstick could be picked up in the prison commissary.

Two girls conveniently occupied each cell, but public dating was popular. "The girls," she recalled fondly, "would date each other for the prison movies on Saturday nights or they'd visit after dinner before lights out, a two-hour interval."

There was none of the compulsion reported in institutions for juveniles. "For the few who didn't want to," she said, "nobody bothered them. But practically everybody is compatible—temporarily, anyway—once they're in jail, even if they're not really lesbians. I met married women, in jail for thirty days, who had a ball with other girls and then went eagerly home to their husbands."

Converts learned, too, of the places they could meet girls like the ones they had met in prison. And when they got out of stir, despite boy-friends or husbands, many found their way to the Greenwich Village bars. For the first time in the history of American bars and joints, the lesbian was going a-cruising.

Like the rest of the female world, she was finally branching out on her own, ready for anybody who was equally ready.

BARS AND COUNTRY CLUBS

For many lesbians, the gay bars were a combination town- and country-club. While some preferred an all-girl bar, others would often settle for a mixed homosexual bar, where they could count on not being bothered.

In these bars, in their own way, as loners, they often made friends and influenced people—and not all of these friends were women. But just as often as not, they would take their own girl-friends to their lesbian haunts, sharing together the excitement of being exclusively with their own kind.

From Key West to San Francisco, these bars were the show-cases for some of the most startling beauties and the plainest Janes. In some bars, men could not enter unescorted by women; others were teeming with male curiosity-seekers, sailors and Johns, subtly excited by a sexual challenge they did not even begin to understand.

Hard-jawed bouncers guarded the door at some lesbian spots, keeping out unwelcome males or routing them to distant tables where they would not disturb the girls. Each place was a little different. I have seen bars jammed with a hundred females all wearing slacks and shirts, and others where lesbians were as well dressed and groomed as any model stepping out of the pages of the fashion magazines. And often, ironically, it was that very model.

It was not unusual to find lesbian barmaids toiling in lesbian-owned bars, whereas in the male homosexual bars, the operating homosexuals were generally only a front.

Many of the bars, deliberately bleak to discourage passing trade, operated back rooms in which the lesbian clientele, okayed by the bartenders, could dance, drink, and otherwise cavort to the endless music of the juke box.

The dancing was often cheek to cheek and "bumper-to-bumper," as the lesbian expression went. And it was often possible to distinguish the "men" from the "women" by recognizing who was leading.

Some lesbian bars had a cover charge and were packed nightly, while costly entertainment at a neighboring straight-night club without a cover charge played to empty tables.

Beer was the staple, more for economy than preference, and the prices, both for beer and booze, in the dingiest lesbian bars were often higher than at the Stork Club or El Morocco. "We're giving the customers a better floor show," a lesbian operator said blithely—"themselves."

Many of the younger, prettier lesbians—the baby butches and femmes—who often didn't seem to know which way to turn sexually, were the magnet for many males. In one bar along Key West's sin-struck Duval Street, I saw sailors with tallow hair and corn-fed faces posturing amorously with lesbians—barmaids and customers—on both sides of the mahogany bar.

As a barmaid served a bottle of beer, one sailor impulsively threw his arm around her and then reached up and kissed her lips. She smiled brightly and said, "Seventy-five cents, please."

An old Duval Street hand had taken me to the bar. "Do you think that boy knows what's going on?" I asked.

"Of course. The whole atmosphere of the place feeds on sex—distorted or otherwise—and the air of excitement communicates itself to the boys." He looked up as two older men walked in. "And to the Johns, too," he added dryly.

We stood at the bar for ten minutes before the female bartenders noticed us, or we noticed them. And then we saw two girls with aprons around their waists embracing outside the kitchen door.

Our guide laughed. "I'll bet that's the first time you've had to wait for a drink because the bartenders were busy kissing each other."

Without female guides, lesbians or otherwise, I would have been unable to get into many of the bars, and would not have been admitted to the back rooms of others. Some of the bars were so inconspicuous that for years neighbors merely thought of them as places where young secretaries, receptionists, and schoolteachers gathered for quiet talks among themselves.

Yet the streets outside some of these places in Greenwich Village were often lined with out-of-state cars from Massachusetts, Connecticut, New Jersey, Pennsylvania, Delaware, Maryland, etc. Inside were some of the prettiest residents of these states, expressing their secret inclinations in a lost weekend in a strange city.

There were often as many curiosity-seekers in some of these haunts as there were curiosities. On one typical jaunt, for instance, I was accompanied by a lovely young society girl and her boyfriend; both had expressed some interest in "seeing the sights."

Virginia was particularly intrigued by the prospect of mingling with this strange breed of woman. "I don't think I've ever seen a lesbian," she said.

Her boy-friend smiled tolerantly.

And so, on a Saturday night we headed for Greenwich Village and a bar favored by younger lesbians who were, I understood, mostly secretaries, students, and would-be artists and writers.

We could hardly push our way into the place. The bar itself was lined two and three deep with girls standing around with drinks in their hands, watching every newcomer as she came in. There were a handful of men, but, like Paul and myself, they had evidently brought their own female escort.

Many girls were sitting around at small tables beyond the bar, and still others were dancing in a back room, twisting and twirling with one another. The joint was jumping.

We managed to find a table and a young waitress to serve us. She was in slacks, wore glasses, and had her hair pulled back over her ears. She looked like a nurse or a schoolteacher but turned out to be only a student. "Well, Princess," she said, turning to Virginia, "what will it be?"

She called me "Prince," and Paul "King."

"Give the King the check," I said.

She laughed. "No checks. You pay before you get the drinks." It was a rule of the house.

The drinks were $1.25 each.

"What is this—the Stork Club?" the King growled.

The waitress giggled and, with a sweep of her hand in the direction of the dancing girls, said, "Can you get this at the Stork Club?"

She flounced off for the drinks, weaving through the dance floor, past a pair of young men who, like the girls, were dancing cheek to cheek. Noticing us, they smiled self-consciously but kept on dancing.

As the waitress set our drinks on the shaky ice-cream table, Paul pointed to the dancing homosexuals. "Are those lesbians, too?" he inquired wryly.

"Lesbians?" the waitress said with mock surprise. "We have only the loveliest young debutantes. They 'come out' here." She chuckled at her own joke.

The music from the juke box made conversation difficult. Paul turned to a young, mannish figure with a crew cut slouching half out of his chair. "Say, bud, do you know how to cut that down?"

The youngster coolly spat on the floor, but a feminine-looking girl at the table came over to us with a murmured apology. "She thought you were being smart," the girl said in a whisper.

We looked more closely at our neighbor. Considering the male haircut, the masculine attire, and the studied hardness of face, it was still hard to take *him* for a *her*. Yet it was a *she*, all right.

But he—or she—was the exception that night. Other girls with even the briefest haircuts still looked like girls, and some, like a neighboring girl with bold black eyes and a mop of jet hair, looked even more feminine than the girl we were with. She appeared to be studying the King, who was a good-looking bachelor of thirty or thirty-five. But when Virginia disappeared into the ladies' room, the dark, black-haired girl also disappeared.

The Princess was away so long that the King began to nervously check his watch. When she finally reappeared, her eyes were bright with excitement. "You should see that ladies' room," she announced. "They have telephone numbers all over the place, even on the toilet tissue."

As Virginia was talking, the dark girl returned to her table, her hips swaying in a tight skirt and her smoky eyes holding an enigmatic smile.

Virginia lowered her voice dramatically. "She asked me if I wanted to mix."

"And what did you say?" The King laughed.

Virginia blushed. "Some other time." She giggled nervously. "She told me she came in here about every other night."

We sidled out to the bar for a nightcap, followed by a pair of bold, black eyes. The bar had thinned out a little, but dozens of girls were still there. Standing near us, in a dirty sweatshirt, was a fair-haired blonde with regular features and a well-scrubbed look. "She looks like the girls I used to play field hockey with in school," Virginia whispered.

The pretty blonde was talking animatedly to a dumpy-looking girl with horn-rimmed glasses and a coarse-grained pimply face, who was lightly holding her arm. Virginia was startled by the contrasts. "They can't be friends?" she exclaimed incredulously.

The blonde, noticing our attention, turned her head away. "I shouldn't stare," Virginia said, "but I can't get over that pretty hockey player with that other one."

Two sophisticated-looking girls sitting quietly at the bar had observed Virginia's wide-eyed interest with amusement. "Maybe we can help you tourists get your bearings a little," one said pleasantly.

Easily, with consummate charm and irony, they picked out the interesting personalities. There was a young colored girl sitting down at the end of the bar alone. "There's no segregation here," the blonde said, "she's just waiting for her special friend—a charming young lady from a good Southern family."

She looked around the room again. "Not many baby butches here tonight." She smiled. "They're a riot with their fly-front slacks and their leather jackets. Some of them even smoke those little Mexican cigars."

Virginia frowned prettily. "What," she asked, "are fly-front slacks?"

The other girl laughed. "You are innocent, aren't you?" She explained. "They're like men's trousers, and a lot of places, particularly in California, won't let the girls wear them. They have to wear girls' slacks—the kind that zip on the side."

The two blondes looked as though they had stepped out of the tailored women's band box. Their slacks were gabardine, an olive drab neatly creased, their blouses were colorful but conservatively cut, and their shoes were narrow and obviously expensive. They looked enough alike to be twins.

As the tall, good-looking bartender served one of the blondes a fresh drink, she observed carelessly, "He's a fag. The girls feel more comfortable with a homosexual behind the bar, and the management knows he won't bother the customers."

She turned to a girl who was standing behind us, staring with a fixed expression into space. Her face was pale and stark-looking. She wore a dark jersey top and heavy black stretch pants that reflected the severity of her aspect. Her hair was a sort of Dutch-boy cut, with bangs across the forehead and the hair straight all around the face, like that of a knight in King Arthur's court. "That one has a Joan of Arc complex," the blonde whispered. "She's always alone, always with that suffering look. She comes here to suffer all the temptations of hell, but she never talks to anybody. She orders a drink, and when she leaves, it's still untouched."

Not all the girls were in slacks. I had noticed a studious-looking girl of twenty-four or -five in high heels and a simple dress sitting at one of the tables facing the bar. Her hair was piled high on her head in a huge bun. She was well proportioned, and she might have looked sexy if she had not been wearing a pair of heavy tortoise-shell glasses. She was sipping her beer slowly and staring zealously ahead. Studying her, our blond interlocutor laughed. "You can just bet that she can see everything—and everybody— out of the corner of her eye." She looked again. "She's new at it —timid."

Soon a pretty young girl in slacks slipped over and sat down next to her; their conversation was desultory, and the girl in slacks moved on to talk to another girl. A second girl sat down, but the girl in glasses only smiled politely.

Our blond observer laughed. "The problem," she whispered, "is that nobody can figure out what she is: butch, femme, or out for her jollies like"—her look took in Virginia—"your friend there."

Soon an older woman, perhaps forty or forty-five, in a turtle-neck sweater and gray flannels sidled over to Miss Timid. The girl with the glasses smiled and then, with a deft gesture, removed her glasses and put them in her bag. She lit a cigarette and offered one to the other woman, and soon they were talking.

The blonde commented dryly, "I guess she's intrigued by the older type: they're discreet and they know what it's all about." She grinned. "You see, girls do make passes at girls who wear glasses."

As we were saying our good-bys, three middle-aged women with scowling faces stomped through the bar. They were evidently look-ing for somebody who wasn't there. But as they marched out, cast-ing disdainful glances around them, they collided at the door with two incoming girls. By their very momentum, they bore the two girls out into the street, and one of the three women lunged angrily at one of the girls. She had found the object of her search.

"I warned you to stay away from my daughter!" she shouted. Then, pointing to the second girl, she turned to a man standing by sheepishly. "You're her father," she screamed, "why don't you make her behave?" The man shrugged helplessly, but the daughter stepped forward, eyes flashing defiantly, and cried, "Just leave me alone, that's all I ask."

The mother regarded her with a withering glance. "You're no good," she spat out, "just like your father."

As a police car nosed around the corner, the midnight tableau ended as suddenly as it had begun. And the three women stiffly marched off, the frail, bedraggled figure of a man trailing a step behind. And as we turned, we saw the girls walk off by themselves, their eyes blazing and their heads held high.

It had given us all a bit of a start.

On the way uptown, Virginia was strangely silent. If the row had disturbed her, she did not show it. "Do you think," she said at last, "that those two blondes at the bar were lesbians?" She groped for the right word. "They seemed so . . . so normal."

I could only shrug. But two weeks later Virginia had an unexpected opportunity to further judge the two girls' normalcy. She ran into them while window-shopping on Eighth Street in the Village. And though she was with her fiancé, they had invited her to their apartment for tea.

"Did you accept?" I asked her.

"Oh, no," she said quickly, "they didn't include Paul." She laughed uncertainly. "I guess," she said, "they're not as normal as I thought."

In some bars, it was often hard to distinguish the sights from the sight-seers. As Virginia was still curious, one week night we visited a lesbian bar that featured a jazz combination and dancing. A trio of musicians was performing bravely as we entered about ten o'clock, early for a lesbian bar, and filed past the searching gaze of a vigilant bartender. Two or three couples—men and women—were engaged in the twist, and several girls were dancing together. They seemed wrapped up in each other. But as we took a small table in a corner, couples—girls—sitting nearby began to leave, until we were practically alone except for two or three couples like ourselves. Virginia bristled as she looked around. "Maybe," she said, "they think we're contagious."

At the bar, however, there was still some activity. A tall butch who looked like a truck driver had her arm carelessly draped around the shoulder of a lovely brunette whose soft eyes and long hair made her look like the acme of femininity. She could have been no more than nineteen. As she watched them, Virginia's eyes widened. "Don't they get the darnedest types together?" she said. "You would think a beautiful girl like that would have a strong, handsome-looking butch, or whatever they call it."

She studied them closely. "I don't think she really likes that butch," she said, "she's only being polite." At this point, the lovely teen-ager reached up and fondly kissed the butch on the lips.

Virginia gasped. "I guess love is blind." She was through being an authority.

With the place nearly empty now, a short, dark man with a friendly smile introduced himself as the proprietor and sat down with us. Shortly he asked Virginia to dance. They returned in a few minutes, panting from exertion. As he went back to the bar, Virginia giggled. "He thought we were cops. Imagine me a cop! I told him you were a professor checking on Kinsey." The disappearance of the girls was at last explained.

She looked around the dismal room. "I think I'll drop around some weekend," she said, "when it's livelier. This is no fun."

A week later she had apparently struck it rich. "I've never seen so many good-looking girls together in all my life," she called to report on a weekend tour of her own. She had been particularly affected by the beauty of two models. "They wouldn't give me their names," she said, "but we danced together and they took my phone number." She laughed. "Each one asked me not to let the other know what she was doing."

"You had a good time, then?" I asked.

She shrugged. "Paul got angry when I danced with the girls, and he stomped out of the place." She was annoyed with him. "And the funny thing is, he had suggested going there." She never heard from either of the girls, though a strange male voice started calling her unlisted number and hectoring her at all hours of the night. "Do you think," she asked, "that they would be putting this man up to it?"

The calls stopped when she changed her number.

Many gay bars were often fronts for more sinister activities. One lesbian bar in Los Angeles, for instance, was a well-known gathering spot for pimps, procurers, and drug addicts, preying on the lesbian trade. And young hoods prowled the dark streets near the club attacking girls as they emerged alone in the early hours. One girl was pushed into a hall and brutally raped, but, typically, she never reported the incident. "The police would have asked me where I had been, and that would have been the end of that," she said. "They don't like lesbians."

In the mixed bars frequented by female and male homosexual alike, there was a reasonable facsimile of normal atmosphere, with males and females often equally in attendance, though not with each other. Perhaps because of the semblance of normalcy, however, both sexes behaved with more regard for convention, and outsiders would have had to look closely before realizing they had wandered into a less than conventional bar.

In one mixed bar just outside Los Angeles, the lights were conventionally soft, the music low, and a charming chanteuse sang songs of love, while pretty girls held hands under the table and male homosexuals laughed gaily at the bar.

At the booth next to ours, two pretty young girls were self-consciously looking around the bar, while the chanteuse was looking at them. "They could be anything," my lesbian guide Lee said, "cruising or curious, or just taking in the sights." She laughed. "Some of these kids start out being curious, and the next thing you know, they're finding excuses to come back. They're cruising without knowing it." She dismissed them contemptuously.

Lee's eyes were on the singer, an attractive brunette with a husky voice and a commanding eye. "Every dime she makes," she said, "is lavished on some pretty little femme who twists her around her finger." Lee looked at her speculatively. "She must be hard to live with, they don't last very long."

As she spoke, a pretty blonde entered with two young men.

"Watch her go after the girl." Lee grinned. "That's just her type —the wide-eyed, frou-frou girlie who's so ultra-feminine she can't stand men." She snickered.

"How about her escorts?" I asked.

She gave me a pitying look. "They're gay," she said, "and she will be before she knows it."

The singer had noticed the newcomer, and had sidled over toward her. Her eyes held the girl's, like those of a snake mesmerizing a bird. Her voice soared, sending forth its special message to the girl who sat watching her with rapt eyes. "My personal possession . . . my very precious love . . ." That was how the song went.

Lee snorted. "She's really giving her the business. And then she'll sit back and let the little frou-frou fall breathlessly into her web."

As the music stopped, Lee's eyes wandered down the bar to a girl sitting in black contrast to the bright young thing fluttering like a moth around a candle. As the girl reached for her glass, I noticed she had only one arm.

Lee's face twisted in sympathy. "The poor thing," she said, "she's a cripple."

Marking her unhappy, discontented face, I said, "She's crippled in more ways than one."

Lee turned on me angrily. "I'd hate to read your book if that's how you think."

I didn't understand.

"You implied she was a cripple because she was a lesbian." She was quite upset.

"Not at all," I said. "I meant she was so maladjusted that even as a lesbian she couldn't enjoy the lesbian environment."

She was somewhat mollified. As we finished our drink and left the bar, the young thing was applauding the chanteuse, and the gay boys were crying "Bravo." The one-armed girl with the unhappy face paid her check and walked out—alone. The strains of "My Funny Valentine" trailed her out into the night, but she stared grimly ahead. As a taxicab sailed by, she hailed it and I overheard her tell the driver "Try the —— bar."

Lee shook her head. "She's going to make the rounds until she meets another object of sympathy. And then they'll find each other."

Not all lesbian entertainment was as obvious as the chanteuse deliberately made herself. The proprietor of one night club, who was originally from Greenwich Village, boasted that he could distinguish a dike, as he put it, a mile off, and wouldn't have one in his place. Opening a tourist trap in Miami, he hired six beautiful singers and dancers with an eye to their physical attributes. "They couldn't sing and they couldn't dance," he recalled, "but they were sexy-looking, and I figured they would draw."

One of the girls quit and a replacement turned up in the line. She had been hired by an agent.

"She's really stacked," the owner said to the bartender. "I want to talk to her." He had noticed the newcomer as soon as he walked in.

"You don't want to talk to her," the bartender said. "She's not your type."

Owner Ben bristled. "What's the matter: you saving her for yourself?" As rank prevailed, the girl sat down with the boss, and they started chatting amiably.

Soon the manager walked over. "Ben," he said quietly, "I got to talk to you." He had been summoned by the bartender.

"It can wait," Ben snapped.

"It's urgent," the manager insisted.

"Okay," Ben sighed. "Run along, kid." He bestowed a benevolent pat on the girl's *derrière*. "I'll see you later." He turned to the manager. "So what's so important?"

"That girl, Ben—you're making a fool of yourself."

Ben exploded. "First the bartender," he said, "now you. What are you guys doing—protecting your interests?" He glared sourly.

"Ben, we're trying to protect you."

"From whom?"

"From yourself. That dame's a dike."

Ben's voice rose incredulously. "Don't kid me," he said. "I've made a living off dikes all my life. I know one when I see one."

The manager laughed hollowly. "Well, I've got news for you: you haven't heard anything yet."

He motioned toward the bartender. "Gus there burst into the dressing room last night between shows and surprised the whole six of them." He had the grace to blush. "I'd hate to tell you what they were doing."

Ben summoned the bartender. "I can't believe it," he said. "You must be dreaming."

Gus solemnly crossed his heart. "It's true, boss," he swore. "I never saw anything like it." He shook his head in bewilderment.

Ben rose to his feet in disgust. His face had a stricken look. "What kind of a joint," he said, "do you guys think I'm running?"

12

THE INNOCENTS

The aisle was jammed with girls trying to find a table or a seat at the counter. They were young, nearly all in their teens—all apparently intent on looking like Brigitte Bardot. Their make-up was stark, their hair bleached or jet black, pulled back behind their ears, their faces powdered but not rouged, their lips garishly smeared in white lipstick. Only their eyes were made up, heavily lashed, and they stood out like black coals in the head of a snowman.

"Have you seen Rickey?" I asked the man guarding the restaurant's cash register.

He surveyed me coolly. "What do you want her for?"

"She was to meet me here between ten and eleven," I said. It was now nearly eleven. He studied me carefully and evidently decided I wasn't a cop. "She was here earlier, but she left."

I had noticed two girls eying me curiously as I talked to the manager. And now as I ordered a Coke at the counter and stood there looking around, one whispered to me, "Don't say anything now, but meet us outside. We'll help you find Rickey."

The evening had suddenly taken an adventurous turn.

I paid my twenty-five cents for a watered-down Coke—a reasonable price in a Greenwich Village joint catering to lesbians—and sauntered out into the street. There, on a crowded sidewalk, three obvious lesbians, one a good-looking bleached blonde in a leather jacket, were exchanging four-letter pleasantries with a handful of young hoodlums cruising the Village on a Saturday night for kicks.

"Oh, your father's mustache," hooted a young tough, while his comrades roared. The blonde's retort was unprintable, reflecting obscenely on her adversary's antecedents.

When he continued to jeer, she delivered such a fusillade of sulphurous language that the toughs visibly recoiled, hurling a few hollow epithets in a faltering retreat to the corner.

When the two girls came out, I observed them curiously. Neither was more than eighteen or nineteen. The taller, who had spoken to me, was a dark, Spanish-looking beauty with long, shapely legs and deep-set black eyes. The second was blue-eyed and demure, resembling a Hollywood star whose name cropped up repeatedly in the lesbian grapevine.

"Are you Rickey's father?" the dark girl asked me.

I shook my head.

"Oh," she said in evident embarrassment, "I thought you were her father." Her voice had a slight metallic ring.

"What made you think that?" I asked.

"Because so many parents come down here looking for their daughters." She grimaced. "And I know how parents feel." Her voice was sympathetic.

"Do you know Rickey well?" I asked.

Both girls nodded emphatically. "That's why I spoke to you," the dark girl said. "I heard you asking for her and I felt bad because I thought you were her father."

Wondering why they were so concerned about my status, I explained that Rickey was helping me with a project.

"Really?" They seemed intrigued. "We know where she is," the dark one said brightly, mentioning a nearby lesbian spot. "Everybody is there tonight: it'll really swing." She looked up invitingly. "We're going there anyway."

It was only a few minutes away. Girls were streaming in and

out of the place. I found Rickey sitting at the bar with a lovely blonde. Her mood was gay, in tune with the lively jazz combo that could be heard above the cacophony of female voices. She was not in the least embarrassed about not keeping the appointment. "I forgot," she said with an unconcerned air. "Maybe I can see you another time." With that, she got off the stool and strolled down to the end of the bar. The interview was over.

My two guides were now more curious than ever. "Exactly what are you doing with Rickey?" the dark one, Marie, asked in a whisper as they followed me out into the street.

I wondered what had got into Rickey.

Marie sniffed. "Oh, they're all like that. Maybe it's the wrong time of the month."

She was more curious than ever about my interest in Rickey.

"Oh," I finally answered, "she's done some writing and I'd like to see what she's come up with."

Marie's eyes opened wide. "Wish I was a writer," she said: "what a book I could write!"

"It's remarkable," I said, "the way you two were able to take me right to Rickey."

They beamed with pride. "After a while," Marie said, "you know just where the regulars will be." She laughed. "There's only four or five places to go."

"Do you see much of Rickey?" I asked.

Both nodded emphatically. "We've been trying to take her out of it," Marie said. "She's a terrific girl, but she doesn't know what she's headed for."

I frankly didn't know what to make of the two. I had found them in one lesbian hangout and they had taken me to another, yet there was nothing to indicate they were anything but completely feminine. I was also perplexed by their desire to help me.

They seemed agreeable when I suggested coffee together. "I can't get over it," mused Marie as we settled down in a small restaurant, "why I thought you were Rickey's father."

I was more curious about another point. "Why were you so careful about meeting me outside the first restaurant?" I asked.

She smiled. "I didn't want them to think I was picking anyone up, and, besides," she sniffed, "it's nobody's business."

The other girl had hardly spoken except to mention her name —Dorrie.

"How long have you girls known Rickey?" I asked.

"About a year and a half," Marie answered.

Like Rickey, they came from a middle-class section of Brooklyn and journeyed almost every Saturday night to the Village to tour the lesbian bars.

"I know how my parents would feel if they knew about me," Marie said. "That's why it hurt me"—she touched her heart expressively—"when I thought Rickey was your daughter."

She seemed awfully solemn and sincere and terribly concerned. And I was pleasantly surprised that she seemed willing to talk about herself as well as Rickey.

Both Marie and Dorrie were clerks in a Manhattan office, making about sixty dollars a week. And their Saturday nights in the Village were the bright spots of an otherwise drab routine. "Drinks are very expensive in these places," I pointed out, wondering where the money came from for the pub crawlings.

"Oh, we have one drink and sit on it," Marie said. "That way we can spend considerable time in each place."

"Who buys the drinks?" I asked.

She shrugged. "We pay for our own."

"In a lesbian relationship," I asked, "doesn't the butch usually buy the drinks?"

She laughed. "It's the same way as with men and women: whoever has the money pays."

It was obviously a different world from my own. "Neither you nor Dorrie have very much money, I should think."

She smiled. "Oh, something always turns up," she said airily, and then swerved the conversation off into other channels. "Why are you so interested in Rickey?" she asked again, as though not quite accepting my earlier explanation.

"She's helping me with a book."

"What kind of a book?"

"About girls who like the Village bars."

"You mean about lesbians?" She gasped. "That's wonderful. I'm glad she's helping. I'd like to help, too. Maybe I could do some good."

"What kind of good?"

"It might be a warning to keep a lot of kids from getting in too deep."

"Were you in it yourself?" I asked, not knowing how she would respond.

She smiled at her friend, who smiled back faintly. "Deep in it," she said. "I was a stompin' butch, as Dorrie can tell you, but I've been coming out of it."

"You don't look very butch to me."

She laughed pleasantly. "You should have seen me—the short hair, the slacks, the jacket, the whole bit. I even wore a chest strap under my shirt to keep me flat." She motioned with her hands to illustrate what she meant, and it was obvious that she was no longer wearing one.

I turned to her friend. "And what about you?" I asked. "Were you a lesbian too?"

I could hardly hear her answer. "I guess so," she said, barely above a whisper, but she did not elaborate.

"We're both getting out now," the dark girl said. "Anyone can if she isn't in too deep." She seemed the spokesman for the pair of them.

"What were you doing tonight, if you're out of it?" I was slightly bewildered.

Marie laughed, her face suddenly aglow. "It's exciting to watch the girls make their plays even when you're not in it yourself." Her dark eyes sparkled and then abruptly clouded over. "But it's no good," she said, "it only complicates things."

They looked, both of them, as though they were the kind of girls who should have been spending Saturday night at some neighborhood dance with a couple of nice boys. And yet they seemed very content with each other, and with what they were doing.

Though the next question was clearly indicated, I still hesitated over it. "Have you two ever had a relationship?" I asked finally. "Between the two of you?"

As Dorrie blushed, Marie answered coolly, "Not any more: we're just friends now." She looked casually at Dorrie, who nodded her confirmation.

They were really unusually attractive girls in almost every respect, and it struck me as odd that they shouldn't be surrounded by swarms of eager young men.

"That was the trouble," Marie said with a grin. "There were too many of them." It developed that both girls had had unpleasant experiences with young men and felt they had been given the wrong end of the stick. "I had this one boy-friend," Marie recalled, "who told me one night he wanted to marry me, and asked me to prove my love." The next day, while she was dreamily visualizing how she would look in white, her boy-friend called to express his regrets: he had been drinking and didn't realize what he had been saying. She admitted herself that his commitment had been made in the heat of passion, but it had been a shattering experience. Nevertheless, she still thought of him fondly and he remained her beau ideal among males. "I guess," she said, "I was trying to be like him when I started dressing like a man. I admired him so much, I wanted to be just like him."

This didn't seem to agree with the psychology of imitating what you hated, unless, of course, she wasn't reading her own responses correctly. "How about your father?" I asked. "Did you get along with him?" I was searching for the malignant male influence in her life.

"All right," she said indifferently, "but he was always getting drunk when things went wrong, and leaving everything up to my poor mother."

She seemed to sense what I was driving at.

"I like men," she said. "I certainly liked George." He was the boy-friend.

"Weren't you pretty young," I asked, "to be thinking of getting married at that time?"

She smiled. "I was going with boys when I was fourteen and was as big then as I am now."

"Then, when did you first begin to realize you were a lesbian?" I asked.

The question seemed to startle her.

"I don't know if you'd call me a real lesbian," she said. "I think I just went through a stage."

"Well, when did you first think you might be a lesbian?"

"I stayed overnight with my girl-friend one night. I guess I was sixteen then."

"And what happened?"

"Oh, we just kissed and fooled around a little. We had pajamas on, and neither of us knew what it was all about."

"Do you know now?"

She bowed her head. "I think so."

"Did you become butch right away?" I asked, hardly believing that this pretty girl with the shapely figure and sultry eyes could ever have looked anything but feminine.

Marie smiled. "Not until after I was brought out." She motioned to Dorrie. "As a matter of fact, we were both brought out by the same girl." She giggled, thinking of the coincidence.

The other girl frowned and contradicted her. "No," she said slowly, "your cousin was the first."

Marie stood corrected. "That's right," she said with a smile, "I started going with my cousin after you had gone with her."

My head was beginning to spin. "You mean," I asked, "that your cousin was a lesbian?"

Marie nodded. "For a while," she said, "she had the mistaken idea she owned me. That's the trouble with relatives."

"Was she a close cousin?"

"A kissing cousin." She smiled. "Our mothers were sisters."

"Where did all this take place?" I asked.

Marie shrugged. "Oh, we just slept over at each other's houses. Nobody thought anything about it." She giggled. "It made our families feel good thinking we weren't messing around with boys."

It seemed incredible that, living at home, she could have become a stompin' butch without her family surmising.

"Oh, I lived away from home for a period," Marie explained, "especially that period."

She was not sure whether her mother knew about her. "Some woman in the neighborhood," she related, "once came around to the house and accused me of bringing out her daughter, but my mother told her I was a respectable girl and couldn't do anything like that. She was properly horrified." An impish gleam came to Marie's eyes.

"And had you in this case?" I asked.

She shook her head. "No, it was my cousin."

The cousin, only twenty, was apparently quite active. "There must have been a whole crew of you," I said.

"Only six or seven." She began ticking them off on her fingers. "I guess eight."

"How many girls have you known yourself?"

"Five or six," she said, "but really only one."

"What do you mean by that?"

"You know, all the way." She groped for a way of expressing herself clearly.

I was frankly puzzled. "What about the others?"

"Oh, we'd just neck and mess around the way you would with boys." She paused. "I didn't do any more than this when I was married."

This was a surprise. "Married? Married to whom?"

Marie seemed to enjoy the spotlight. "Oh, nobody like George. I married this girl I had been going with. We exchanged rings in a regular ceremony."

Originally, she had thought in terms of a church ceremony. "I went to the priest in my parish and asked him to marry me," she said simply.

I was dumfounded. "You mean you actually asked a priest to marry you to another girl?"

She said with a smile, "Well, I was a Catholic and thought I'd like it that way."

The priest had assumed she was planning a conventional marriage and had told her she was too young for so vital a step. He was still surprisingly patient when he learned more about her plans.

"Didn't he tell you you were committing a sin?" I asked.

She nodded. "Yes, but he didn't get too worked up. I guess he thought I was going through some sort of silly phase."

"I don't think he believed you," I said. It did seem incredible. "And so you were married anyway?"

She laughed. "We were married by a minister."

At my evident astonishment, she corrected herself quickly. "I mean by a girl posing as a minister. She really wasn't a minister."

"Where did this take place?"

"On Gay Street in the Village, in a little areaway."

"Gay Street?"

She laughed uproariously. "We thought the name would be appropriate, since we were all gay."

It had been a double-ring ceremony. But I noticed she no longer wore a ring. "The whole thing only lasted three or four weeks," she explained apologetically. "She was too jealous and possessive."

But with all regard for Dorrie, who was listening silently, Rose was the most attractive person Marie had ever known. "She was a beautiful redhead with a figure to match," Marie said reminiscently. "I was butch then and she was femme. She wanted to try on my chest straps for kicks, but I wouldn't let her—not with that figure. She was like a doll—too pretty to touch, even."

"Why was it," I asked, "that only one of your relationships was fully consummated?"

Her lip curled in disapproval. "I didn't like it," she said. "It did nothing for me."

Had Rose been the one and only?

She shook her head. "I had already discovered it didn't appeal to me." It was a "kissless" honeymoon.

"Were you the aggressive partner?"

She appeared momentarily puzzled. "Do you mean did I take the lead?"

I nodded.

"I told you," she said, "I was a stompin' butch."

We had now been talking more than an hour, and coffee had given way to Seven and Seven, a rye highball that many lesbians seemed to fancy. The two girls opposite me were a study in contrasts. Marie, the complete exhibitionist, obviously enjoyed analyzing herself, while Dorrie brooded silently, occasionally nodding or shaking her head. They were probably compatible for this reason.

It was quite difficult drawing Dorrie out, but I kept plying her with questions. "Did you have trouble with boys, too?" I asked.

She made a face. "I guess so. One, anyway."

"Maybe that's why you turned to girls?"

She shook her head glumly. "I had a girl-friend before my trouble with Frank. And I fooled around some with boys after Frank."

"Perhaps," I suggested, "your family was so strict they built up sex fears."

"We were never allowed to discuss sex," Dorrie said, "and if we asked about the birds and the bees, my mother would tell us to put evil thoughts out of our minds."

Her parents had recently separated, and she no longer saw her father. "He drank too much," she announced. "In fact, he was always drinking. I guess that helped him forget he had a family."

"And what happened with Frank?"

She blushed faintly. Her experience was similar to Marie's. "I thought he felt the same way I did. He told me he loved me, but after that one night, he never called again and wouldn't come to the phone when I called him. But I still care for him."

"How can you girls be lesbians if you fall in love so easily with young men?" I asked.

Marie laughed easily. "That's what the boys say. They can't believe those stories about me being a lesbian after they've made out with me."

"Made out?" I frowned. "Exactly how many relationships have you had with men?"

She hesitated briefly. "Just one."

"Your boy-friend, I suppose."

"Oh, I don't count that one." Marie seemed to enjoy my surprise. "No, this was a married man."

"Where did you meet him?"

She became suddenly vague. "Oh, through friends."

"Did you meet in a bar?" I asked.

She shook her head. "I don't think so. I can't remember where we met. But it didn't last long. He still keeps calling me, but I won't see him." She grimaced. "I guess I was drinking."

"It must have been a bar, then?"

She nodded. "I guess so."

Had he given her any money?

She darted a quick glance at Dorrie. "Oh, just some presents," she said carelessly.

Her connotation of the phrase "made out" was far different than mine. She laughed disarmingly. "Oh, it only means kissing and necking." That had not been what it meant when I was younger.

"Oh, that's what it means now," she said easily, but I had the feeling she was already regretting a slip of the tongue.

The interview didn't seem to be getting anywhere, and the girls were apparently adrift in semantics. "The expressions you girls use are not what they were twenty years ago," I said.

"What do you mean?" Marie asked.

"Well, I get the impression at times that you're contradicting yourselves."

Marie smiled imperturbably. "You'd understand," she said, "if you had children our age."

"I have a boy in the Army," I said.

Dorrie's eyes widened. "You have a son that old?"

"What's so surprising about that?" I said. "You thought me old enough to be Rickey's father, and she's only nineteen."

Marie laughed lightly. "Oh, it's just from the way you said you weren't Rickey's father that we didn't think you had any children —that's all."

"Yeah," echoed Dorrie, "that was it."

I decided to concentrate on the less agile Dorrie. "What," I asked, "is the reason for your sudden reform?"

"What reform?" she asked.

"From lesbianism."

She turned a pair of innocent eyes on me. "My religion," she said. "I wasn't able to go to confession or receive communion, and now I can receive the sacraments again."

"You don't seem like a terrible sinner. Curiosity and love and human frailty might easily excuse the mistakes you have made."

She shrugged. "I just didn't want to tell anybody about it."

Marie, however, was more than willing to discuss her rehabilitation. "My reform was due to my brother," she said brightly. "He had been going with this girl and was so considerate that it opened my eyes. He sent her flowers, perfume, and things like that, opened doors for her, and made her feel like a great lady. It was a good influence on me seeing a relationship like this."

"That's hardly enough to make you change overnight," I observed.

"It wasn't overnight," she said. "I'd been thinking about it before. My other brother was killed in an accident and that made me feel I wanted to be a better person. We had so many family problems. My father kept getting drunk and pounding the walls. But my mother didn't cry once, though my brother was her favorite. And I didn't want to do anything that would let her down." It was a touching story, if you could believe it.

From what I could read between the lines, I was beginning to think they were a couple of delinquents. "I really don't think that you girls are lesbians," I said. "I'm sure you will both marry and have children someday."

"Do you really think so?" Marie said. "There's nothing I'd like better." And Dorrie faithfully nodded agreement.

Before we separated that night, they decided they would like to talk to me again. "If other girls knew what we've been through," Marie said, "not so many girls would slip into this sort of life."

And what had they been through?

Marie had the answer. "Always being afraid, afraid you'll be found out, afraid to go to church and"—she hesitated—"afraid that the one you like might like somebody else." She sighed. "And what future is there in it? I'd like somebody to worry about me for a change."

Before I heard from the two girls again, I met up with Rickey in the Village.

"Where did you find those two?" she asked. Her voice was heavy with disdain.

I explained that they had mistaken me for her father.

She seemed startled. "For my what?"

I repeated how I had met them.

She laughed until the tears streamed down her face. And then she backed off and looked at me. "Don't you know," she said, "when you've been picked up?"

"Picked up?" I frowned. "Why should they bother with me?"

"They were hustling you." She seemed to be enjoying herself.

"What do you mean, 'hustling?' " I asked.

"They thought you were a John." She seemed terribly amused.

"That doesn't say much for you," I said.

She scowled darkly. "I don't get it."

"After all," I pointed out, "I was looking for *you*."

She shrugged indifferently. "That wouldn't have anything to do with it. They wouldn't even think about that. "They were just doing what comes naturally—for them."

"How can you be so sure?" I demanded.

She gave me a long look. "You wouldn't be the first."

"But what for?" I asked.

"For money," she said, "what do you think what for? Is there anything else?"

"You mean they're prostitutes?" I was understandably incredulous.

She snorted. "Don't dignify them with such fancy names. They're creeps."

"But they seemed eager to help me."

She jeered. "Can you imagine when they found out they had

picked up a reporter? The only thing worse would have been a cop."

"But they could have dropped me easily enough."

"Oh, they just wanted to con you a little for kicks and hear themselves talk."

"I wasn't convinced they were really lesbians."

She grunted. "They're not. They're escapees, beatniks, looking for excitement—and they're dumb enough to think they will find it in the Village. They'll do anything for kicks."

I wondered how much of their story was true.

"They're too dumb to lie straight," Rickey said derisively, and then guffawed at her unconscious pun.

"Do you think Marie actually married another girl?" I asked.

"Oh, sure, I knew the other one—Rose. In fact, Rose invited me to the wedding." She laughed. "She's just as bad as those beauts you were with. I told you: they'll do anything for kicks."

I put another question to the expert. "Do you think there's anything between Marie and Dorrie?"

She laughed. "Of course—what do you think they're together for all the time?"

"What makes you so sure?"

She shrugged. "They let other girls know whose baby they are: it saves time and trouble in the long run."

"They told me they had reformed."

She snickered. "They have: no more outsiders except for Johns, and they're fair game, not fun."

But how could they hit it off when both appeared to be femmes?

"When I first met Marie more than two years ago," Rickey said, "she looked more butch than me. She's playing it cool now, but she's still butch."

"How about Dorrie?"

"She does what Marie tells her."

"They insist they are just friends now."

"That's a howl," Rickey said. She gave me a pitying glance.

"Did you ever have anything to do with them?"

"Don't insult me," she said sharply. "I wouldn't bother with those delinquents."

"Do you think they'll marry someday—some young man, I mean?"

She shrugged. "Why not? When they get tired of working and knocking around, they'll find some sap who'll support them. And they'll convince him they never liked any guy before, and they'll be right."

I still found it difficult to believe I had been picked up. "After all," I said, "they did take me to you."

She snorted. "And they left with you, too."

"Even so," I said, "what would they gain by it?"

She looked at me compassionately. "Besides the kicks, that's how they finance their relationship. It costs better than a buck a throw for a drink at most of these lesbian joints, and who can afford that on their take-home pay."

And the kicks?

She smiled. "Just think: while you're buying for them, they're romancing each other." She frowned. "But when they think they're fooling the Johns, they're only fooling themselves. The Johns are getting what they paid for, and that's all they care about."

There was something else that puzzled me. "Why did Marie bother to get married?"

Rickey threw up her hands. "Why do they do anything? Because they're bored and have to keep doing new things all the time for excitement."

It was hard to believe that these seeming innocents were little more than street walkers. "When I see them again," I said grimly, "I'll have a few more questions for them."

Rickey appeared to be amused. "What makes you think you'll see them?"

"We made an appointment for Saturday noon, outside Bloomingdale's department store."

Rickey snickered. "Want to bet? I'll give you ten to one you're stood up. When they get to thinking it over, they won't want any part of a reporter, believe me."

The day before the scheduled meeting, I received a phone call from a girl with a strangely familiar voice. It was Dorrie. "We won't be able to make it this week," she said. "Marie had an emergency appendectomy this morning and is in the hospital."

"Why don't you make it alone?" I suggested. "We can discuss a few things between ourselves."

Her voice was barely audible. "She wants me with her," she said.

"Then, why not meet me later?" I said. "You'll only tire her if you visit too long."

She hesitated. "I really should go home with Marie's mother when I leave the hospital. She'll be there, too."

This seemed a pretty obvious pretext. "You sound as if you're afraid to see me," I said.

There was an awkward pause. "In a way," she admitted finally, "I am a little nervous about it."

"You have nothing to worry about," I said. "You can talk about anything you like, and later, when Marie gets out of the hospital, we can all get together."

She seemed to be weakening. "All right," she said, "I'll meet you at Fifty-ninth and Lexington at one o'clock."

I arrived ten minutes early to avoid a slip-up, and waited for forty-five minutes at the Bloomingdale corner, not really expecting Dorrie to turn up, but giving her the benefit of any doubt, as I was to discover that Rickey was right on at least one score.

That night I phoned the hospital and asked for Marie. There was no patient there by her name and no appendectomies. The escapees were still adrift in a world of make-believe.

"They don't do anything right," Rickey observed scornfully. "Like I told you, they're complete frauds."

13

BUTCH AND BABY BUTCH

She was a stompin' butch of the baby-butch variety.

Her hair was cut close over her ears. She wore a sweatshirt, fly-front slacks, and hobnailed shoes. She bellied up to the bar for a drink, straddled the bar stool, her legs dangling carelessly off the floor, and boldly surveyed the room. She was not unattractive, despite her efforts to purge herself of femininity. Her skin was clear and high-colored, her dark eyes luminous, and her face had a nice contour. Though she was a little heavy, even the roomy sweatshirt could not hide the suggestion of a good figure. She wore no make-up and a cigarette hung limply from her lips. She could not have been more than nineteen or twenty.

She had stared curiously when I took a small table opposite the bar with a pretty companion. From time to time I caught her studying us. There was nothing offensive in her stare; it was almost friendly, and when I caught her eye once, there was a glimmer of interest.

She did not speak, however, until my companion, a pretty girl who was with me out of curiosity, had briefly retired to the ladies' room. And then, her eye catching mine again, she said, "That's a very pretty girl." She smiled pleasantly, as though commenting on the weather.

When I invited her to join us, she seemed a little taken aback. "I didn't mean anything," she assured me. "I don't fool with straight girls."

When I asked her her name she seemed a little uncertain about it. "Call me Marty," she said finally. "That's my name for now."

She seemed to know just about everybody in the bar, waving casually as they passed. "Are they all friends of yours?" I asked.

Her lips curled in disdain. "I haven't looked twice at anybody in six months."

"Do you have a special girl?"

She looked at me with dark brooding eyes. "I have nobody," she said emphatically. "I'm looking for a job so I can eat and go to school."

She had worked in a doctor's office, gone through high school, and had a semester of college. "I'm having trouble getting up the tuition money," she said.

"You won't find a job in here," I said.

She gave me a hard look. "I can't stay home all the time," she said half defiantly.

"Do you live with anybody?" I asked.

She smiled mirthlessly. "I live alone—and don't like it."

Occasionally her eyes roved to my companion's pretty face. "Don't think I was trying to be personal," she said. "I just thought she was pretty."

An older woman who had been talking softly to my companion put in a disclaimer. "She's beautiful," she said. "Look at that profile."

"Oh, knock it off!" Marty said rather roughly. "She's straight."

"Are you both butches?" I asked, my nod taking in her friend.

"Yeh," she said, "she's an old one." There was no friendliness in her voice.

"You would be pretty too," I ventured, "if you didn't try not to be."

"I get plenty of whistles," she said coldly.

I didn't quite understand.

"From guys," she said. "Sailors, Johns, and the rest of them. They're all degenerates." She seemed bristling with hostility.

"You don't have to answer any questions," I said.

She grimaced. "I don't mind. What difference does it make?"

Studying her closely across the narrow table, I could see that the contour of her nose was imperfect. It was flattened slightly on one side, near the bridge. "How did you break your nose?" I asked.

She shrugged and looked away.

"Did you fall down?"

"No, I had a fight."

I was surprised. "Did some fellow hit you?"

"No, my girl-friend." Her voice sounded disinterested. "She just poked me." She paused. "It isn't that bad. I'll get it fixed sometime."

Her casualness intrigued me. "I guess it makes you look more manly."

She gave me a sharp, incisive glance. "What are you, a psychiatrist or something?"

Like so many teen-age girls I had found in lesbian haunts, she didn't seem to fit any familiar lesbian pattern. "Have you always been a butch?" I asked.

She folded her arms. "What else?"

"How long have you been a lesbian, then?" I asked.

She winced. "Don't use that word," she growled. "I can't stand it."

"You're a good-looking girl," I said. "Why do you wear your hair that way?"

"To keep it from falling in my face, that's why."

She had an apartment by herself in the Village, while her parents lived a few miles out on Long Island. "When was the last time you saw them?" I asked.

"Last week," she said, "for the Jewish holidays. I went home on account of my father." She was half Jewish, she said, but followed no faith herself.

"What did your father think when he saw you?"

She shrugged. "I wore a scarf over my head, and a dress. I can look as good as anyone when I want to." There was a note of belligerence in her voice. "I don't care what a lot of creeps think. Let them make all the remarks they want: they're still creeps."

Suddenly her eyes engaged mine. "Do you know where I can get a job? I need a job. I got no money and I have nothing to do."

"What did you do this afternoon?" I asked.

"Went to a movie on Forty-second Street."

"Were you looking for someone?"

Her voice flared angrily. "I was looking for a movie," she said. "Don't you understand? I'm not interested in anybody right now. There hasn't been anybody in six months."

"Why not?" I asked. "Did you have a bust-up?"

She had begun to study me curiously now. "What are you," she said, "some kind of investigator?"

"I'm a reporter," I said, "trying to find out about girls like you."

"You're kidding," she said.

I shook my head. "I'm writing a book."

She hooked a finger in the direction of my companion. "And how about her?" she said. "Is she a decoy?"

"She was just interested in coming along."

Marty looked at me with new interest. "So you're a writer?" she said. Her face seemed to have brightened considerably. "I've written a lot myself. Maybe we can collaborate."

"What have you written?" I asked.

"You know, mood poems, essays, vignettes about the Village, that kind of jazz."

We arranged a date for me to go over her material. "You're sure that you'll be there?" she said. She was almost pathetically eager.

But her attention soon wandered back to my companion. "I like to watch pretty girls," she said, and then she laughed lightly. "She's the picnic type, the kind you see running along the beach with her hair trailing in the breeze." She held up a protesting hand. "But don't get me wrong: I never cut in."

"Then how," I asked half humorously, "did you get your nose broken?"

She remained unruffled. "Just a difference of opinion."

I could see that something was puzzling her.

"What made you get interested in all this?" she said. "You'd have to be sick."

I mentioned that I had already done a book on male homosexuality.

Her ears perked up. "What was it called?"

"*The Sixth Man.*"

An expression of incredulity crossed her face. "You did that?" she said. "You really did?" She seemed to regard me as a celebrity.

I offered her an ID card.

"Why, I just finished that book," she said. "It was all right as far as it went."

It was my turn to be curious.

"You didn't go far enough," she said, "particularly in Hollywood: that's a real cesspool." She had been in Southern California for several months. "I was all over the place," she said. "They really dug me out there." She frowned. "But there's too many fags. Whatever I am"—and she looked across at me challengingly—"I'm still a woman."

When it was time to say good night, she said, "Don't forget, you're going to look over my writing." She turned to my companion. "You're a real pretty girl," she said, "not beautiful, but"—she groped for the word—"but elegant."

Marty and I made our date and shook hands on it. Her clasp was firm and dry, like a man's, and her gaze level. We were to meet in a Village restaurant one night. But after one or two broken appointments—par for the baby-butch course—we finally sat down together two weeks later in her fifth-floor walk-up.

As she ushered me into the front room, through a maze of small boxlike rooms, she announced, "You're the first man that's been up here."

"How about girls?" I asked.

"Not for six months," she said.

The apartment was dingy, with a few scattered pieces of patched-up furniture. In the half-darkness, I had the uncomfortable feeling of things crawling on the dark walls. "Why don't you live at home?" I asked.

She made a face. "I can't get along with my mother. We just argue all the time. Ever since I was fourteen I've been running away."

For twenty years her mother had a boy-friend, and everybody knew about it, including her father. "I felt sorry for him," she said, "but what can you do?"

At fifteen she had been sent to a children's shelter. "Some shelter," she said. "I got kissed by a girl for the first time."

"What did you do about it?" I asked.

She smiled. "I liked it."

Later, judged a delinquent because she continued to run away from home, she had been sent by the court to a private agency-controlled school for girls. "It cost them five thousand dollars to give me an education," she said with a trace of pride, "and I got a good one."

She had started writing and painting in school. "Would you like me to read for you?" she asked.

As I nodded, she drew out a sheaf of poems. Many described her loneliness; others were mood portraits of the city. They were not at all bad. "A lot of tripe, aren't they?" she said in a deprecating tone.

She seemed pleased that I disagreed. She showed me her paintings, some water colors, others in oil. They were not good. "You don't like them," she said.

"Not as much as your poetry," I said.

"You know, I never talked to anybody like this before." She ran a hand through her short hair. "But you just have to talk to somebody sometimes or blow your stack." She mentioned her job quest again.

"You can't look for a job that way," I said, looking at her butch-cut.

She understood immediately. "One trip to the hairdresser—I have a special one—and I'll be all woman," she said.

"Do you think you can work yourself out of being butch?"

"I'm already doing it." She looked at me crossly.

"Would you become femme then?"

She looked at me as though I were out of my mind. "I'd bust any butch in the nose that came after me." She rolled her husky shoulders, and I could well imagine her doing it. "I'd just like to get out of this whole grind," she said, "and be a woman."

She took me by the elbow to a wardrobe closet, sliding open the door, and proudly showed me a rack of clothes. "Guess where that dress is from," she said. "The best shop in town. Guess."

I mentioned a Fifth Avenue shop.

"Right you are," she said.

She examined the dress critically. "I was wearing that dress when I met —— [she mentioned a celebrated movie star] in Sardi's. You should have seen her look." She laughed, apparently relishing the memory. "I was feminine that day, but she got the message. She knew I was butch."

"How would she know that?" I asked.

She shrugged. "It's all done with the eyes, and you don't have to think about it any more than a fellow or a girl have to think about what they're thinking."

The star was known for her romances with athletic-type men. "She likes both," Marty explained, "athletic men and athletic women."

I asked her what had happened.

A shadow fell across Marty's face. "Nothing," she said, "a big nothing. I was shy then, and the next move was up to me, and I didn't know enough to make it."

She liked talking about Hollywood and Hollywood stars. "I had a real ball there," she said, "just one party after another." Her party-going companions read like a Who's Who of Hollywood —both male and female. She mentioned a lovely, young, unmarried star whose name was constantly being linked to rich, eligible males by the gossip columnists. "What a laugh," she said. "The only men around are the queers who decorate her parties. And the person she's most likely to marry is her secretary—a real dike."

She had been to many of the star's parties. "She could have

about any girl she wanted," she said, "but she still pays girls to come out to her house."

That seemed rather odd.

"She does it for kicks, just like a John likes to pay a prostitute."

I was genuinely curious about this much publicized siren of the screen. "Would she be butch or femme?" I asked.

"She's both," Marty said, "but"—she sniffed—"if she didn't have to think of her adoring public, I think she'd probably go butch. That's what most of them are out there."

In New York, too, she had been to many parties, particularly those given by a famous star with a deep, throaty voice that was guaranteed, according to two generations of billing, to send males into ecstasy. There were nearly always men at these parties—homosexuals, of course, who didn't disturb the girls. "If anybody should drop in unexpectedly," Marty pointed out, "it wouldn't look so bad."

She described a typical party. "They're very elegant," she said. "People quietly disappearing in two's or three's, the girls usually with the girls and the boys with the boys, but occasionally they mix things up a little." The more conservative quietly arranged little tête-à-têtes for the future.

I wondered how, in so cautious an atmosphere, she, an unknown, happened to be asked to the home of a star who had so zealously guarded her secret for years, even to maintaining a husband she trotted out expeditiously on rare occasions.

There was a system in both Hollywood and New York. "It's done through theatrical agents," she said. "They okay the girls and send them on. And if it doesn't turn out right, they may lose a client."

She had savored the high life in Hollywood, and was familiar with Beverly Hills, Bel Air, Westwood, Brentwood, all the fashionable suburbs of filmland, and Venice, Newport Beach, and Santa Monica. "The only thing I didn't like was all the queers," she said. "The area is just crawling with queens."

"Maybe you just don't like men of any kind?" I suggested.

She was immediately scornful. "You call them men?" She mentioned the name of a great box-office star she had met at many of the parties. "He's a real lady, that one," she said, "playing the big, tough hero. What a laugh."

Her voice took on a sarcastic edge. "And what they've done to television . . . On one program there's five or six, all big queers with brawny arms and the whole masculine bit, and the dumb little dames all over the country swooning over them. It's a riot."

"You only know the faggot type," I suggested, "the stereotypes who flaunt their homosexuality."

She shrugged indifferently. "They're all that way when they can get away with it."

"Many lesbians," I pointed out, "not only get along with homo-sexuals but date and marry them."

Her face tightened. "Don't ever call me a lesbian," she said. "I don't like the word."

"You don't like the stigma of it," I said.

"Whatever it is, I don't like it, and I'm getting out. But I need a job."

Why hadn't she remained in Hollywood, where she had known so many influential people and jobs might have come easy?

Her face darkened. "You won't believe it," she said, "but one star [she mentioned a young blonde just then making a reputation for herself as a new Marilyn Monroe] offered me a sports car to stay with her."

"Why didn't you take it?"

"She wasn't my type, and nobody buys me."

I still didn't know why she had left this homosexual utopia.

"I didn't go out there," she explained patiently, "to get mixed up with a lot of lesbians: it just happened that they were avail-able." She looked up at me challengingly. "One of the richest young men in California brought me out there, and I was visiting his family for a while."

"Did he know you were—"

"How would he know," she cut in, "unless I wanted him to?"

"Was there anything between you?"

Her voice grated harshly. "Whaddya mean, was there anything between us." She was mimicking my voice.

"You know what I mean."

"Not him," she said. "He was a decent kid."

"So there was somebody?"

Her eyes suddenly smoldered. "I'll get even with that guy," she said, "if it's the last thing I do."

This was the first intimation of a romance.

"A fine romance," she said. "He raped me."

I remembered what police—and medical—friends had often told me: "Nobody can rape a big strong girl if she doesn't let him."

"Let him!" she said. "The bum knocked me out while we were walking along the beach. I didn't even see the punch coming."

"If you're a butch," I said, "what were you doing on the beach with a man at night?"

She hesitated a moment. "I met him at one of those interracial meetings that liberals are always advocating, and he seemed to be a fine, dedicated person. He knew what I was—a minority like himself—and it never occurred to me he was thinking anything like that."

"Was he a Negro?" I asked.

She nodded. "But that had nothing to do with it. He just wasn't decent."

She had hurried back to New York for a hasty rabbit test. "I wasn't taking any chances," she said grimly.

I suddenly felt the need of fresh air. Marty volunteered to walk with me to a cab. "I think I'd like a Coke or something," she said.

As we walked through the lower Village toward Sixth Avenue, we passed a group of girls on a neighboring stoop. Two of them started to titter, and I could almost imagine what they were saying. Out of the corner of my eye, I could see Marty's jaw harden. "If you dressed like a woman," I said, "you wouldn't expose yourself to things like that."

She turned on me fiercely, extending two fingers. "I could have those two just like that," she snapped. "Just like that." She jabbed her fingers into my face.

On Sixth Avenue, as I looked around for a cab, I suddenly spotted an old editor friend. He was with an attractive, fashionably dressed girl in her thirties. I looked around to introduce Marty. She was a quarter of the way down the block, standing on the curb, staring aimlessly into the street. With her short hair and man's sweatshirt, she looked very much what she was, even from where we stood.

"I see you're doing a sequel to *The Sixth Man*," my editor friend said.

"What makes you say that?" I asked.

"It's not only logical, but"—he pointed down the street—"also very evident."

His companion showed sudden interest. "You mean," she said, craning her neck, "that she's a lesbian? How exciting!"

I felt a surge of sympathy for Marty.

As we said good night and they moved off, I caught up with Marty. "How about that Coke now?"

She looked at me tensely. "What did they say?"

"Why didn't you stay around and listen?"

Her voice dropped deprecatingly. "Because I knew what they would think."

There appeared to be two Martys, perhaps three or four: one sensitive to the core, wanting desperately to belong somewhere; the other defiant, acting with bravado, determined to punish herself.

She was living in a masochist's paradise. As we strolled down the street, we noticed a young couple embracing ardently without the least concern for passing pedestrians. Marty quickly averted her head. "If you just look cross-eyed at their girl," she said, "some guy is liable to give you a bash." She was unusually depressed and glum.

I had noticed, too, with some amusement, that she automatically walked on the outside, near the curb, as a gentleman would with his lady, doing a side step, if she had to, to retain this position.

Like so many lesbians, she was volatile, and didn't keep any mood long. As we entered a nearby restaurant, favored by lesbians, she seemed to become jubilant again. As a man would, she took the end chair at our small table. Almost immediately, several girls trooped over to pay court. There was almost as much table-hopping as there would be on a busy night at the Stork Club. "What did you do with those drips?" Marty gaily called across a table to a plain-faced girl who had long hair and was clad in dungarees and a white shirt. The girl waved back cheerfully. And soon she had bounced over to our table. She regarded me inquiringly. "He's not a John," Marty said dryly. "He's a clean-cut red-blooded American newspaperman."

The conversation was not very illuminating, dealing with a Broadway character named Phil—presumably one of the "drips"—who had taken Marty's friend, Peggy, to a World Series game the day before. "You should see the way he throws hundred-dollar bills around," Peggy said admiringly.

"That's Phil," Marty said. "He's a big John." She seemed to be enjoying herself. "I'm starving," she said, "and he's throwing away C notes."

Appraising her solid figure, I said, "You hardly look like you're going hungry."

Both she and Peggy laughed in chorus. "You're a real square," Marty said. "That's an expression."

With her spirits now fully restored by the attention of the congenial stream of girls, butch and femme, Marty seemed eager to talk about herself again, as Peggy drifted off. "What kind of story you going to do about me?" she asked.

"I think I'll put you in with the baby butches," I said.

She seemed affronted. "Whaddya mean, 'baby butches?'"

"Oh, they're the kind that are trying hard to be butch but don't know quite how to behave." I laughed. "Somehow, the more frightened and insecure they are, the tougher they seem."

"Don't worry about me," she said. "I'm doing what comes natural for me."

I wondered where her food money was coming from. "When are you getting that job?" I asked.

"Nobody'll give me a job looking like this," she said, pointing again to her close-cropped head.

"Then let it grow," I said. "That's no effort."

"I got to get personal things straightened out first," she said. "I need somebody I can talk to, who feels about things like I do."

"How about a fellow?"

She shook her head. "I got a block."

"What kind of girls appeal to you?" I asked.

She answered shortly, "Good-looking ones."

She mentioned the name of an outstanding beauty whose face and form graced the pages of the slick fashion magazines. "Do you know her?" she asked.

I nodded, having interviewed the lady in question in Hollywood. She became immediately enthused. "Do you think you could arrange an introduction?" she asked.

I looked at her in some surprise. "What for?"

"I can tell she's that way."

I expressed my doubts. "Even so," I said, "why should she be interested in you particularly, or you in her? You might have absolutely nothing in common."

She laughed good-naturedly. "I just happen to be the type those people dig."

Witnessing the easy conviction with which she spoke, I recognized with a start that all this was very familiar. She was talking like a cocky college sophomore who felt that all he had to do was smile and his quarry would swoon. "You're that sure of yourself?" I said.

"With girls I am," she said. "I have a pretty good record."

As more girls continued to wander over to our table, I said good night. Marty was so engrossed in her friends that she hardly knew I was leaving.

The next time I saw her was quite by accident. Walking down one of those vague, winding Village streets lined with attractive renovated brownstones, I saw her sitting on a stoop with a young girl of striking appearance. They were holding hands. The other girl, even younger than Marty seemed tremulous and agitated. Her eyelids fluttered like a frightened fawn's. She withdrew her hands as I stopped.

Marty greeted me pleasantly and introduced her friend. "Meet Lucy," she said.

"Does she have a last name?" I asked.

"Nobody has a last name," Marty said.

Lucy had been staring at the sidewalk. She suddenly glanced up, and her eyes met Marty's. They seemed oblivious of everything else.

"Be here tomorrow," Marty said.

Lucy half nodded, and her dark, pretty face flushed. "All right," she said, "but I'll have to think of a reason."

Marty guffawed, and turned to me. "She's got parents," she said, as if that explained everything. The girl blushed again, rose quickly, acknowledged me with downcast eyes, and, with a last lingering look at Marty, tripped off down the street for the nearest subway.

Marty seemed pleased with herself.

"I guess you've finally found a girl-friend," I said.

Her face crinkled in scorn. "She's only seventeen—jail bait."

"Then why all the hearts and flowers?"

She shrugged. "She's a good kid. I dig her for kicks. These straight kids always affect me that way."

I saw Marty two or three times after that, exploring the Village bars with her. And one day I dropped down to meet her with a Broadway personality considered an authority on baby butches and beatniks.

As they looked at one another, a curious expression came over both their faces. Jack spoke first. "You're Marty," he said. "I wouldn't have recognized you, you put on so much weight."

During the evening she was strangely quiet, and I found her eying my companion covertly from time to time. "It sure is a small world," she sighed once. And when we finally said good-by, she seemed relieved.

On the way uptown, Jack waxed philosophical. "She's not a bad kid, just a little sick, that's all."

"What do you mean?" I asked.

"She's a young, healthy, good-looking girl," he said. "She ought to be in school or out working somewhere."

"She's looking for a job so she can go to school," I said.

He snorted. "When I first met her two years ago, she was looking for a job to go to school." He had been a close observer of the Village scene since the days Edna St. Vincent Millay wrote the poetry that the Village beatniks were now trying to emulate. "The trouble with most of these kids," he said, "is that they reflect all the worst weaknesses of our generation. They're moochers, they lack integrity, they don't have any morals, they don't stand for anything, and they're out to get whatever they can without working for it. They see all the bad things of our society and that's what they copy. They're destructive, and they destroy themselves while they're at it."

This was quite a speech from a Broadway character. "Do you think she's a real lesbian?" I asked.

"Who knows what she is?" he said. "If she's with girls she's a lesbian."

"She's had a pretty rough background," I pointed out.

He snorted again. "They all have hard-luck stories, but other girls have the same stories and don't turn to girls or go looking for hand-outs. They pull out somehow."

One phrase had struck me. "Did you give her any money?"

"A few dollars," he said. "Nothing much."

"Do you think she's doing anything for money?"

"Oh, sure," he said. "She's giving the boys a good time."

"You mean she's having relations with them?" My surprise was obvious.

"Oh, no," he said. "That would be giving somebody something for his money. She just gets the boys excited talking to them and mooches a few bucks: that's as far as it goes. She's an escapee, like the rest of these baby butches."

As they grew older, the baby butches progressed in different ways. Some underwent a feminine transformation, as the lesbian psychologist had; others, as had so many friends of Marty's, got engaged and married; some became playthings of rich men, disguising their inclinations; still others became prostitutes and addicts. Many others, however, with the courage of their convictions, became confirmed butches and organized their lives along lesbian lines, looking for a partner with whom they could maintain a semblance of orderly home life. Many of these practicing lesbians seemed content with their decision, particularly after having unhappily passed through a heterosexual interlude that reinforced their conviction that only another woman could make them happy. "What a relief it was," a gratified butch told me, "to see your partner cheerfully doing the chores around the house that you hated to do for your husband."

Once they settled down, their social lives seemed as unexciting as the next couple's. I had attended several "family" parties, and the proceedings were anything but wild. The girls interchanged partners, dancing cheek to cheek, twisting to the hi-fi, and drank beer and highballs; there was some flirting, but it seemed almost a mimicking of heterosexual parties I had been to, and there was no attempt by anybody to walk off with another girl's partner—butch or otherwise. At one party in Burbank the butches conversed pleasantly with each other, as did their femmes, exchanging small talk as one might on a weekend night in suburbia. Some even discussed their children.

There was no necking, no kissing, no whispering in the corners. And I couldn't help wondering aloud whether everybody was on their good behavior for my benefit.

"Not at all," said Sandy, a former butch who had invited me. "This is the way this group acts all the time—dullsville."

Sandy was now a femme herself, her hair long, her face made up like any woman's, and she was wearing a smart form-fitting dress. There were ten girls at the party—five butches and their partners—and even the butches looked feminine at times. The explanation was simple. "They all have jobs," my hostess said, "and so, while they can cut their hair short and bob or shingle it, they can't afford to look mannish."

There was a lone exception, a tall, husky girl with brawny arms, whose hair had been combed back severely and who, despite her ample proportions, wore slacks and a sports jacket that was several sizes too large. Dottie had followed my questioning of the girls with sardonic humor as she moved about the room with the decisive motions of a man. "There's nothing complicated about me," she said. "I just don't like men."

"Then why do you get yourself up like one?" I asked.

She smiled. "Because that's what the girls like."

The party conversation was desultory, concerning homes and mortgages, outdoor life in Southern California, jobs, husbands and ex-husbands, the problems of being a lesbian and yet not letting it be known. "I'd like to proclaim it out loud," a good-looking girl in shorts told me, "but I'd lose my job and probably have to move out of my happy home."

As it approached midnight, the party thinned out, the girls explaining that they had to be up early in the morning. And so they got into their cars—jointly owned, for the most part—and headed for bungalows in which they also shared ownership. The not-so-gay Gay Party was over.

I was finally alone with my two hostesses. "Not very exciting," the butch member of the team commented, "but I thought it was one aspect of lesbian life you may have overlooked."

As a knowledgeable butch herself, she knew the field well. "As a former bartender," she said, "I'm probably the world's foremost authority on butches—not these baby butches who don't know what the hell they are, but the ones who are butch because they know what they want and like it."

Somewhere I had read that the true butch is about the only lesbian type that hasn't had heterosexual relations. "Don't make me laugh," my hostess said. "The great majority of stompin' butches have been married, several have kids floating around somewhere, and not a few engage in extra-income activities with the good old opposite sex. Many live in Hicksville—those large frontier-looking, half-industrial, no-sidewalk, lots-of-railroad-track, too-many-beer-joint clumps of communities to the east and southeast of Los Angeles (El Monte, City of Industry, La Puente, Baldwin Park, Monrovia, Covina). They have large tracts that are now rented with option to buy, because people with means won't live there. They are straight neighborhoods, but many of the stompin' crowd find work in their factories, rough beer bars, and are accepted as part of the ugliness of the surroundings."

It was certainly a different picture of home-owning suburbia, one that the local chambers of commerce weren't talking about. "Exactly what," I asked, after making a mental note about the surrounding real estate, "is a stompin' butch?"

Sandy had a prompt description handy. "Oh, they're generally more male than the men, the truck-driver type, or 'big diesels,' 'bull-daggers.' They have more style than just plain ordinary dikes, more swagger and *élan*, and they're rough and ready with their women, sort of cave-man type. And they like to stomp around in heavy boots."

Dottie, earlier, had struck me as the stompin' variety.

My hostess couldn't quite agree. "Not really," she said. "As for myself, I'm a simple, plain, uncomplicated dike. I can pass as a femme by letting my hair down a bit, or as a straight when my job—and the company—calls for it."

She looked over at her roommate, an older femme, with a smile. "But I can't fool Ethel: she always finds out what I am." Ethel permitted herself a wry smile.

Sandy had appeared a lanquid clinging vine next to Dottie. "There's one," I persisted, "that would have nothing to do with men." It seemed so obvious, as I recalled those brawny arms and quick masculine movements.

Sandy roared with laughter. "She must have done something: she has a daughter eight years old."

The girl often stayed with Dottie and her partner, Nancy, and they took her to ball games, Disneyland, picnics, and movies. The child was almost as fond of her "Aunt Nancy" as she was of her mother and knew nothing about their lesbianism—as yet.

Dottie was comfortable only when wearing slacks, and fortunately, in her job as an industrial-plant foreman, she was quite at home in this attire. She wore an "engagement ring" on her right hand, recently given her by Nancy as a souvenir of a holiday trip to the Black Hills of the Dakotas. Though she normally shied away from publicity, she was willing to discuss her background to clear up a few common misconceptions about people like herself. "Few outsiders know what it is all about," she said. And she was not sure how many lesbians understood their problem. "You have to keep thinking about it," she said. The genesis of her own lesbianism continued to intrigue her. "You might say," she said, hitching her gray flannel slacks a bit, "that I had my first affair in the orphans' home."

She had been eleven and the other girl twelve. "She brought me out," Dottie recalled, "but there really wasn't much to it. It was more curiosity and loneliness than anything else." She thought a moment. "I don't know whether she's gay now or not. Of course, I didn't know what I was doing was gay at that time either, but when I was put in the county home later, I never saw her again."

Early in life Dottie had acquired a strong feeling of rejection. She had not got on well at home, and her mother had placed her in the orphanage. "She said I was a troublemaker, and she couldn't work and keep track of me too. She kept my older sister around, though." The parents were divorced, and she couldn't recall her real father.

Her mother had married again, and when Dottie was nine or ten, she recalled, her stepfather had molested her. But when she went to her mother, she was accused of lying and eventually put out of the house. She had bitterly resented her mother but had later found the Home pleasant; a social worker took her to the beach and parks, and seemed interested in her. She had crushes on many of her woman teachers, including the social worker. "I had these crushes all through school," she said, "but then everybody has them, they say."

As Dottie grew older she was put into a foster home, and while going to high school she worked summers full time in defense plants. The war was on, and with the male shortage, many women were thrown together for amusement. "I met Betty at the plant," she said. "She was very feminine then, and I brought her out, but she was more than just curious. She's butch now, but before she turned butch she got married and had a couple of kids." Apparently the experiment with normalcy had failed, just as Dottie's had.

After Betty's marriage, Dottie began going out with men. "It was the thing to do," she explained. "Everybody else did it. I didn't know about the gay life then, and thought an affair with a woman was only incidental."

She was not butch-looking herself then. She was slimmer and prettier and attractive to some men. When one proposed, she agreed to marry him, though with some misgivings. "It was the thing to do," Dottie said. "I never felt strongly one way or the other about him, but in my heart I knew I really didn't want to get married." But Bill had hurried ahead with plans for a wedding and honeymoon in Las Vegas. "On the way to Las Vegas I told him to turn back," Dottie recalled, "but he said we'd gone too far and what would our friends think." She shrugged. "So I thought, what the hell, I can always try it."

She had no favorable recollections of her marriage. "He was a slob," she said. "He was just downright dirty, and the only time he would bathe was when he thought it would do him some good"—she grimaced. "That's the kind of guy he was, always thinking of only one thing."

After her marriage, she ran into Betty again, and this time Betty, now safely married, introduced her to the gay crowd. "Until that time," Dottie said, "if anybody had suggested I was gay, I would have thought they were nuts. I knew I didn't feel like other women, but I didn't know there were so many other women who felt like me."

Bored with her husband, enjoying Betty's crowd, she finally decided to tell Bill she was a lesbian. "The marriage was on the rocks anyway," she said, "and I didn't mind the slob knowing I preferred a woman." In fact, she looked forward to the interview.

Bill was not upset. "He didn't seem to mind one way or the other," she said, "nor was he surprised. Then we separated—we're not divorced—and worked out an arrangement. He keeps my daughter, but she spends most of her weekends with me." She reflected quietly a moment. "She's better off with him, even if he is a slob. I don't want her to be influenced by the type of gay friends that come around the house. I want her to have every chance. I really wouldn't be doing her or Bill justice if I continued living with them. But I know she loves me"—she paused— "she really does, and I love her enough to want her to have every chance."

She didn't consider herself a real stompin' butch, since she didn't swagger around defiantly advertising what she was, nor did she approve of flaunting tactics. She was more, she felt, the uncomplicated dike type, like my hostess, though she could hardly look as feminine with the thirty or forty excess pounds she was carrying. "I personally do not like to associate with the stompin' crowd or the ones that hustle," she said. "They give gay life a bad name."

She was a living refutation of those who say that lesbians can't be happy. "I was miserable married," she said, "and now I'm as happy as a clam." Dressing mannishly at work was no problem as she worked with straight girls who wore convenient capris and slacks. And she sported conservative gabardines when she went out with Nancy. "I've never had any cracks made about me when I'm out," she said, "and Nancy, of course, wears feminine clothes, and her hair is long."

How permanent was her present role? Just as she once wouldn't have considered herself gay, could she not visualize a time when she might be straight? "If you met a pleasant, non-aggressive male you enjoyed being with as a friend," I elaborated, "would you ever consider marrying again?"

She didn't hesitate a second. "There wouldn't be any reason to. Men just leave me cold. I don't have anything against them, but there's nothing for me to respond to, and once I knew this was the way it was, my life became relatively simple."

Her social life was not exclusively lesbian, though. "We do have some straight friends, some couples I knew when I was married. They know about Nancy and me, but it doesn't make any difference to them, since their concept of my personality was formed before they knew I was a lesbian, and their opinion of me was already fixed."

She thought lesbians were born, not made, since so many of her gay friends, like herself, had yearnings for the same sex at a very early age. Yet anybody who had made a study of lesbianism would have wrung his hands gleefully over the case she presented for "made-at-home."

To this day she resented her mother and the stepfather who was all that the traditionally horrible stepfather could be—and more. "I was pretty young," she recalled, "when he began fooling around with me. And I didn't like her for staying with him after I had told her what he had done."

Admittedly, this childhood experience had influenced her attitude toward other men. "I was always afraid of them as a kid." Her older sister, Chris, had not been immune to her stepfather's attentions. "But she went running to Mother, and he didn't get anywhere with her." She smiled bleakly. "Of course, Mother believed her." So far as she knew, her sister had no tendencies. "Isn't one in the family enough?"

But Dottie wasn't at all sure that the trauma of incest had anything to do with her lesbianism. For even before her mother's remarriage, she had peculiar urges. "I never did want to play with dolls, while Chris always loved dolls and all that jazz. I wanted boots. My dream was to have a pair of boots with a knife pocket in them." She laughed. "I sure did want a pair of boots like that."

She stuck out her feet and took a hearty drag on her cigarette. She was proudly wearing a pair of heavy boots, complete with knife pocket. If nothing else, Dottie had fulfilled her childhood ambition.

POTENTIALS
The Lesbian in Society

PROGRAM

FRIDAY

8:00 p.m. Reception for out-of-town guests to be held at 527 Hazel St., Glendale, California. This will be convention headquarters for the evening. Telephone: 242-1023, area code 213.

SATURDAY

Saturday sessions are open to the public.

8:30 a.m. Registration at the Orient Room, Hollywood Inn.

9:30 Address of Welcome - Jean Nathan, president, Los Angeles Chapter, Daughters of Bilitis.

"About DOB" - Jaye Bell, national president, Daughters of Bilitis.

10:00 "A Study in Minority Action" - a research paper presented by Mrs. Susanne Prosin, San Fernando State College.

10:45 PANEL DISCUSSION on "The Place of the Lesbian in Organized Religion and the Effects on Mental Health" with Dr. Evelyn Hooker, sociologist and researcher, University of California at Los Angeles, acting as moderator. Panelists are:

Rev. Rollo M. Boas, rector of the Episcopal Church of Our Saviour, Los Angeles.

Dr. John D. Brown, minister, First Baptist Church of Beverly Hills, California.

Dr. Zoltan Gross, psychologist, Los Angeles.

Rev. Brooks Walker, minister of the Unitarian Church of Canoga Park, California.

12:30 p.m. LUNCHEON in the Orient Room.

Leon Mayer, attorney from Los Angeles, will give an address on "The Model Penal Code."

2:30 "A Sociologist Views Some Aspects of the Homophile Movement" - Dr. Paul K. Rowan, professor of sociology.

3:30 PANEL DISCUSSION on the topic, "Is the Lesbian Being Portrayed Realistically by the Mass Media?" Ron McCoy, of Radio Station KFI, will act as moderator. Panelists are:

D. K. Miller, motion picture and television producer.

Jess Stearn, author of "The Sixth Man" and staff writer for "Newsweek" magazine.

5:00 Cocktails on the Patio.

7:00 BANQUET in the Orient Room.

Main speaker will be Thane Walker, mentor-analyst and dean of The Prosperos Academy, Honolulu, Hawaii. "The Golden Mean of Sex."

Three-day program for the Daughters of Bilitis' national convention in Los Angeles.

14

THE CONVENTION

As I looked around the big meeting room, the scene reminded me of numerous other meetings I had covered over the
years. Like other convention-goers, the delegates and guests wore
name tags on their lapels, and eagerly participated in the convention agenda. They sipped cocktails between sessions and exchanged friendly greetings with other members from around the
country.

They looked like the ladies' auxiliary of some typically American organization—more so perhaps, like a militant women's
group, which they actually were. For this was the second biennial
convention of the Daughters of Bilitis, a predominantly lesbian
organization, meeting in open conclave in the Orient Room of the
Hollywood Inn in downtown Hollywood.

Save for an extremely short haircut here and there, there was
nothing to suggest that any of the women were lesbians. Their
faces were bright and shiny with the expectation of a good meeting, and their conversation was that of any comparable group
of businesswomen, except, of course, when they got on the subject
that had brought some of them hundreds of miles. Many had
driven all day and night to get there for the first rap of the gavel.

There were as many different types in the assembly as there

would have been at a heterosexual gathering, and their professions too, were as varied. Their ages ranged from the early twenties to the late fifties, and while a few wore slacks, the majority were in smart suits and dresses. The weather was balmy, comparatively free of Los Angeles smog, and the delegates' cheery attitude seemed to reflect the sunny skies.

Many were short on sleep from having attended a reception for out-of-town visitors at the local chapter house in nearby Glendale, but the prospect of a stimulating program had worked them up to a keen pitch.

Even before the morning session got under way, some were milling around in the hotel's coffee shop, where I had a chance to study the three-day convention program over breakfast. I had noticed my own name included as a participant in a panel discussion headed: "Is the Lesbian Being Portrayed Realistically by the Mass Media?" The forum was to be moderated by Ron Mc-Coy, a well-known Los Angeles radio commentator, and a fellow panelist was D. K. Miller, described as a motion-picture and television producer. I later learned that while his credentials were correct, he was using a pseudonym.

This discussion was to take place after lunch, for which I had been given a card, just as at any other well-organized convention. The morning discussion was to be given over to "The Place of the Lesbian in Organized Religion and the Effects on Mental Health." Moderator was Dr. Evelyn Hooker, a psychologist at the University of California at Los Angeles.

The religious panel included the Reverend Rollo M. Boas, rector of the Episcopal Church of Our Saviour, Los Angeles; Dr. John D. Brown, pastor of the First Baptist Church of Beverly Hills; and the Reverend Brooks Walker, a Unitarian minister of nearby Canoga Park. There was no Roman Catholic or Jewish clerical representation.

Practically every phase of the lesbian problem was to be explored by the convention. At a luncheon meeting, Leon Mayer, a Los Angeles lawyer, was to discuss "The Model Penal Code" as it concerned the homosexual, and Dr. Paul K. Rowan, a sociology professor, "A Sociologist Views Some Aspects of the Homophile Movement."

The dinner meeting was to feature a talk by Dr. Thane Walker, psychoanalyst and head of a metaphysical group, The Prosperos Academy of Honolulu. His topic: "The Golden Mean of Sex." It looked like a busy day.

Sipping my coffee, I had just leafed through the program when a pretty dark-haired woman of thirty-five or so introduced herself as the president-elect of D.O.B.'s Los Angeles group, and plunked herself down at my table.

"You have no idea," she said breathlessly, "how much detail there is in a convention like this." She sighed. "We've just got through billeting most of the members around town."

She had anticipated a record-shattering enrollment for the convention. "At the last convention in San Francisco two years ago," she said, "only eighty registered, but one hundred and twenty attended. But we feel a greater percentage will register this time. Many of the teachers and other professionals who had just come to look around have more confidence in the group now, and less fear of exposure."

She nodded pleasantly at the groups of girls who were wandering in and out of the restaurant, meanwhile casting an anxious glance at her watch. As we talked, I had noticed small clumps of clean-cut boys and girls meandering out to the hotel's patio for breakfast. "Are they with the convention?" I asked.

She laughed. "Lord no, they're high-school kids from Mississippi, or some such place, on a tour of Hollywood, I suppose."

In the convention hall itself, I was placed next to a lean, lantern-jawed girl of thirty with short sandy hair, glasses, and a nervous fidget. I was soon calling her Jackie and she was calling me by my first name. She had a critical outlook and a caustic tongue. There were perhaps two hundred persons in the assembly when Jean Nathan, outgoing president of the Los Angeles chapter, delivered the welcoming remarks. Many in the audience, surprisingly, were male. "They're observers," Jackie advised me, "and some homosexuals trying to learn something."

Unlike Jean Nathan, who was using a pseudonym, Jackie was using her own name, plainly written on her lapel. "It takes a lot of nerve," she said, looking around the room, "to put your name to what you are."

At this point, there was a special announcement from the convention platform. With a smile, an official dryly announced, "Because a group of impressionable teen-agers is stopping at the hotel, the hotel management has asked us to be careful about leaving programs and other literature lying around."

There was some mild laughter, but Jackie regarded me with a pained expression. "I suppose that's one way of telling us not to go near the kids," she said sharply. "I don't know what the hell some people think we are."

On the dais, a tall, attractive girl was telling the assembly something about the origin of the Daughters of Bilitis. She was Jaye Bell, D.O.B.'s national president, and her friends called her "Shorty." She came from San Francisco.

She explained the derivation of the organization's name, assumed when it was formed seven years before. "In the Pierre Louÿs book *The Songs of Bilitis*," she said, "Bilitis first thinks of herself as a heterosexual woman, then drifts into a bisexual existence, and later becomes a convert to Sappho, living contentedly on the Isle of Lesbos with women exclusively."

A tall, handsome woman dressed severely in black was next introduced. She was Dr. Hooker, the religion moderator. She briefly discussed the celebrated Wolfenden Report on English homosexuality, in which the Anglican Church and the Catholic Church in England, she said, had relegated homosexuality to the area of "private conscience." And then, after giving the Wolfenden group an approving pat, she introduced the religious panel.

The Reverend Boas, a tall, kindly man with a red face, was the first protagonist.

Mildly self-conscious, it seemed, at finding himself on the platform, he immediately made it clear that his views were his own and not his church's. In the past, he pointed out, he had worked with other problem groups, such as alcoholics. Jackie's lips turned down as he ambled on. "I wonder," she whispered hoarsely, "what he could do for an alcoholic lesbian?"

Happily unaware of his critic, the minister explained that his church did not automatically reject lesbians or any other sinners. "I have learned," he said, "that there is no stereotype concept of homosexuality by clergymen. If I can say anything about the church attitude, it is that we do seek to meet homosexuals as persons."

Jackie sniffed. "That's big of him," she said. "He admits we're human."

Continuing his parallel with alcoholism, the pastor said that he would like to see a program similar to that of Alcoholics Anonymous for those lesbians who wanted help. "However, if the homosexual—the lesbian—is not seeking to change herself, the church will counsel her, and I, as an individual, will do nothing to try to change the homosexual's way of life."

As the Unitarian minister succeeded the Episcopalian, Jackie beamed expectantly. "I like those Unitarians," she said, grinning. "They're so damn broad-minded."

The Reverend Brooks Walker, a good-looking, soft-spoken young man, said nothing to disappoint her. In judging any human relationship, he said, the question should be properly asked: "Does this relationship enlarge or enhance the human personality?" As he made a plea for greater tolerance and understanding for the homosexual, the Reverend John Brown, a Baptist fire-eater, seemed to draw himself erect in his chair. His eyes glinted angrily as the Unitarian suggested that the Ten Commandments, dated by the centuries, no longer directly applied to the problem of present-day sexuality. "I feel it my Christian duty," Reverend Walker stressed quietly, "to help anybody and everybody I can."

With an air of uneasy expectancy, the audience watched the Reverend Brown follow the Unitarian to the microphone. "Watch him give us hell," Jackie said. She laughed harshly. "When he accepted the invitation, he thought we were a penitent group like A.A. It just never occurred to him that we could be lesbians and like it."

Like his namesake, who crusaded against Negro slavery, the Reverend Brown was an angry man. "You are all sinners," he thundered, "and by recognizing your sin you become free." His voice carrying over the murmur of protest in the audience, he pointed out that sinners, in keeping with Scripture, were welcome in his congregation but could not participate in certain other activities of the church. They could not, for instance, sing in the choir. "We must have clean vessels administering the functions of our church," he said sharply.

Many of the women sitting around me visibly flinched. Jackie's voice vibrated with indignation. "Does he think we're going to corrupt his damn old choir?" she demanded.

But, like a prophet of old, the Reverend Brown pounded home his message. His eyes burned with a strange intensity, and his voice rang out like Judgment Day. "Jesus," he cried, "said it was better for the sinner never to be born than that he should cause an innocent person to stumble." It was obvious who the sinners were.

The audience reacted as though it had been violently slapped. In the taut silence, Jackie said between clenched teeth, "Why the hell do we have to listen to his insults? He's worse than the Catholic Church. They told us we were all broken reeds and they wouldn't sanction the presence of a priest at the meeting." She eyed the speaker darkly. "I wish he had stayed away, too."

But the Reverend Brown had more to say.

Invoking Scripture, he pointed to the destruction of Sodom and Gomorrah for the sin that gave sodomy its name. "God," he bellowed, "gave them up." He surveyed the tense assembly with an angry glance. "What is wrong with celibacy?" he demanded. "The priests and the nuns practice it." And then, eyes smoldering, he cried, "If a person cannot live a normal life, perhaps it is better that he did not exist at all."

You could have heard a pin drop in the big hall.

Angrily, Jackie demanded of her neighbors, "Who invited that guy?"

"Oh, let him have his say," another girl rejoined calmly. "After all, we asked for it. At least we're finding out what the churches think about us."

Jackie's voice dripped with sarcasm. "Jesus didn't seem to mind us terrible sinners."

To many sighs of relief, the Reverend Brown resumed his seat, sitting stiffly erect and staring rigidly over the heads of the audience.

"Maybe," Jackie scoffed, "he thinks it's contagious."

Next was Dr. Fred Goldstein, a Beverly Hills psychologist described as a former rabbinical student. He was an added starter, and was clearly sympathetic to the problem. Jackie relaxed noticeably. "Psychology," he droned sonorously, "is concerned with the individual as a human being, not as we would like him to be, but as he is. The punitive pronouncements of the churches are not the answer to the problem, and the churches won't make headway with this problem until they recognize that people are human, not divine. Hypocrisy is not unique in the homosexual world. And as for the charge of promiscuity so often leveled against the homosexual, infidelity is not unique to homosexuality."

There was a murmur of approval as he continued. "To ignore pressures resulting in homosexual drives is not being divine, it is being blind." Breakups in homosexual relationships, he pointed out, with their resulting emotional upheavals, were just as demanding of assistance as other breakups.

And the world, too, had some responsibility for the homosexual's emotional problems. "The homosexual is in constant conflict, since he is brought up in a world that makes it especially difficult for the non-heterosexual to adjust. It is much like a Jew trying to attain acceptability in a Nazi society. And he will experience conflict as long as he tries to function in a society that rejects him."

As he paused, moderator Hooker asked with a significant glance at the gentlemen of the cloth, "What kind of religion, if any, promotes mental health in the homosexual?"

"Any religion," Dr. Goldstein replied mildly, "that builds up the self-respect of the individual."

As he sat down, there was a generous round of applause, but Jackie did not join in. "I don't know about him," she said. "He was saying the other day that he had cured six lesbians who came to him for help." She looked up at me. "If it's society that's sick, not the lesbian, what did he cure them of?"

I laughed. "Maybe he dulled their sensitivity."

She snorted. "I don't want anybody telling me I'm sick. I'd almost rather have the Reverend Brown telling me I'm going to hell."

As the clergy sat around, crossing and uncrossing their legs, Dr. Hooker summed up the discussion. "Although most homosexuals would like to be accepted in some church group," she said, "it appears that the chief source of their moral condemnation are the very groups in which they would like to find acceptance. Perhaps there is a need for an effective, non-authoritarian religion that will understand every human need and work toward the mental health of all people, not only the homosexual." As she finished, the applause was thunderous. If nothing else, it was clear where the sympathies of the audience did not lie.

Lunch was next on the agenda, and it was attacked with vigor. As the dessert came on, attorney Leon Mayer, a youngish, even-tempered man, brought the meeting up to date on the so-called sex laws, pointing out that California law, which forced even minor offenders to register as sexual psychopaths, had been unfair to many, many people. "If you want to change this legislation," he said, "write your assemblymen and state senators." He was clearly for the orderly processes.

As the girls listened intently, he explained the controversial police policy of deliberately entrapping homosexuals, but could offer no prospect of relief. "A law officer," he observed, "can legally give a person the opportunity to commit a crime, provided the idea of that crime originated in the mind of the individual and not the officer."

Many of the girls obviously thought this an injustice, and Jackie, still my neighbor, clucked impatiently, "Just as if any of those damn cops would admit what was in their minds."

Mayer got a perfunctory hand.

The dearth of information of almost any kind about the lesbian was noted by sociologist Paul Rowan. "We can hardly discuss the lesbian problem intelligently," he said, "when we have no body of information about the lesbian and nobody working on it." He pointed out that because of lesbianism's strong taboo, even the psychologists and sociologists undertaking special studies risked putting themselves under a cloud. "Yet," he stressed without rancor, "the medical profession can study any subject they like without being subject to suspicion."

Looking around the room with a glint of humor flickering behind his horn-rimmed glasses, Professor Rowan poked around at the root of the group problem, "Most of you want something of society or you wouldn't be here," he said, "and what you want is legitimacy. You want to be accepted, but only as your group wins acceptance and interacts with other groups can you get your message across."

As a sociologist, he was alive to the difficulties of organization action. "You find yourself rubbing elbows with some girls you wouldn't have in your front room." There was a ripple of agreement in the assembly, and Dr. Rowan sat down to polite applause.

Next was the panel on mass media, in which I was to participate. On my right was a girl named Tracy, an attractive redhead who had been added to the panel. "For your information," she said as we were introduced, "I'm not only a former newspaperwoman but a former lesbian newspaperwoman."

"Does that," I asked, "make you a former newspaperman?"

She did not think it funny.

D. K. Miller, the producer, was a pleasant-faced young man who soon confided that his name wasn't really Miller, and talked compassionately about the entire homosexual problem. "I wouldn't dare use my own name here," he said. "I'd be hounded out of the business." He looked at me with spaniel eyes. "Now, I ask you, how fair is that?"

As the convention listened politely, moderator Ron McCoy, a widely known heterosexual, recited the formal question: "Is the Lesbian Being Portrayed Realistically by the Mass Media?" and, with arched brows, asked, "Is the lesbian being portrayed at all?"

"You must understand," somebody on the platform rejoined, "that this is practically a virgin field."

A roar greeted this apparent faux pas, but newspaperwoman Tracy was in no mood for levity. Grimly, she lashed out at males for the currently unrealistic picture of the lesbian. "It is mostly men who write about lesbians, despite the old saying that 'it takes one to know one.'" As the members applauded, she added tartly, "And I might say that 'it takes one to write about one.'"

There seemed an obvious rebuttal. "One of the reasons we don't have any real material on the lesbian is the lesbian herself," I suggested. "She is unwilling, generally, to co-operate unless she is an exhibitionist of some type. To get a good cross-section of any group, you must also take in the people who don't jump at the chance of being interviewed. But most lesbians are reluctant to stand up and be counted—even privately."

Tracy was unimpressed. Without any concession to the men, she also objected to the lesbian image developed by women writers. "I'm getting tired," she said testily, "of lesbian literature that continually paints the lesbian as drowning in her individual well of loneliness. She is forever haunted by black despair, always grieving over being jilted by some little minx, always contemplating suicide, and"—she clipped her words off angrily—"that just isn't the case. We all know lesbians who are happy, well adjusted, and lead useful lives. These are the lesbians I would like to read about—and write about for a change."

Tracy got a big hand, and it seemed a lost cause. But I nevertheless observed mildly, "I still think that the most objective study of lesbians could be written by somebody not directly involved if the lesbians would only co-operate."

"This sounds like male superiority," Tracy said shortly, again drawing applause.

"Just male detachment," I corrected.

Tracy was indomitable. "I get so tired," she said, "of that wonderful heterosexual sunset, in which the homosexual—the lesbian —has to align himself. It apparently never occurs to the people who make some of these movies, for instance, that homosexuals— lesbians—have lives of their own, and problems of their own. They should be portrayed honestly, with less emphasis on the sex distinction itself, and more on their special ideals, frustrations, hopes, and dreams."

"Exactly," interjected producer D. K. Miller. "The homosexual movies all have phony endings, prompted by the outmoded moral code of the motion-picture industry, which makes it essential to keep the homosexual basking in the heterosexual sunset, which actually he wants no part of."

It seemed to me that the discussion was getting nowhere. "There's no point to any publicity," I said, "unless you know what you are trying to do. If you are seeking a realistic picture of the lesbian, showing her to be a human being above all, then, of course, you must settle for the bad as well as the good."

Moderator McCoy interjected curiously, "If you portray the lesbian realistically," he asked, "would it be interesting?"

"It depends," I pointed out, "on the available material. As matters stand, we don't even have the slightest idea how many lesbians there are. And you certainly can't do a book about lesbians, ignoring the heterosexual world and its attitudes."

"I would like to see a book," Tracy cut in, "that would be realistic without either condemning or approving." Her eyes flashed, and she looked at me challengingly. "I would like to see us pictured as human beings, without resorting to all the tired, worn-out stereotypes by which the public now knows the lesbian."

This seemed reasonable enough, particularly since the most subtle aspects of lesbianism were also the most fascinating. However, the popular conception of lesbians was rapidly changing, because of the recent homosexual upsurge extending to all classes and groups. It was getting so in California at least, a woman pointed out from the convention floor, that when two girls danced together, people immediately began to suspect them as lesbians. As the audience murmured its assent, moderator McCoy interposed blandly, "Do I have it right? If two people dance together, it's homosexuality. If three dance together, it's folk dancing."

With this remark, lustily cheered by the convention, the discussion ended, and Tracy turned to me. "You know," she said pugnaciously, "I was told to take it easy on you because you were a guest."

"Were you upset about something?" I asked.

"That damn book of yours, *The Sixth Man*," she said.

I still didn't understand.

"Then I'll remind you," she said warmly. "Your observation that the lesbian combined the worst features of both sexes."

"That was somebody else's observation—a male homosexual's," I responded. "I only recorded it."

She grunted uncompromisingly, and then flounced off into the crowd with an "I'll be seeing you."

As the meeting broke up, a large girl with glasses approached me and held out her hand, introducing herself as an officer of the New York chapter. "I didn't know you had an active New York group," I said.

"We're not very active now," she conceded, "but we hope to be soon." She looked up brightly. "You know, we're getting the national convention in 1964, and that should help."

I penciled the date into my calendar.

The next big event on the agenda was the evening banquet, and I was pleasantly surprised to note the Reverend Brown at a table with a sweet-faced, gray-haired lady who was obviously Mrs. Brown. Many of the lesbians seemed heartened by his appearance. "Feeling the way he does," my friend Jackie conceded, "it was sporting of him to come back."

I was seated next to a middle-aged woman, with thick-lensed glasses, who was introduced only as Miranda. She was a Midwesterner, and had been drawn to California by her interest in the Daughters of Bilitis. "But she has to go back soon to collect a disability pension," Jackie pointed out, "and I can hardly wait." She shuddered. "She thinks everybody should like her because she's a lesbian."

I looked for Tracy, and my eyes found her at a neighboring table. She looked feminine, bursting with appeal in a red evening gown, and she waved merrily as she spotted me. "You really got the prize," she whispered a few minutes later, "sitting next to Miranda."

Miranda didn't look particularly forbidding, though she was admittedly plain. "All she can think of is Belle," Tracy said. "She can't take her eyes off her." Belle was interested exclusively in a woman she had been living with for many years. They were considered an ideal match. "Even if this weren't so," Tracy said with a laugh, "who would want poor Miranda? She's a dud."

Just before dinner was served, a little convention ritual was observed. Each banqueter, in seating order, stood up and called out his—or her—name.

With some surprise, I marked the laughter as a tall, distinguished-looking Negro woman rose and with a smile called out, "Elizabeth Taylor."

"That's quite a coincidence," I said to a neighboring woman. The woman laughed. "Oh, that's just her convention name. She has a responsible position in San Francisco and has to be careful." Her eyes twinkled. "Don't you think it's a little funny—Elizabeth Taylor at a lesbian convention?"

Dinner proceeded cheerfully, with the announcement of a special event. Lisa Ben, songbird of D.O.B., was to entertain. To hearty applause, an attractive woman with pale blue eyes and long black hair curling at the ends stood up and took a bow. "This song I wrote myself," she said in a soft, pleasant voice, "and it means very much to me." She folded her arms over her chest. "I hope it will mean as much to you."

Her voice pealed out like a bell. She sang without accompaniment, with a haunting sweetness that captured the audience:

"Scattered are we, over land over sea
How many we number will never be known.
Each one must learn from the start,
She must wear a mask on her heart,
We live in a world set apart—
A shy secret world of our own."

Her voice seemed to gather volume, and looking around the tables, I observed many of the women dabbing their eyes. Her own eyes were glistening.

"Here's to the day that we yearn for,
To give of our hearts as we may,
Love's always love in sincerity given
Despite what the others may say."

Now her voice rang out boldly:

"The world cannot dare to deny us,
We've been here since centuries past
And you can be sure our ranks will endure
As long as this old world will last."

She threw up an eloquent hand, and there was a tender smile in her eyes as she continued:

"So here's to a fairer tomorrow,
When we'll face the world with a smile
The right one beside us to cherish and guide us,
This is what makes life worth while."

As she repeated the last two lines, there was a deafening ovation, and with a modest little bow, Lisa sat down. The musical interlude was over.

After the applause, the program continued. The toastmistress, an attractive blonde, discussed the problem of lining up convention speakers. "I didn't think I could do it in such a short time," she said, "but lo and behold, we sent out letters, uttered a small prayer, and before we knew it, we had a program together." She laughed infectiously. "Which just goes to show," she said, with a fond look at her partner of long standing, "that lesbians who pray together, stay together."

Looking around the room, I noticed that the Reverend Brown —and his wife—had joined in the general laughter. They appeared to be enjoying themselves at this point.

Next came a special awards ceremony.

The toastmistress announced with a flourish that four special friends of the D.O.B., all males, were to be recognized fittingly for their interest and help. "And so," she said, "we accept them into the honorary order of the Sons of Bilitis—S.O.B.'s."

The audience roared at her sally. And a tall man with a clean-shaven head, who was wearing a red-checked dinner jacket, rose to make a brief speech. As he spoke, one of my neighbors said, "I hope he recites some of his poems." As though reading her mind, he promptly complied. His first offering was innocuous enough; his second was vaguely addressed to "My Darlings," and the import, rather impudently delivered, appeared to be that it didn't matter, My Darlings, how one dressed, behaved, or thought: it was up to him—or her—to please himself. "It is what we think and know of ourselves that counts"—that was the burden of it.

I could see the Reverend Brown stir restlessly, his face a grim mask. And then, abruptly, taking his wife by the arm, he strode from the chamber. Many eyes followed him out of the banquet room. "I guess," my neighbor said softly, "he didn't like the poetry."

Some regretted his precipitate departure. The featured speaker, Dr. Thane Walker, a handsome, middle-aged man with a ruddy face and snow-white hair, rising to his feet, said he would have liked to have acknowledged the Reverend Brown's contribution to the convention in the Reverend's presence. "It took a great deal of understanding and courage," he said, "for this minister to take such a fundamentalist stand in front of a group that his whole religious training had taught him to deplore." He looked around the room. "And all of us should remember," he said, "that we too came from homes where the fundamentalist views he expressed were a familiar way of life. It should be a reminder of our own origins, and we should never put that completely away from us."

Dr. Walker spoke modestly, without oratory. He had abandoned his scheduled address on the Golden Mean of Sex and talked instead about the meeting itself. "Just think," he said, "as you sit around this room, innocently conversing and enjoying yourself, what the public reaction would be if they knew a group of lesbians was meeting in this hotel. They would undoubtedly imagine the worst depravities." His scrutiny took in the whole room. "It is our job—your job," he said, "to let them know how wrong they would be in their appraisal of you."

As the banquet concluded, I still knew nothing about the Golden Mean of Sex. "Thane Walker," a convention-goer volunteered, "believes in the basic ambisexual nature of mankind. Heterosexuality or homosexuality is only an exterior through which the energy force of this ambisexuality is channeled. And what becomes important then is not whether the individual is heterosexual or homosexual but whether his creative force is best expressed one way or the other, and at what times."

"In other words," I said, "what seems to make him most useful or most enhances him is right for him?"

"Something like that," the interpreter agreed.

"But who," I asked, "is the best judge of what is most useful?"

My interlocutor looked startled. "Why, the individual, of course."

The next day I lunched with a D.O.B.er named Elsie.

"That was quite a song that Lisa Ben sang," I said.

She laughed. "It created quite a controversy later." Lisa had offered the song as the group's official anthem, and after due consideration, the offer had been turned down. "Some were afraid," Elsie explained, "that a club song would make them look like a fraternal organization instead of a serious self-help group."

I was surprised that Elsie had skipped the day's round of D.O.B. business meetings, since she was evidently in the inner circle.

She groaned. "You're lucky," she said, "that these meetings are for members only." She laughed. "But I don't think some of them mind my not being there. I'm not very popular today."

There had been some discussion of the poetry recital that had apparently precipitated the Reverend Brown's departure. "I thought that guy should never have been allowed to make that spiel," Elsie said. "And yet some girls thought it was cute."

Others had been appalled—and unprepared—for what they considered a thinly veiled contemptuous flouting of convention. "My Darlings," Elsie indicated, had been an unexpected encore. "It was bad public relations," she said.

She was very solemn. "How," she asked, "can we present a desirable picture to the public, as we're trying to do, when we approve something that would suggest we are different from other people?" She grimaced. "Anyway, I was against it as a matter of taste."

"I'm sure," I said, "that others felt as you did."

She nodded. "Quite a few, but some of the others are so damn absorbed in themselves that they live in a world of their own." She was clearly exasperated. "We might better have accepted Lisa's song," she said. "At least it meant something."

Lisa herself was not as concerned. When I spoke to her about it later, she thought it all a tempest in a teapot. "What was wrong with his poem?" she said indignantly. "I got the message."

The Ladder

JUNE 50¢

2nd National Convention

Hollywood, California

June 23-24, 1962

☆purpose of the

Daughters of BILITIS

A WOMEN'S ORGANIZATION FOR THE PURPOSE OF PROMOTING THE INTEGRATION OF THE HOMOSEXUAL INTO SOCIETY BY:

1 Education of the variant, with particular emphasis on the psychological, physiological and sociological aspects, to enable her to understand herself and make her adjustment to society in all its social, civic and economic implications——this to be accomplished by establishing and maintaining as complete a library as possible of both fiction and non-fiction literature on the sex deviant theme; by sponsoring public discussions on pertinent subjects to be conducted by leading members of the legal, psychiatric, religious and other professions; by advocating a mode of behavior and dress acceptable to society.

2 Education of the public at large through acceptance first of the individual, leading to an eventual breakdown of erroneous taboos and prejudices; through public discussion meetings aforementioned; through dissemination of educational literature on the homosexual theme.

3 Participation in research projects by duly authorized and responsible psychologists, sociologists and other such experts directed towards further knowledge of the homosexual.

4 Investigation of the penal code as it pertains to the homosexual, proposal of changes to provide an equitable handling of cases involving this minority group, and promotion of these changes through due process of law in the state legislatures.

The Daughters of Bilitis' monthly magazine, *The Ladder*, defines the purpose of this predominantly lesbian organization.

15

DAUGHTERS OF BILITIS

As I watched her across the banquet table, my eyes caught her ironic smile. "Are you enjoying the convention?" she asked dryly, as her companion, a much younger woman, regarded me impassively. I smiled back, squinting to make out the names on their tags.

"They're not our real names," the older woman remarked with amusement.

"Are you members?" I asked.

"Just looking." She shrugged, and then said, as though on impulse, "There's something I'd like to ask you later." She looked around the table significantly.

Her friend closed her eyes with a long-suffering look.

But over cocktails, later, the younger girl had thawed out considerably. "I've been telling my naïve friend here," she said, "that it is all a big camp."

"I think they're quite serious, don't you?" the older woman asked.

I regarded them both evenly. "Why not find out for yourselves?" I asked. "They're looking for new members."

The younger woman scoffed. "You bet they are."

"I think they're very silly, trying to change the world," the older woman said, "but I did think they meant well and I wanted your opinion."

To the Daughters of Bilitis, this was a familiar reaction. "We're used to suspicion," one of the founding "fathers" told me, "both from homosexuals and heterosexuals. It's just another thing we have to overcome." She spoke cheerfully.

Launched in San Francisco in 1955 by eight women who were tired of congregating in lesbian bars, the D.O.B. has proved a happy revolving door for hundreds wanting to do something about their lesbianism. Besides helping lesbians to understand themselves, the D.O.B. has embarked on a program of educating the public about the average lesbian. Ignoring stigmas and taboos, they have ventured on television and radio, submitted to interviews, and compiled surveys, helping reporters and social scientists seeking information about the lesbian.

In the area of public education, the D.O.B. has tried to make people aware that the lesbian is no threat to morality. Since many lesbians are teachers, it is particularly pertinent that the "myth" of child molestation be dispelled. Within the D.O.B. organization, no minors are permitted, and D.O.B. spokesmen stress that lesbians are exclusively interested in adult relationships. "Many lesbians," one authority pointed out, "don't even like children. And those who work with children often find greater rapport with even the young masculine mind."

As lesbians, they feel that they should be measured by the same yardstick as the heterosexual. "We believe," one D.O.B. official stated almost as a club credo, "that the practical solution to the problem is to judge sex activity on the grounds of whether or not society is harmed. Homosexual activity between consenting adults in private is not harmful to society. However, there must necessarily be protection given the public against offenders where assault, force, or violence is involved, and against indecent public behavior. We are not asking for license but rather a realistic approach to an ever-growing problem."

The average woman who joins the D.O.B. generally is motivated by a need to help herself. However, part of that self-help program appears to involve plunging into the areas of social reform rather loosely espoused by the D.O.B. "It is hard to feel sorry for yourself," a veteran D.O.B. officer said, "while fighting for such things as the right to adopt children, recognition by the churches, and the right to serve in government and the armed forces without fear or restraint."

Even more, the D.O.B. would like to see the time come when lesbian couples will be invited to friends' homes and other social functions with no more thought about it than if they were heterosexuals. "This, of course," one leader said with a smile, "is the utopia, which is obviously not just around the corner."

The founders of the organization are not dreamy-eyed idealists. Most of them have been successful in their careers and are socially popular, even when they are suspected of being lesbians. And they have tried to cast their organization along the heterosexual lines they are clearly familiar with.

Even as "organization women," they have observed a noteworthy prudence. Incorporated in the State of California, the Daughters of Bilitis is not strictly a lesbian organization, since it is open to any woman who is twenty-one or over and interested in the lesbian problem. "In that way," a leader pointed out, "membership doesn't automatically incriminate the member." Even the staunchest members, for fear of losing jobs or offending families, often do not use their actual names. But many cling stubbornly to their last name while grudgingly altering the first.

The D.O.B. has more formal sanction than California alone can give. It is also recognized by the federal government. Established for the high-minded purpose of promoting the integration of the homosexual into society, it qualifies under federal statute as a nonprofit, do-gooder corporation, and all contributions to its by no means bursting coffers are tax deductible.

From the standpoint of numbers, the D.O.B. is hardly a public menace. There are seldom more than thirty or forty members in any chapter at any one time, and there is no active proselytizing. "The membership," a D.O.B. member summarized, "is made up of women interested in the problems of the homosexual, some mothers, some heterosexual women with curiosity, and of course the lesbians themselves." The membership is perhaps ninety per cent lesbian. "Ideally, the lesbian joiner," an official said, "would tend to be the thoughtful, public-spirited, responsible type, with the capacity to absorb the philosophy helping her to help herself."

As a form of group therapy, Gab 'n' Java sessions, originating with the San Francisco chapter and spreading to other chapters, have been fruitful fun. Discussing their problems openly, the girls have often found, to their surprise and relief, that they are by no means unique. And they often find a reassuring togetherness even as they listen to guest sociologists, psychologists, and journalists tell what is wrong with them—and the world. And after the serious discussions are out of the way and the coffee gone, they may pull back the rugs and dance, play dominoes or checkers, or just get acquainted. "But these are definitely not camping sessions," leader Del Martin emphasized. "The girls, if they arrive alone, generally leave alone, and if they arrive with a particular girl, they leave with that girl. The D.O.B. may be a substitute for gay bar life, but it is certainly not a replacement."

Extending its coffee session to male homosexuals, the D.O.B. is now encouraging leaders of male homosexual organizations to discuss their common problems. "One of the troubles, of course," a D.O.B. officer sighed, "is that so many of these boys are trying to change the world, not themselves."

Variety often spices the D.O.B. schedule of events. One evening, for instance, there might have been a talk on "Self-Acceptance" by the D.O.B.'s favorite psychiatrist, the late Blanche Baker; a few days later, group bowling at the local sports center, or a debate on the controversial "We Walk Alone," by Ann Aldrich, or perhaps even a gala St. Valentine's Day party—bring your own sweetheart. The lighter get-togethers often have the added value of simulating normal activities. In September 1962, fully recovered from hosting a national convention, the Los Angeles chapter sponsored a fall fashion show. "As you well know," a membership announcement explained, "one of the purposes of the D.O.B. is the advocation of a mode of behavior and dress acceptable to society." And then came the intriguing query: "Well, what is a mode of behavior acceptable to society that you will like too?"

The show had a special theme—"A Gay Weekend"—and the clothes, furnished by a smart new shop which catered to the lesbian of taste, were modeled by D.O.B. members at a special garden party. The show was a grand success, and some of the proceeds went gratefully to the Blanche Baker Memorial Scholarship Fund.

Out of respect for this eminent San Francisco psychiatrist, who had the idea that homosexuals were *people*, the D.O.B. had thought that it would be a fitting tribute, after her recent death, to start the scholarship fund. The first scholarships were to be awarded in the summer of 1963, and one was earmarked frankly for a lesbian, the other for whomever could qualify, regardless of sexual tendencies. The lesbian scholarship was the secondary one, permitting a young lesbian to improve her earning power by sending her to a good vocational trade school. The other was open to any bright young woman over twenty-one who was already in college or graduated.

Like the late Dr. Baker, whom it venerates, the D.O.B. feels that the law unjustly discriminates against homosexuals, and that homosexuality in itself should not be a crime any more than heterosexuality. To put this belief into practice, the organization has embarked on an educational program that is making the California legislators sit up and take notice, even if they sit right back down again. During a recent legislative inquiry, for instance, Assemblyman John A. O'Connell, chairman of the California Assembly Interim Subcommittee on Constitutional Rights, was apprised by the D.O.B. that the cause of homosexuality was largely speculative, and not a matter of choice but of development. "Homosexual incidence," an open letter pointed out, "cannot be controlled by legislation, and the fear and insecurity imposed upon the homosexual by prejudiced and outmoded laws hamper the therapist in his efforts to help the individual make his adjustment to himself and society. Legal discrimination against the homosexual," the letter stressed, "benefited no one but the black-mailers."

Entrapment by police, the bugaboo of the homosexual, was roundly scored, even though male homosexuals, not lesbians, are its principal target: "We also call to your attention the tactics of certain law-enforcement agencies where the use of decoys is employed to entice individuals into engaging in an overt homosexual act leading to arrest. It would seem to us that the first duty of the police is to prevent, not to punish, crime—certainly not to incite or create crime for the sole purpose of its prosecution and punishment."

Despite their efforts at re-educating the public, D.O.B. leaders are more intent on reversing their own public image than on revamping society. And it is for this reason that they take the risks involved in appearing publicly, and in changing that image itself by intensive field work among lesbians who have withdrawn bitterly from society. Rehabilitation is a slow process, because it depends almost exclusively on personal association. "Doing anything significant through correspondence is difficult," Del Martin pointed out, "because we have often found we are spoofed by male voyeurs. And help by telephone is limited, not only because of the fact that our office in San Francisco is not always open, but because of limited knowledge of the actual circumstances." However, like Alcoholics Anonymous, individual members have responded at any hour of the day or night to help a lesbian in distress. "Many a time," one of the founders reported, "I have managed to talk some poor girl out of suicide, until somebody could get to her."

They do not baby supplicants. "They're already bogged down in self-pity," Del said, "and we try to take them out of it so that they can stand on their own two feet, without groaning or complaining, once they understand that virtually everybody has problems, and how you meet them is what counts."

There is also a library—perhaps the only lesbian library in the world—for the intelligent deviate with a wish to understand her problem. The titles of the books here are often revealing: *Odd Girl Out* and *Women in the Shadows*, by Ann Bannon; *Carol in a*

Thousand Cities, by Ann Aldrich; *Stranger on Lesbos,* by Valerie Taylor; Paula Christian's *Another Kind of Love* and *Love Is Where You Find It; The Third Sex* and *This Bed We Made,* by Artemis Smith. There is also a record library, featuring the "gayest songs on wax"—anything to make the lonely lesbian feel less alone.

Though it has formed new chapters in several states and is contemplating others, the D.O.B. is not interested in building up a big membership. "Girls get what they can out of the organization," Del said, "and they move on."

Del herself and her partner, Phyllis, editors of the D.O.B.'s mouthpiece, *The Ladder,* have been considered classic examples of what the D.O.B. can do for the woman who discovers that she is society's greatest taboo—the female homosexual. "In our own cases, of course," Del said, "it was so much simpler to adjust, because we found ourselves so busy trying to be helpful that we didn't have time to think of how cruelly the world was treating us." Her voice was faintly ironic.

To ease public disapproval of the lesbian, the D.O.B. has concentrated on altering the traditional conception of the lesbian as a brash parody of a woman; but admittedly they have had little influence on the bulk of lesbians who look and act that way. The D.O.B. feels this group to be a small, unrepresentative minority, and deplores the majority suffering in silence because they dare not become vocal enough to reveal themselves. But little by little, leaders feel, they are making converts to their way of thinking, and are sending out as emissaries of femininity girls who were as stereotyped as the next butch until they discovered the D.O.B. "We believe," Del Martin said, "that one of the first rules for social acceptance must necessarily be self-acceptance. And it is much simpler for girls to start learning self-acceptance in a group where the women are in varying stages of self-acceptance because they have finally found a group that will accept them for themselves."

I wondered how this therapy worked in practice.

Del cocked an eye at me. "Did you meet Tricia at the convention?"

I recalled a pretty girl with a Peter Pan haircut who looked as though she had been turned out by a smart eastern finishing school.

Del's voice reflected her amusement. "As Phyllis will bear me out," she said, "when Trish first came into the group, she was so belligerent that nobody would have anything to do with her—except, of course, Phyllis and myself." She laughed. "We're old hands, and, like psychiatrists, we don't take personal reactions very seriously."

"But how did she make herself so odious?" I asked. "She was certainly attractive enough."

Del chuckled. "Oh, we had a party, for instance, and the donation was the same whether you drank a Coke or a beer, and she complained about this inequity, since she drank nothing stronger than orange juice, and she felt she was being put upon. Since she had considerably more money than the other girls, many thought this was pretty small. Of course, as we older girls understood, she was only transferring her antisocial feelings to our group. It was up to us to win her over by showing her that things weren't any worse for her than for anybody else." She laughed pleasantly. "Just think, she was feeling sorry for herself, when one of our brightest and best girls is a Negro who is blind. This girl had everything against her. And yet, through gaining acceptance within the group, she has found contentment, and learned to express whatever she feels in poetry."

I recalled the quote that had been admiringly attributed to the blind girl by a pretty femme. "She looked at me," the femme had related, "and then turned to some other girls and said, 'Just remember, girls, I *saw* her first.'"

Trish, too, I had heard about. "Wasn't she the girl who blamed her lesbianism on a lesbian, saying she would never have been one if this girl hadn't brought her out?"

Del nodded. "We soon straightened her out on that, merely to reduce her resentment and also to get her to see things in proper focus. She was intelligent enough to know that if that one girl was all there was to it, she wouldn't be coming to us for help."

It took two years before Trish got over her hostility to the

D.O.B. "But she kept coming around," Del said, "because she didn't have anyplace else to go, and she knew in her heart that we were sincerely trying to help her live with herself."

Only recently, after two years, she had joined the group. "She is now very pleasant and personable, as you can see," Del observed, "and this attitude conveys itself to others outside, and makes life a little easier for her—and them."

Trish had consulted a psychiatrist before going to the D.O.B., and this had only seemed to complicate her problem. "They can say what they will about the head-shrinkers," Del said, "but the girls we generally have the most trouble with are the ones who have been seeking psychiatric help."

One of the most striking converts to normalcy was a young butch from out of state who had journeyed to San Francisco to learn more about the D.O.B. "When she first came to town and met us," Del recalled, "she was in full drag—men's clothes entirely. About a year and a half later, Phyllis and I made a date with her to go to the theater. She was to meet us for dinner first. Well, she arrived in a dress, hat, gloves, the works." The transformation was more than superficial. "She was indeed proud of herself, but, above all, she was comfortable with herself. She had learned to accept herself as a woman, though gay."

In the D.O.B., they have an expression known as "homo-cide," which is more than just a clever play on words. "For the homosexual to meet prejudice with whining, or to openly antagonize the public, or to cower in fear of authorities is," Del pointed out, "an act of homo-cide." The homosexual—the lesbian—limits herself terribly by identifying her role in life wholly with her sexuality. It reminded Del of a noted English playwright, a homosexual, who had visited the homosexual paradise in Fire Island and then turned away in disgust. "I'm a playwright who happens to be a homosexual," he said. "They're just homosexuals."

From working with girls who have turned from society, Del and her cohorts have learned: "If homosexuality is a disease, as some insist, it is not contagious, nor need it be crippling. With less public pressure, there would obviously be less crippling effect, but the lesbian's affliction stems more from the concern with the self—from self-pity, self-consciousness, self-abasement. It would be better if another 'self' were mustered—self-awareness, self-knowledge, self-observation. Then the homosexual would find that much of the rejection she feels is self-imposed. The lesbian who cries out, 'I am different, you don't understand me,' is setting into motion a chain reaction of doubt, guilt, and fear which will paralyze her life until she realizes, 'Yes, I'm different, so what?'"

I wondered how the D.O.B., by merely speaking a few simple truths, could make a girl listen, when a skilled psychiatrist might not do as well.

Del smiled. "It's not quite that simple," she said. "It's a sort of combination effort. The girl listens to what we have to say, and then she has a chance to see how it works with us, and on us." She laughed pleasantly. "Not many psychiatrists can do this for her."

In Del's own case, she had married young, had a child, and was reasonably fond of her husband. "There was nothing wrong with the sexual phase of our marriage," she said, "or not so that I noticed it. But I wasn't ready for the female responsibilities of marriage. I didn't like to do housework." She regarded Phyllis tenderly. "And I still don't. I didn't care too much about building up the male ego, which is one of the major chores of the good wife. I wanted the same little things done for me that my husband wanted."

A woman of culture and refinement, she was horrified at the implications of her self-discovery. But it was years before she finally made her first move—out of the marriage. And it was long after that before she made her first timid ventures into the world of lesbiana, and found herself drawn inevitably to cheap, tawdry bars completely foreign to her nature. "I didn't know where else to go—just to test myself, if nothing else." It was in the bars, of course, that she found the swaggering, rough-talking butch whose prototype the D.O.B. is now trying to change.

"There was not only a complete depreciation of femininity in those situations," she said, "which made the gay bars demeaning as a way of life, but they were making conformists out of girls who thought they were being nonconformists."

For many this was a rebellious phase. The confused girl, discovering with shock that she was a lesbian, denied all that was feminine and heterosexual about herself, recognizing that the world of convention would never accept a way that she herself would not have accepted in another. "In this first awareness of her own lesbianism," Del pointed out, "the neophyte tends to accentuate her masculine qualities and discard the feminine."

As Del saw it, from her own experience, girls in this stage were in flux; they could either flounder in a backwash of fear, guilt, and hostility, through not being able to adjust emotionally with their prior conditioning, or they could make their peace with themselves, and permit their personalities to roam beyond the inhibiting borders of conventionality. "As they expressed themselves freely, so would they learn, not only to live with what they were, but to profit by it, and emerge from the welter of conflict that had hemmed them in."

And so had it been with Del and Phyllis. They had kept their womanhood, and they had found each other, but only after they had first found themselves. "Above all," Del said, "I tell girls, 'You are a woman, and never do anything that would be unbecoming to you as a woman.'"

Del herself was a serious-faced woman of middle age, a few years older than Phyllis. They had lived together comfortably for years, had responsible jobs, and managed to share each other's personal and family problems. Neither looked the way most people would expect a lesbian to look, but Del's hair was shorter than Phyllis', and she appeared to be the butch, if so crude a term could be used to describe so gracious a lady. In the strength of their own relationship, both seemed to have found the necessary strength to be tolerant, and even humorous, about the lesbian's lot. As some lesbians practiced it secretly, they openly advocated a togetherness with society. "How often," Del said, "have we heard the homosexual decry the dual role which society has foisted upon him or her? But think of the many roles the heterosexual is forced to play, and the compromises he must make." She regarded me with a benign look. "I remind the girls that society makes the same demands on heterosexual and homosexual—consideration for others and decorum in public."

Through the public-relations media, while trying to change the face of lesbianism, Del was also striving to convince the public that this new face was harmless. "Sexual activity between consenting adults in private," she observed, "is not harmful to society, and for the first time in United States history, the State of Illinois so stated in 1962 in its revised penal code." She hoped this marked the beginning of a legal break-through.

Progress was admittedly slow. "We can't very well hope to overcome the prejudices of centuries in a few years," Del said, "but we can keep trying."

During the D.O.B. convention, I was given an indication of how the group uses the mass media to win acceptance for lesbians, if not the lesbian way of life. The president-elect of the Los Angeles chapter, the same winsome brunette who had briefed me in the hotel coffee shop, told me with suppressed excitement that she was being interviewed on television by Paul Coates, a Los Angeles newsman with a considerable tv following.

"What for?" I asked.

"Oh," she said, "so that millions of people can look and listen to a real live lesbian and perhaps get over the idea that we're all some sort of monster."

"Won't you be blindfolded?" I asked.

"Oh, no," she said, "I have nothing to be ashamed of." She hesitated. "I'm not using my own name, but that's only because of my family. I don't want to hurt them if I can help it."

On the evening of the scheduled broadcast I was with friends in Beverly Hills. "Do you mind," I asked, "if I turn on the Paul Coates show?"

My hostess, a transplanted Southern belle, asked casually, "Who is he interviewing tonight?"

"A girl I just met, a lesbian."

Her eyebrows went up in surprise. "A lesbian!" she exclaimed. "Don't tell me they're on tv now?"

"Wait a few minutes," I said, "and you'll find out."

"Not me," she drawled, "and I don't think the children should watch it, either." The children were old enough to have children. "Why, it's sickening, just the thought of it."

The man of the house humored his mother. "Our guest has to watch it," he joshed, "it's part of his job, and so we might as well." He was as curious as most young men about lesbians.

His mother looked up with spirit. "I don't know what's gotten into the young men these days. In my day the men were interested in women who were glad to be women, and knew what to do about it."

She was still grumbling when the program came on, but had permitted herself to be cajoled into watching the show. But she stirred uneasily in her chair as the black-and-white images formed on the screen, and we saw an attractive woman, her hair swept back, sitting at ease with her interviewer.

"That's not her," my hostess said. "She doesn't look like a lesbian to me." There was doubt and suspicion in her voice. And then, as a close-up of the girl was shown, the superimposed lettering over the image spelled out: HEAD OF A LESBIAN ORGANIZATION.

She clucked her tongue incredulously. "Can you imagine that?" she said, "right on our own television, bringing this awful thing into the house?" She turned to her son. "What about the children: don't they think anything of them?"

He glanced at his watch. "All good children should be safe and snug in their beds by now, Mother."

She tossed her head, but her eyes were glued to the screen. "She certainly doesn't look like a lesbian," she repeated in wonderment.

Her son, a veteran of theater life, was amused. "Mom, the most beautiful girls in the world are lesbians. I've worked with them."

She looked at him in shocked disbelief.

The announcements were out of the way, and the interview had begun. My hostess sat with pursed lips, still shaking her head.

The pleasant-faced brunette was introduced as Terry. Her voice was well bred and her diction good. She spoke forcefully and to the point. She was obviously well educated. In response to the questions, she gave a brief rundown of the organization and its avowed purposes.

"How many members are there?" Coates asked.

"Oh, between one hundred and twenty-five and one hundred and fifty."

Coates seemed puzzled. He looked at her closely. "Did you mean to add the word 'thousand' to that figure?"

She smiled, shaking her head.

The expression on my hostess' face darkened. "My word," she said, "a hundred of them running loose is bad enough."

Nobody had any idea how many lesbians there were, Terry pointed out, and she made an appeal for fair play for a minority group. "Our aim," she said, "is integration of the homosexual into society, and we advocate for lesbians behavior and dress acceptable to society." She certainly looked a model of acceptability herself.

My hostess' eyebrows lifted sharply. "Everything," she said in her Southern drawl, "is integration these days. That's all they think about."

Interviewer Coates registered surprise that the D.O.B. would dare meet in open convention. "Aren't you inviting a disturbance?" he asked.

Terry smiled easily. "Not at all," she said. "We have received official recognition from law-enforcement officials and professional people. We are a serious group."

The talk got around to gay bars. As Coates agreed that the gay bar was perhaps helpful in isolating the homosexual—male and female—my hostess couldn't restrain herself. "You mean," she said, "there's whole bars full of them?"

On the screen, the interviewer and the interviewee had squared off. "Don't you think," he said, "that gay bars may have an adverse effect on innocent youngsters?"

Terry smiled sweetly. "Innocent youngsters," she said, "don't belong in bars."

And then she pointed out that the D.O.B. permitted only those girls who were twenty-one or over to any of its functions, social or business.

Terry seemed to be having the better of it. When she described herself as a college graduate, Coates nodded, and my hostess rose to new heights of indignation. "Is that what they teach them in college these days?" she demanded.

The questioning continued, with a reminder that lesbianism was a great stigmatizer. "Why, then," asked Coates, "did you come on my program?"

Terry said calmly, "Because you asked me."

Coates was mildy annoyed, and my hostess exploded. "The hussy! She knew what he meant."

Coates rephrased his question slightly.

"Because," Terry answered, "I believe in what the D.O.B. is do-ing educationally, and because I'm the least vulnerable. I own my own business, a poodle-grooming shop, and so I can't lose my job if somebody should happen to recognize me and not like the idea."

As the interview ended, my hostess snapped off the television set with a flourish. "Just never let me have my poodle groomed at that shop," she said.

"But, Mother," her son said, laughing, "you don't have a poodle."

She was unreconciled. "Well, that's one animal I will never own."

"You would have never known she was a lesbian," I observed, "if she hadn't told you."

She snorted contemptuously. "All the more reason to be alarmed," she said. "You can't tell who's decent any more."

In D.O.B. circles, the interview was considered a great triumph. Tapes were made of it, and it was played back at D.O.B. functions. Proudly it was announced that millions of viewers had tuned in to the show.

"Do you think the interview served any useful purpose?" I asked a D.O.B. official.

She nodded emphatically. "It gave the girls a sense of accomplishment—and status—and was a symbol of acceptance."

I wonder what my hostess in Beverly Hills would have thought of that.

16

CLIMBING THE LADDER

A small office in downtown San Francisco is the Singapore of the lesbian world. It is the crossroads of lesbian news and views, the distillery of virtually all thought and activity in the lesbian grapevine. It is headquarters for *The Ladder*, a publication by lesbians for lesbians.

It is sold on the newsstands in the larger cities where homosexuality is regarded with indifference, and it is sent through the mails, its right to be heard defended by a recent ruling of the U. S. Supreme Court.

It is an important voice in lesbian affairs, and its subscription lists number many secret lesbians whose only association with the forbidden world of lesbians lies in the multigraphed pages of this handy-sized publication. From reader response, the editors have realized that their humble publication is a heartening voice in the lesbian wilderness—as useful in its way as the forums of ancient Rome. "It is evident," observed chief editor Del Martin, "that *The Ladder* helps many realize they are not alone, and that there are others who share their problem."

Not all *Ladder* subscribers are lesbians. Many are sociologists, psychologists, educators, novelists, and journalists, and they read it as avidly as any lesbian. And though the circulation is but a few thousand, the editors proudly estimate that many times that number read their publication in virtually all the states and the civilized nations of the world as it is eagerly passed around each month.

In it, those interested in lesbians can find practically everything they want. Every facet of the lesbian problem is explored in *The Ladder*—a title symbolic of the D.O.B.'s crusade to elevate the lesbian colony in their own eyes and the eyes of the world. Lesbian humor, sometimes Rabelaisian, more often rueful, is sprinkled liberally through *The Ladder's* twenty-eight pages. Reports of homosexual conferences and of D.O.B. activities are carried to its readers. The progress in public acceptance, if any, is duly noted. Books about lesbians and homosexuals generally are reviewed. A few erotic poems by amateurs are printed without comment.

And the emanations from readers are equally revealing, reflecting the spread of the lesbian grapevine from Alaska to Florida, from the rock-bound coast of Maine to sunny California, where a flourishing grapevine has been wryly dubbed another "grapes of wrath."

As it has grown, *The Ladder* has shown a notable flexibility. In a pioneer issue in September 1957, *The Ladder* advised its readers that they had nothing to fear in joining the Daughters of Bilitis. "A person is as secure in the Daughters of Bilitis," noted Kenneth C. Zwerin, a San Francisco attorney, "as he would be in any other fraternal or social organization that makes certain demands of its members and requires that they accept certain beliefs in order to become members."

Pointing out that the D.O.B. was a legally chartered organization in the nation's largest state, Zwerin had the reassuring word: "Forget about the mailing lists or membership lists being turned over to the police or postal authorities: it won't happen."

Lesbian security, job-wise and socially, was stressed in this comforting message for D.O.B. members: "As far as the security of your job is concerned, any employer can fire without reason. But if you do your job, you will have little to fear. But if you're worried about your private life all the time, you probably won't do good work and will get fired." Attorney Zwerin agreed, as have so many

others, that the female homosexual had it all over the male counterpart in respect to built-in security. And he listed three basic
reasons: "By her very biological nature, she is not promiscuous;
she prefers a quiet domestic type of life; she does not solicit in
public places."

She was also in a far superior position, legally as *The Ladder*
noted: "'The law prohibiting oral-genital contact has never been
applied to two women in the State of California,' he [Zwerin]
said, 'only to two men. There have been no cases reported in
California involving homosexual charges against two consenting
adult women.'" [But since 1957, when this statement was made,
women have been involved in such cases.]

But with time, learning to be practical, *The Ladder* was not so
sure about the wisdom of gratuitously revealing oneself regardless
of police immunity and constitutional rights. To encourage contributions to *The Ladder*, there were new assurances to anonymous
readers. Together with this assurance came a denial that the
D.O.B. was a clandestine organization: "'Clandestine' means 'secret,' 'hidden,' or 'underhanded.' Those who would question the
existence of our organizations would seem to infer the 'underhanded' definition. They base the accusation upon the fact that
the organizations have declared quite openly that with the exception of national officers, the anonymity of members and subscribers would be protected."

It was a hostile society that made this step strategically necessary, *The Ladder* explained. "This would seem to be very logical
under the circumstances in which we live in this society. Ignorance
breeds fear and hostility, and until education in this field relieves
the necessity, concealment of identity is only practical. Just as
many authors who have broached a controversial subject have
chosen to use a pseudonym, many members do likewise. This matter is left entirely up to the individual."

But while discretion often seemed the better part of valor, *The
Ladder* nevertheless ranged boldly over every conceivable subject of
interest to lesbians, including the rapidly growing problem of
lesbians living together in a state approximating marriage. Three

years after his reassuring words on security, attorney Zwerin was exploring for *Ladder* readers the ticklish legal problems of the lesbian couple. He was now casually referred to as "Ken" by *The Ladder,* indicating the confidence and trust in which he was held. His discussion of the problem was made quite openly at a banquet sponsored by the D.O.B. in downtown San Francisco, and was engagingly reported by *The Ladder.* "Ken," the editors announced, "said that in the first instance the problem was to find a 'couple.' And then came the description of how to become legally entangled, if you were lesbians and felt that certain way together. He did make it clear that there was no such thing as community property (not even in California) and that the thing to do was to leave everything to one's estate and to have an attorney draw up the will. He stated that 'holographic wills' were legal, but that those drawn up by an attorney were safer. Among Ken's many delightful sayings, this one stands out: 'Hell hath no fury like a dispossessed heir.' "

For couples sure of staying together, there was sound practical advice: "Mr. Zwerin suggested too that lesbian couples purchase property and hold their bank accounts in joint tenancy: in such cases the property automatically goes to the survivor. While there would be an inheritance tax, he did not feel this to be a deterrent."

The lawyer was not advocating any particular way of life, the editors stressed, but merely trying to help the principals anticipate the problems they could expect—legalistically.

In every field, *The Ladder* reflected the homosexuals' rising interest in the fight for equal rights—such equal rights, for instance, as rest-room privacy. In June 1962, in its special convention issue, *The Ladder's* headlines trumpeted a new victory: "COURT RULES FOR REST-ROOM PRIVACY." Very objectively, the story followed:

"The California State Supreme Court ruled early last month on the right of privacy in a rest room. The Court issued writs prohibiting the Los Angeles Superior Courts from trying three men charged with 'infamous crimes against nature,' because police obtained evidence against them by watching through a 'spy-pipe' while they were in a public rest room at a Long Beach amusement park.

"The 'spy-pipe' operation constituted illegal search in violation of the men's constitutional rights, the Court held unanimously. An opinion written by Justice B. Rey Schauer said: 'Authority of police officers to spy on occupants of toilet booths—whether in an amusement park or a private home—will not be sustained on the theory that if they watch enough people long enough some [illegal] acts will eventually be discovered.'"

Blandly, *The Ladder* concluded: "Police said they kept the rest room under surveillance at the request of the amusement-park proprietor 'to do something in regard to the homosexual activity going on inside.'"

While it stayed out of politics, as an objective publication should, *The Ladder* was extremely sensitive to the growing clamor by the homosexual minority for representation at the polls. And it was obvious from *The Ladder* pages that the lesbian was beginning to think of where her best voting interests lay as a lesbian, as well as a woman and as a member of the general electorate. In July 1960, while the two major parties were deliberating over their presidential nominees, *The Ladder* pondered the importance of "the homosexual vote": "Is there or could there be a homosexual voting bloc? How much voting strength does the homosexual minority have? To what extent does that or can that vote influence an election?" Such was the probing tone of the article.

In a special reference to the 1959 San Francisco mayoralty election, the magazine pointed out that homosexuality unfortunately had been one of the central issues, and may inadvertently have had some bearing on the final result. It noted without heat: "There was a strong feeling among the homosexual minority in this city against the incumbent Mayor George Christopher—*until* his opponent, Russell Wolden, charged the Mayor with harboring 'organized homosexuals' in his midst. Christopher won the election, and it was interesting to note that there were some nine thousand votes cast in that election where the voters abstained on the issue [certainly the most important] of Mayor."

And so *The Ladder* speculated judiciously, without forming any broad opinion: "What actually does this mean? Did the homosexual vote defeat Wolden because of his attack on their group? Or were the people of San Francisco too wise and too sophisticated to take the charges seriously?"

Preoccupation with "the homosexual vote" continued to develop, perhaps in keeping with that vote. Before the November 1961 elections in San Francisco, *The Ladder* noted that a liberal candidate, quietly favored by many homosexuals, was being offered to the electorate: "Among the many candidates running for supervisor in the San Francisco November elections is Jose J. Sarria, who declared simply that he is concerned with 'equality before the law.' Rumor has it that he is the 'homosexual's candidate,' the idea being to tally by secret ballot the voting strength of this minority group in the city of San Francisco."

Sarria himself had nothing to do with this support, and was defeated. The election was inconclusive.

The Ladder is by no means insular in its political interests. It is a strong supporter of women's rights everywhere, and generally favors anybody favoring full emancipation of the so-called weaker sex. There has been some support recently for President Kennedy because he felt that women should get their due in the workaday world. In May 1962, for instance, *The Ladder* pointed alertly to a Kennedy move to give working women vocational equality, and was not greatly concerned whether these women were lesbian or not. "A commission," *The Ladder* reported, "to study discrimination against women, particularly in wages and promotion, has been set up by President Kennedy. The President told the commission to make a nationwide study of laws that affect women's status adversely, and to publicize its findings. Kennedy said that nine out of ten women hold jobs at some time in their lives, and 'we want to be sure they are able to move ahead and perform their functions without any discrimination by law or by implication.'"

The Ladder was happy to report progress toward ending male favoritism: "The Civil Service Commission immediately called on all government agencies to review their policies on hiring women. The Commission said that from now on, agencies seeking top-management personnel and specifying men—as happens ninety per cent of the time—would have to show cause for the restriction."

The matter of a lesbian's religion is a touchy one, and *The Ladder* has frequently aired this preoccupation of lesbians with church groups that shun them. And, with equal faithfulness, the publication has reproduced the views of the very clergymen who find overt lesbians difficult to fit into their conception of God's scheme. Occasionally, however, *The Ladder* permits itself a little irony. In discussing the opinions of the Reverend Fordyce Eastburn, an Episcopal chaplain of San Francisco, the magazine noted that the Reverend Eastburn had been a minister for twenty-six years, was married, with three children, but "had no real experience with homosexuals in his counseling except for one admitted lesbian."

And then *The Ladder* took off mildly on the worthy Reverend, who had expressed his views at a D.O.B. meeting. "Having admitted that homosexuality was an unknown island to him, Reverend Eastburn proceeded to inform us that he felt that homosexuality was a 'primary disorder of the Divine Plan.' However," the magazine observed slyly, "he was charitable, since 'God accepts, we must also.'

"A practicing homosexual could be accepted into the church," the article went on, "but how long such a person could continue in his actions once he had accepted Jesus Christ was a burning question to Reverend Eastburn. Chastity or marriage were the only alternatives a true Christian had, in his eyes."

With almost brutal candor, *The Ladder* summed up the clergyman's dark hopes for the lesbian: " 'Homosexuals,' he told us, 'were (1) afflicted with a disorder of nature; (2) must attempt to stay away from their sources of temptation; and (3) should take therapy and attempt to make a heterosexual adjustment to life.' " And then *The Ladder* editor wryly observed for her lesbian audience: "If you can't make number three, I presume that leaves you celibate, presuming further that you're capable of remaining celibate and retaining your sanity."

The readers, too, got into the act in the perennial controversy of the lesbian with her religious past—and present. With perhaps a little more equanimity, *The Ladder* published a countering view from a Paris reader whose unconventional position was countersigned only by the initials "P.L.": "I believe it paradoxical, in a world in full evolution, that our attitudes, our prejudices, all our ethic continues to stem from a medieval Christian code which took over ancient Hebrew laws all of two thousand years ago. The Hebraic law against masturbation and homosexuality was required in order to permit the extension of the race (as with polygamy), but they don't have a place in our modern society. In our too peopled world, sexuality doesn't mean reproduction, and homosexual practices are a natural means of birth control."

Of all publications, only *The Ladder* has ever discussed the problems of lesbians bringing up children—by previous marriages, of course. After frank discussions within the D.O.B., guided by a guest authority in parental education, *The Ladder* carried the comforting headline for its many married and unmarried readers: "RELATIONSHIP NOT SO DEVIANT IF CHILD HAS LOVE AND SECURITY." The story was equally reassuring, as it pointed out that only love was required—that and the child's feeling wanted: "In referring to children raised in a deviant relationship, it was pointed out that anything that strays from the sincere feeling or true values can be said to be deviant, and there can very definitely be deviant heterosexuals as well as deviant homophiles. The emotional stability of parents will determine the background of the child. Love and security overshadow almost all other factors. If a child knows love, gives love, and receives love, and knows he is wanted, chances are that he will be normal and well adjusted."

However, one concession was made in the summary. "Both male and female children need strong contact with both male and female figures to balance out their life." There was no suggestion as to where that male figure was to come from. But there was a warning to the butch or femme mother openly living with a lesbian partner. "In any third-person relationship, the child will turn to one or the other; he will try to pit one person against the other. He does this because he cannot focus on the situation as a whole. All this is part of growing up." In other words, "Auntie," too, had a responsibility for little Johnnie.

Unlike the male homosexual, the lesbian could often enjoy a laugh at her own predicament and the picture she offered a scoffing society. And she could poke fun similarly at the weak chinks in the heterosexual armor, particularly on the score of love and amour, a common interest.

And so, while generally thoughtful, devoted to serious issues, *The Ladder* reflected this almost undefinable impishness of the lesbian, as it seized on homosexuality and heterosexuality as a target for its sense of the absurd. Its tongue-in-cheek treatment of the Eddie Fisher, Elizabeth Taylor, Richard Burton triangle at its sizzling peak reflected a tolerant view of heterosexual hi-jinks and was perhaps a sly bid for similar tolerance:

"From the New York *News*," *The Ladder* deadpanned, "came the report that Elizabeth Taylor's real love is her movie director, Joseph Mankiewicz, not actor Richard Burton.

"The report that the Taylor-Fisher-Burton triangle is really a square, with Burton acting as a decoy to cover up Mankiewicz's involvement, was denied by studio sources.

"Mankiewicz, wisecracking, declared, 'The real truth is that I am in love with Burton, and Miss Taylor is the cover-up for us.'

"Meanwhile, back at the ranch (in the U.S.A.), husband Eddie Fisher was being questioned by reporters as to whether or not he intended to marry Natalie Wood, who had recently separated from her husband, Bob Wagner.

"Fisher reported impatiently, 'Of course not, I'm going to marry Bob Wagner.'"

And so *The Ladder* saluted the great Hollywood romance of our times.

From Herb Caen's column in a San Francisco paper, *The Ladder* dredged up a chuckle or two at the lesbian's expense. "In a

Sausalito (San Francisco's Bohemia) bar, two mannish-looking girls were discussing a mutual friend, and one said, 'I can't stand her voice: it's so effeminate.'"

And again: "'Just before the raid on the Taybush [a bar],' reports Ralph Barrie, 'two of the customers [female] were having a terrible argument, which ended when one screamed at the other, "Don't you dare lower your voice to me."'"

Although the literary content of *The Ladder* has been criticized by readers and writers alike, some of the verse and prose clearly convey the universal message of love. That message is often equally illuminating to the non-lesbian, not only of lesbian literature, but of lesbian life. For instance, the tone poem "I Love Her" begins quite eloquently: "I love her fragrant hair with its flaxen strands that sweep backwards from a wide, clear forehead, and the curly tendrils that form an intricate design upon her slim neck."

And then, after further revealing the tenderness of her heart, the poetess soars into poetic heights somewhat reminiscent of the Songs of Solomon, and certainly as graphic as anything the most literal-minded could demand:

"I love her mouth with the flexible corners and the genuine smile that goes deep and sincere . . . and is void of mere surface qualities . . . and her voice that passes through smooth, well-moulded lips, with a richness that is a delight to the ear and a caress to the soul. The same voice that can scale an octave; the higher keys in moments of gaiety . . . and then recede to the pit of her being in moments of stronger emotion."

And it continues warmly, with all the fervor of a spring day, indicating perhaps the lesbian idyl, the dream of all girls whose love image is another girl:

"The slender hands I love with their grace in motion and beauty in repose . . . the way they paint colorful pictures in the air with their expressive gestures . . . the fingers slim and warm with feeling, I truly love above all else . . . fingers that twine about yours in a firm clasp and the knowledge of sincere friendship that flows through me when the grip is close and true."

For those in a different mood to read of love, there was *nik's* couplet, indicating the cynical attitude of the lesbian who has found love not all it is cracked up to be:

> Many have I, but none to please me,
> Many have me, but none completely.

Or, by the same author, reflecting the feeling of futility of so many lesbian lovers:

> I have given my body,
> I have given my love.
> I have flung my soul
> At the moon above.
> I have poured out my thoughts
> To a secret friend.
> And I have nothing left
> At this long day's end.

The burgeoning market in lesbian literature does not pass unnoticed. From time to time the leading fiction and non-fiction dealing with lesbian themes are reviewed and discussed, and some sample fiction, necessarily short, is printed. And many professional writers, some quite distinguished, have used the pages of *The Ladder* to discuss their own ideas about the treatment of homosexuality in serious works.

In the July 1960 issue of *The Ladder*, Artemis Smith, a pseudonym for the female author of *Odd Girl* and *The Third Sex*, knowingly discussed the trials and tribulations of a writer stereotyped as the author of lesbian fiction.

The Ladder was tacitly sympathetic: "She told how one of her novels was turned into a lesbian novel, against her wishes, by the publisher. She mentioned that while this was probably one of the best times to get a lesbian novel published, she had some truly good ones in her closet that her publisher wouldn't take. It seems that a stereotype must be followed in order to make the publisher interested."

But Artemis, as the saying goes, was hankering to go straight, literary-wise, seeking perhaps a broader audience or broader expression. "Artemis," the readers were advised, "is now more interested in making lesbians and homosexuals background characters in heterosexual novels. She feels that more good can be done this way than with the purely lesbian novels she has written and that she could do a higher class of novel and get less blue-pencil editing." The new format was already launched: "She is writing a new book about a young man in the armed services who is neither a homosexual nor a Communist, but who gets branded both by 'association.'"

How does the general writer approach the homosexual theme? When *The Ladder* reviewed one of her books, the distinguished novelist Mary Renault sent in a letter from South Africa, expressing her opinion that homosexuality should be incidental to its setting in a historical novel and not given more importance than the author intended. Pure self-expression was not the mark of the true artist. "Miss Strong [the reviewer] describes the subject of *The Last of the Wine* as male homosexuality, transferred to an ancient Greek setting, and comments on the tolerance of its reception," the author observed. "I think this book was in fact received rather as a portrayal of Athens during the Peloponnesian War, and of some members of the Socratic circle. I hope so, since this was how I wished it to be judged. The love relationship in the book is one characteristic of that society rather than our own; not only because of its recognized public standing, but because the two young men are, like most classic Greeks, fully bisexual. . . . In my view, it is a primary duty of the historical novelist to make his characters people of their era. The writer who exploits a period setting for propaganda purposes, drawing fallacious parallels with his own society, at once sacrifices his integrity not less than by commercial vulgarizing."

The author minimized the homosexual theme in another novel. "In *The King Must Die*, the Amazon bull-girls who attract Theseus in Crete have a relevant purpose. They foreshadow his famous love affair with Hippolyta. They aim to make his youth consistent with his later story. These references are of slight importance in the novel as a whole, the theme of which is primitive kingship. . . ."

The primary loyalty of the artist, the novelist pointed out, was to a basic humanity and his sense of man's place in the universe. "Asked 'what are you?' his spontaneous answer will be 'a writer' (or painter or whatever it may be), because this is the first intention of his will. If in the practice of his craft he cannot learn maturity enough to raise his sights above mere self-expression, or concern for public status of his own group, or even social reform, he submits to a castration of his creative self for which both as artist and human being he will be the poorer all his life."

This rather sound literary advice was printed without comment.

Shunted about by society, hearing disparaging remarks about homosexuality which cut her the more because she dare not speak out, the lesbian frequently compensates by developing an attitude of bland superiority, which often fools not only others but herself. This expresses itself often in scorn of straight society, the "squares," and traditional concepts of marriage, religion, family, whatever normal society rests on, together with the innuendo that the homosexual somehow comprises a knowledgeable elite. "If you are congenitally a homophile (highly doubtful from present knowledge)," reader F.B. wrote with self-conscious authority, "all the guilt feelings and all the psychiatrists in the world are not going to change your needs, any more than they can change the color of your eyes." And then the identification with special distinction: "You have an extra burden to bear as you go through life in an uninformed society, but so—in their own special ways—have artists, poets, or original thinkers of any kind."

By orderly expansion, *The Ladder* plans to spread its message of kinship throughout the world. As the organ of the D.O.B., its pages indicate not only the growth of new chapters but the groundwork necessary for each chapter to become successful. Before the Los Angeles chapter took shape, there was evidence of simmering interest in organized lesbianism in Southern California. "Regarding the establishment of a Los Angeles chapter of the

D.O.B.," V.V. wrote from Long Beach, "I would most certainly be interested in knowing more about the organization and in ascertaining whether my particular talents might be of some use in this very worthy group. Now that a member of your original group will be present to do the groundwork, I cannot help but feel encouraged. At the present time I am taking a course with One Institute in Los Angeles [a homosexually oriented organization] in order to give me more knowledge and perspective regarding the homophile field."

Equally cheering was the correspondence before the Chicago chapter formed, but the Pacific Northwest was a harder nut, as a note from S.J. plainly revealed: "You ask if homophile women in the Pacific Northwest are 'ready' to form a chapter of the D.O.B. in this area. There are a few, like my friends and myself, who are 'ready' and would be willing to give time and effort toward making it a success. However, I have met many others, who are either too fearful to associate themselves with a homophile organization or seem to be too concerned with themselves to be willing to 'give' their time and talents to any organization. The first need more courage and the latter need more unselfishness."

New York, of course, was a natural. "I noted with interest the discussions on raising children in a deviant relationship: is it possible to find out more regarding this problem? Also I noted with interest your plans to organize the New York area. While I would be most anxious to remain discreet and discriminating in social contact, I would enjoy meeting with, or hearing from, others in the general New York area who are genuinely sincere about the organization." Signed "S.B."

And interest was mounting in Texas, Illinois, New Jersey, Pennsylvania, even the Canadian provinces. From Toronto, G.H. lamented: "Too bad I am so far away. I would love to drop in on one or two of those sessions. I don't suppose you have heard of anything akin to your organization in Canada? If we could have such meetings, it would be quite something."

By and large, immersed in their number-one problem, *Ladder* readers look upon the publication as a major treat. From Alaska,

N.J.C. rhapsodized: "Getting *The Ladder* up here is almost like a letter from home," and New Jersey's M.G. summed up reader response pretty well when she wrote: "I think the Daughters of Bilitis is the greatest thing for us girls, who are supposed to be different."

In its sixth year now, *The Ladder* recently showed that it is coming of age. It is beginning to develop a heterosexual look, so to speak. In the footsteps of older, more conventional magazines, the editors announced in July 1962 that their publication was going completely respectable, and might soon be fat and fussy like other women's magazines. "Starting with this issue," the editors proclaimed, "*The Ladder* will henceforth be copyrighted by the Daughters of Bilitis, Inc. This will afford protection to contributors (artists, poets, and authors) under the copyright laws of the United States."

17

THE INTERLUDE

It was apparently love at first sight. "There was something about the way her hair fell over her face, the smudge on her cheek," Cindy said. They were living together three weeks later. "Why wait?" Cindy asked. She smiled. "Nobody had thought anything of my moving in with another girl." Bobbie had been the first and only one. Now, after six months, Cindy was sure there would never be another.

"How do you know?" I asked.

She smiled confidently. "I just know." And then she added quickly, with a smile that dimpled her pretty face, "You would have to know Bobbie to know why I am so sure."

There was no mistaking the feeling in the girl's eyes and voice. It was virtually idolatry. "When you meet her," Cindy said with assurance, "you'll see what I mean."

"You never knew anyone before?" I asked.

Cindy frowned. "How do you mean that?"

"You had no physical relationship before?"

She shook her head. "Not with a woman."

There had been a couple of men—boys—but Bobbie was the first on the distaff side, and the first that mattered. "I was engaged once," Cindy confided, "but it didn't work. It wasn't until I met Bobbie that I knew what living was."

"Don't you think the right young man might have had a similar effect?" I asked.

"I like men," she said, "but they just don't do anything for me. It was like being a spectator at a party."

Born a Catholic, of a middle-class family, she did not strike me as a girl of easy morality. "How long was it," I asked, "before you and Bobbie became intimate?"

"Oh," she said, knitting her brow, "a week or ten days."

Her dark Latin face kept its frown. "I can remember the exact day we met, and every day after that."

"Who was the aggressor?" I asked

"It was mutual," she answered shortly.

"As a neophyte, you could hardly make the first move."

"That's true," she conceded, "but I knew what I wanted."

Hadn't this been an unusually brief courtship?

"Oh, no," she exclaimed, "I knew right away."

"Did she encourage the relationship?"

"Oh, no," said Cindy loyally, "she warned me to think it over."

"Why the warning if the relationship was good?" I asked.

Cindy frowned. "There was an age difference, and personality differences—nothing important." She closed her eyes dreamily. "Bobbie has taught me many wonderful things."

For a lesbian, she seemed strangely miscast. "Which type are you?" I asked. "You don't even look like a lesbian."

She seemed disappointed. "I don't?" She slapped her checked woolen slacks. "I'm not trying to hide it. I just don't think I'm any type."

"Not femme or butch?"

She shook her head. "I guess I'm just a crazy mixed-up lesbian."

Cindy generally did the cooking, sewing, and general housework around the house. "Since Bobbie's older and it's her apartment, she decides who does what. But it varies from day to day."

I had met Cindy in the cocktail lounge of the hotel in which the D.O.B. held its convention. She had been wearing a name badge on her lapel, as I had, and I had thought her an observer, like myself. She seemed no more than twenty; she was of medium height, with dark, flashing eyes, black hair neatly bobbed, and was sturdily proportioned. She had talked so freely that I was afraid she had mistaken me for an analyst. "Oh, no," she explained, "Bobbie says that we should acknowledge what we are, and respect ourselves for what we are."

Cindy had not said much about her family. Her mother was divorced when Cindy was young. There were no men around, except for mother's boy-friend and an occasionally visiting uncle.

"How did your mother feel about your moving out?" I asked.

Her voice went dead. "Oh, she thought at first it might be a good thing."

"How does she feel now?"

"Who knows?" she said, stifling a yawn.

Cindy had a good job as a secretary, and was self-sufficient. "I'm twenty-four," she said, "and my family treats me as if I were fourteen."

Again I couldn't help but note how wholesomely middle class she appeared. She would have been the last person I would have taken for a lesbian. "Did you ever have any indication previously that you preferred girls?" I asked.

"You won't laugh?"

I promised.

When she was nineteen, she used to wait for the bus at the same corner every morning, and her interest was captured by a pretty light-haired girl waiting at the same stop. Without directly staring, Cindy noticed her cute nose, her smile, her clothes. "And then out of the corner of my eye," she recalled, "I saw her studying me the same way."

"And then what?" I asked.

"Why, nothing," she said.

"You mean that was all, and you remember it?"

She smiled. "It wasn't until after I met Bobbie that I realized the other girl was attracted, too. I just didn't think anybody could be interested in me."

"How about the young man you were engaged to?"

She sniffed. "I felt used, like an animal."

She was pleased now that the girl on the bus had faded innocently out of her life. "It is better this way, for it makes Bobbie the first and the last." She spoke with an ineffable sense of satisfaction.

I was even more anxious to meet Bobbie than Cindy was for me to meet her. "She's the greatest," she said, starry-eyed.

Bobbie was attractive but no great beauty.

She was a social worker, working with children. I judged that she was about ten years older than Cindy. She smiled tolerantly at Cindy's faltering attempts to explain what we had been talking about.

"You told me," Cindy said, "that we had nothing to hide."

Bobbie quickly dispelled her embarrassment. "I know, my dear," she said gently. She turned to me pleasantly. "I don't know what Cindy has been telling you, but I'll be glad to fill in any way I can."

She was busy right then, so we agreed to meet later that same night in a nearby Hollywood restaurant. There was an addition to the party when we finally sat down. Bobbie casually introduced me to an attractive blonde a few years older than herself. "You don't mind her joining us?" She smiled pleasantly.

I shook my head.

"She is not a lesbian," Bobbie went on, "but she understands our problem, and might be able to contribute something."

Bobbie and Cindy sat together facing me, their faces a sharp contrast. Cindy was bubbling, as usual; Bobbie was smooth-faced and serene, her eyes watchful. The blonde sat next to me, and she was as cool as a mackerel on ice.

Her name was Laura, and she was connected with a metaphysical group in which Cindy and Bobbie had some interest. She seemed to take charge of things. "Why not ask your questions," she said, smiling in my direction, "and we'll answer the best we can."

"Cindy tells me," I began, "that this relationship is the greatest thing since hopscotch."

The two older women looked fondly at the younger. "It has made a great difference to Cindy," Laura said. "You should have seen her when she met Bobbie, and for weeks after that. She didn't know what she was."

Cindy agreed eagerly. "My hair was even shorter and I was wearing all the wrong clothes. I just felt bitchy about everything."

Laura nodded understandingly. "It has been a good relationship for Cindy."

Cindy guffawed. "That's the understatement of the year. It was the only good thing that ever happened to me."

Bobbie was amused. "Cindy," she explained with a self-deprecating smile, "was not happy about herself. She was lashing out at the world instead of sitting down calmly and asking herself what she wanted of life."

Cindy's eyes gleamed. "Doesn't she have a wonderful way of putting things?"

Bobbie half smiled in embarrassment, and Laura interposed lightly, "To Cindy, Bobbie can do no wrong."

I had found Bobbie an interesting study. She had placid blue eyes set in a fair oval face that freckled easily. Her auburn hair was worn short in a fashionable bob, but it was not butch. She spoke softly, weighing her words, and looked intently at the person she was talking to. I had the impression that as I appraised her, she was quietly returning the compliment.

She had tortoise-shell glasses, which she twisted in her fingers as a lecturer might in class. She seemed very sure of herself.

"Were you aware," I asked, "that you were the first girl that Cindy had known?"

"I assume," Laura cut in with a laugh, "that you mean the biblical 'know.'"

"I was very much aware," Bobbie said quietly.

"Had you ever lived with anybody before?" I asked.

A shadow fell briefly across her face. "I was with Frankie for six years before it fell apart."

At the sadness in her voice, Cindy looked at her reassuringly. "That's never going to happen to us," she said. "Our relationship is going to last."

"What makes you so sure?" I asked.

"Because," Cindy said, "I love Bobbie and she loves me."

Bobbie winced the least bit.

"She also loved Frankie and Frankie loved her," I pointed out.

"The moment I saw her in her blue jeans, with that smudge on her face," Cindy said, "I knew she was it."

"Don't you think," I said, "that you're influenced a little by hero worship?"

"Heroine worship," Laura corrected. Cindy only seemed puzzled. "What he means," Laura said patiently, "is that perhaps you are looking at the relationship out of context, and not seeing Bobbie as she really is."

Cindy still did not follow.

"You are going through a stage, a necessary stage, and when you emerge, you may see things differently." Laura's voice was gently impersonal.

"Never," said Cindy, "not about Bobbie."

"Don't you think," I said, "that you were ripe for lesbianism, and if it hadn't been Bobbie, it might have been somebody else?"

Cindy looked as though she had been stabbed through the heart. "How can you say anything like that?" she demanded. There were tears in her eyes.

Bobbie patted Cindy's arm reassuringly. "Of course, you were ready for something like this, or it never would have happened." She paused. "Do you remember our discussions?" She turned to me. "Cindy and I had many heart-searching conversations before we came to a decision."

"So I understand," I said, adding casually, "Wasn't it a week or so before the relationship was actually consummated?"

There was an awkward silence; the clink of a cup four tables away could be plainly heard. "Cindy," Bobbie said finally, "how could you?" She had flushed to the roots of her hair.

Even Laura, the imperturbable interpreter, seemed to have lost her aplomb.

"Didn't you tell me," Cindy protested, "that we shouldn't be ashamed of anything we do?" She had an injured air.

"There is such a thing as love at first sight," I said placatingly.

Cindy had squeezed herself into a corner of the booth, and was beginning to show a faint resentment. Bobbie broke the tension, finally. "Sometimes," she said half humorously, "I don't know whether to hug or kick her." Laura and she both laughed, but the atmosphere was not the same. Without anybody saying anything, I felt this particular interview was about over.

"I hope you don't misunderstand," Bobbie said.

"I won't," I promised.

Bobbie's eyes searched my face. "I don't want you to get any misleading ideas of our relationship," she said. She seemed to be toying with a new thought. "Perhaps I might see you alone sometime, and continue the discussion?"

Cindy's jaw dropped. "Why do you have to see him without me?"

"Because," Bobbie said gently, "he has the story from your eyes. It might be different from mine."

Laura added her soothing syrup. "Sometimes it is difficult to explain yourself in front of people."

Cindy snorted. "I had no such trouble." She looked about aggressively, and I felt suddenly that the interview might have an unlooked-for postscript.

"You seem a little unsure of your position," I remarked, concentrating on Cindy, "for a girl who has found undying love."

Cindy bridled. "It's just that all this talk sails over my head, and I feel as if I made a faux pas, when I was only trying to express myself." She seemed near tears.

Bobbie laughed. "All the more reason, dear, to look and listen first." She began collecting her bag.

It had not been apparent to me at any time what interests the two girls shared. "What makes you so sure the relationship will last?" I asked Cindy. As I turned, I thought I saw an almost imperceptible smile on Bobbie's lips, but Cindy missed it.

"Other people spend their lives together," she said doggedly.

"Married people are a little different situation," I said. "They can't just walk off."

"That's right, dear," Laura interposed. "Nothing keeps lesbians together but their feelings for each other."

"But there's no reason," Cindy persisted, "for that feeling to change."

"In California, too," I pointed out, "there are community-property laws, and waiting periods for divorce. Children are a consideration."

"We can always adopt children," Cindy said stubbornly.

Bobbie's laugh tinkled out pleasantly.

"Would you consider adopting any children?" I asked her.

She looked fondly at Cindy. "She's all the child I can handle," she said easily.

Cindy's good nature suddenly deserted her. She said petulantly, "All right, treat me like a child. All I said was that we had a great relationship. What was wrong with that?"

"Nothing, dear," interjected Laura, the dispenser of milk and honey, "but life is uncertain at best, and there are all kinds of possibilities to consider."

"And what," asked Cindy, "do you mean by that?"

"Just that we can't be sure of anything," Bobbie said. She sighed ever so slightly. "I was with Frankie a long time."

"Cindy," Laura added for my benefit, "was at a stage where she needed an older, gentler person, and Bobbie helped her over a rather rough spot."

I had thought Cindy's remark about adopting children particularly provocative. "Would you actually like to have a child?" I asked.

"Oh, I dunno," she answered. She was not as communicative as she had been.

I persisted. "But you mentioned it."

"Freudian, perhaps," Laura said with her ready laugh, as Cindy sat sulking.

Cindy stirred herself. "It might be nice," she said, "to live over your childhood in somebody else."

"That's a beautiful thought," Laura said.

Even Bobbie seemed impressed. "You are growing up," she said with the air of a teacher applauding a precocious pupil. "You are beginning to scratch beneath the surface."

Cindy snickered. "What did I say that was so wonderful?"

Bobbie smiled. "Cindy is making progress. She had to get over many of her fears. She has known so little kindness that it made her hostile and resentful, but she's improving every day."

She spoke impersonally, as though discussing a pet which had performed well, or a child who was not in the room.

Cindy's spirits were restored by the unexpected praise. "All I know," she said with a grin, "is that I belong somewhere for the first time in my life." She laughed gaily. "I had no idea there were so many of us."

Bobbie and Laura exchanged quick glances and I knew definitely that the interview was over. When we parted, Cindy said wistfully, "I suppose I won't be around for the next interview."

"Now, don't be silly," Bobbie chided good-naturedly, "you had your day."

Bobbie was her customary cheery self when we sat down alone a few days later. "You'll have to make allowances for Cindy," she said pleasantly. "She's rather impulsive."

We ordered a couple of drinks, and eyed each other frankly across the table. "I have the feeling," Bobbie said, "that you are really interested in the truth."

At the risk of appearing smug, I pointed out, "I find it easier to deal with what actually happens."

She smiled contentedly. "Then we don't have to beat about the bush."

"Fine," I said. "That brings us to your old girl-friend, Frankie. How was she different than Cindy?"

Bobbie's face lighted up. "We were intellectually compatible. We got stirred up over the same things. We could do the simplest things together, knowing exactly how the other was reacting."

I wondered what had happened. "Was there someone else?" I asked.

"Not really," she said. "We had always done things together, and then suddenly she wanted to do things herself."

"That's not uncommon," I said, "even among the most devoted husbands and wives."

Bobbie frowned. "Lesbians are different from ordinary couples. Living together, they do everything together. There are no nights out with the boys." She stared glumly in front of her.

"Who moved out on who?" I asked.

She grimaced. "I moved out and came back, and then she moved out and stayed out."

Even their friends took sides. "We had been idealized among lesbians as the classic couple." Both had good jobs; Frankie was a draftsman. They lived well, in a comfortable apartment, with a joint bank account, and had two cars. They were fixtures at concerts, recitals, plays, and the ballet.

"If it meant so much," I said, "why didn't you try patching it up?"

She smiled wanly. "She no longer felt the same way about things —or me."

"Was there a money problem?"

She brushed that aside. "Like most lesbian couples, we shared expenses." She sighed. "She just seemed to resent every suggestion I made, and there was constant turmoil where it was once so smooth."

It still wasn't clear what had occurred after so many years to alter the relationship, but Bobbie obviously didn't want to go into it right there and then, so I switched to a less sensitive area.

"After Frankie," I asked, "wasn't Cindy a rather drastic change?"

"They're different," she agreed, "but Cindy is a dear. And I do think I have helped her."

"Shouldn't a good relationship be mutually beneficial?"

She gently touched my sleeve. "Please don't get the idea," she said with a plea in her voice, "that our relationship is wholly physical. At this particular stage, Cindy was good for me. She gave me somebody to think about besides myself. And I was good for her at this time."

"In other words, Cindy is a sort of interlude."

Pained protest ruffled her features. "I'm quite attached to Cindy," she insisted, "but she does say the damnedest things. She thinks everything new to her is new to everybody else."

There was an obvious difference in the two girls' education. "She went to high school and a good business school," the college-bred Bobbie said. "That's no problem. She's bright enough."

It seemed likely that she had caught Cindy on the rebound.

She considered a moment. "It was almost a year later. I didn't go anywhere or see anybody for months, just stayed home and stared into a book or listened to music. So I can't agree."

Bobbie's friends, knowing Cindy and learning of her budding interest in lesbianism, had set up the first date. It took place at a New Year's Eve party. "We paired off for the party," Bobbie continued, "and we left together." She smiled. "At respectable lesbian parties, everybody leaves with the person they arrived with." Actually, they had met briefly before the party, when the impressionable Cindy had become infatuated with the smudge on Bobbie's face. "I had been housecleaning," Bobbie explained, "when a friend brought Cindy in and introduced her, and I wasn't looking quite my best."

Apparently, it was good enough.

Cindy's curiosity about lesbianism had evidently drawn her to the party in the first place. "If it had not been you," I asked, "might it have been somebody else?"

Bobbie nodded. "As a matter of fact, she may be fortunate it was me."

"Why is that?"

She smiled. "She is just so anxious to give of herself."

"Do you think she is a confirmed lesbian?"

She shrugged. "I don't think Cindy knows what she is yet. But she is learning and someday may make some very important discoveries about herself." She looked at me inquiringly. "How much did Cindy tell you about her family?"

"Not very much. She seemed to avoid mentioning them."

It was little wonder, as Bobbie told it. "When she was eight, one of her uncles molested her, and when she was fourteen, an older man dating her mother gave her a terrible time."

"Meaning what?"

"Meaning that this was her introduction to the male animal. In time," she added coolly, "she may lose her inbred fear of men."

"Have you discussed these fears with her?"

"We had a long talk before Cindy moved in. I wanted her to be fully aware of her own motivations."

"Didn't she discuss her problem with anybody else?"

Bobbie wrinkled her nose. "She told a priest about thinking she was a lesbian, and he told her to get married." Her face became somber. "Religion is a big problem. Our own faiths won't accept us, yet we have a great spiritual need. Sometimes you would think Christ wasn't interested in sinners."

She had turned to metaphysics, which accounted for her friendship with Laura, and it was a convenient cult. "Laura," she said, "has pointed out the ambivalence of sex. A person should direct his sexual energies in a fashion that best brings out and develops his own personality." Laura, it developed, was a teaching disciple of a group that believed in the "Golden Mean of Sex."

Bobbie attended her classes regularly with Cindy. Laura was their favorite counselor, and mediator. She served as a minister for Bobbie and a priest for Cindy. She was considered expert on personal relations, though apparently not her own. She was not a lesbian herself, and was about to be married a second time. Her first marriage had failed abysmally. "It's too bad," I observed, "that she hasn't profited by her own counsel."

Bobbie shrugged. "We all reach some sort of impasse: the important thing is knowing what to do about it."

Laura had counseled them constantly. And Bobbie felt that she had been instrumental in helping Cindy to get in harmony with her new way. "That's all life is," Bobbie said: "harmonizing with yourself and your surroundings."

She felt in harmony with Cindy—at times. She had been through the same turmoil herself. Like Cindy, she had been engaged and considered marriage. "I didn't think it would be fair to Roger," she said. Her face softened as she spoke of her former beau. But they had remained friends, corresponding long after his marriage. "When I broke off with Frankie, he offered to come out and help me through it."

It seemed odd that he should have known the significance of their relationship. "Then, he did know about you?"

"Long after he had married," she said, "we were reviewing old times, and he said he had one question for me." She had known what was coming but felt she owed him the truth. And so she had told him frankly why she had decided not to marry him.

He was not surprised. "As I got to thinking about it," he had commented, "I could see it couldn't be anything else." And so the male ego was assuaged, and he felt better about it all.

She seemed to have a great fondness for him, and I wondered why she hadn't given marriage a try.

"He didn't complete me," she said, "though I loved him."

"Do you mean the sex relationship wasn't right?"

She shook her head. "Physically perhaps, but inside I felt bleak and cheerless and alone. It made me want to cry."

"And it was different with Frankie?"

She smiled. "In the most exciting way, physically and emotionally."

"And Cindy," I asked. "What about her?"

"She has a niche of her own."

"Would you trade her for Frankie right now?" I asked.

Her eyes twinkled. "That's not a fair question. But every relationship has its own reward."

Neither Bobbie nor Cindy looked particularly feminine, and yet neither appeared conspicuously mannish. They were just two average-looking fairly attractive young women. Bobbie had never been taken for a lesbian except by another lesbian, and neither had Cindy. But Bobbie felt she could always spot one. "I can always tell," she said.

"You mean that you could have picked Cindy out?"

She nodded. "Cindy and the rest."

Identification was subtle but sure, she insisted. "The way a girl smokes—thumbing her cigarette; the way she glances around a room, taking in other girls without appearing to notice them; the piercing look close up, the things she gets embarrassed about. Because of your own sensitivity, you observe these things without even thinking about them and then, after a while, you develop a sixth sense about homosexuality."

Bobbie had had her first misgivings about herself as an adolescent but had not dared discuss the problem with anybody. While in college, she had attended a youth seminar one summer in Colorado. One authority, a young psychologist, had impressed her with the frankness of his views on sex. And, with her doubts still preying on her mind, she had asked obliquely, "How does one discover homosexuality in a friend?"

And he had replied, "Turn that question around: the way you discover it in yourself is in seeing it in a friend."

She had got the message.

As she phrased it, I found the psychologist's statement provocative. "You mean that if a person reacts to homosexuals, he may be homosexual?"

"Something like that."

For the first time she had realized what she was. It was a shock, even though she had played with the idea a long time, but she still didn't know what to do about it. Not long after, however, in a college classroom, her eyes accidentally encountered those of another girl, and stayed there. That had been all that was necessary —that one look. Soon the two girls were visiting each other when their respective roommates were away, carefully charting their schedules. And in their last two years they roomed together. "There was a certain satisfaction in a clandestine relationship under such respectable auspices," Bobbie recalled. There had been no complications. "In every relationship," she remarked, "I have never imputed what wasn't there." And for both girls it had been a sort of coming out, nothing more, and both understood.

With all her lesbianism, she had always thought of herself as a woman—an unmarried woman—and could conceive of the possibility, however slim, that she might one day marry and have children. While she thought that her relationship with Frankie had been closer than any marriage she could contemplate with any man, she still hadn't thought of herself as being bound in marriage even then. "I have never been able to think of lesbians as married," she said, "for they are actually only mocking a normal relationship —and their own femininity in such a concept—no matter how many cars or pieces of property they register jointly. And of course they are trying to kid themselves."

She laughed softly. "There was one pair who wanted to be buried next to each other, their names on adjacent headstones, as husband and wife."

"What happened?" I asked.

Her voice revealed her amusement. "I think the undertaker fainted."

She avoided all the conventional trappings of lesbianism herself.

"You have never worn a friendship or wedding ring, not even with Cindy?" I asked.

She shook her head. "It's only a grotesque attempt to recapture some semblance of a familiar relationship." She obviously considered it beneath her dignity to exaggerate the lesbian posture.

She was tutoring Cindy, she said, not to be a successful lesbian, but to be a successful human being, to recognize her own capacities and weaknesses and to act boldly out of these capacities, overcoming the weaknesses through sheer will and purpose.

It sounded awfully good as she expressed it.

Remembering her own family, she had insisted upon Cindy's maintaining friendly ties with her mother. Bobbie's own father was dead, and Bobbie had been fortunate enough to have a mother who had tried to understand her, when she felt constrained to confide in her. "She didn't understand my lesbianism, or even all of what it implied," Bobbie said, "but she did understand what a trial it must have been for me in my family relationships."

Bobbie's sister was not so broadminded, and had discouraged all contact with Bobbie when she found out. "She's afraid I'll pollute her children," Bobbie said with a laugh. "And yet she has a potential homosexual problem in her husband which she doesn't recognize. And," she added solemnly, "I see signs already in her boys."

Latent male homosexuals, she pointed out, frequently expressed their tendencies in cooking and in helping with domestic chores. "My sister's husband is a great one for barbecues, and nobody thinks too much about it," Bobbie observed. "Of course, if he were as eager around the kitchen, he might get himself talked about."

On the basis of her record as a social worker, and her even disposition, Bobbie had impressed me as a woman who would be good with children.

"I work with scores of them," she said, "and in this way perhaps I escape the usual mother frustration. I am a mother many times over, not womb-wise, which is an expression of self, but through obligation and responsibility."

"But wouldn't it be nice to have a child of your own?"

"That would be purely vanity," she said. "I would be far better with other people's children—certainly more objective."

Considering her sensitive job area, she was surprisingly open. She had given me her true name freely and had not expressed any wish that I not use it, though I took the liberty of disguising it myself. "Do any of the mothers of the children you work with know that you are a lesbian?" I asked.

She smoothed back a wisp of hair that had fallen into her eyes and said with a smile, "They wouldn't believe it if I told them myself. Only recently they signed a petition urging my promotion."

"But if they knew," I persisted, "would they still want you around their children?"

"I would like to think so." She smiled the least bit wryly.

"Oddly," she said, "I prefer working with boys. I guess the masculine in me finds better rapport with the male."

It occurred to me, as we sat talking over a long drink, that I was not able to tell with any certainty into what lesbian category Bobbie fell—not by appearance or anything she had clearly stated, nor by Cindy's attitude or posture. And so I asked, half apologetically, "Do you consider yourself butch or femme?"

"Neither," she said. Patiently she explained. "As a woman becomes aware of her own sexuality, she realizes she is not necessarily bisexual or homosexual or even heterosexual." She paused for a moment. "So why should I put myself into a semantic straitjacket that insists on classifying me when I can't classify myself?"

"You don't think of yourself as a lesbian, then?" This seemed to be what she was driving at.

She shook her head. "I don't deny my lesbianism, but it does not tell the full story of my sexuality, which changes as my personality needs change."

"Then you may be bisexual at times?"

"Perhaps, if that is best at the time for my personality development."

This was apparently the "golden mean of sexuality" explored at the D.O.B. convention. "In any way that I deny myself expression, I become less of a person," she said. Her reasoning was plausible, though some might have thought that she was only trying to rationalize her behavior. "Now that we are in the nuclear age, we may have to recondition our whole view of sex. The world today is far more different from the Victorian era than the Victorian from the biblical. Everything is speeding up and sex is speeding up with it."

As Bobbie coolly imparted her views, I somehow could not imagine Cindy worrying her head about the nuclear age of sex.

Bobbie smiled. "I'm not sure that Cindy thinks along these lines, but she's learning." Her voice softened. "She was terribly immature at first. She wore her hair butch to proclaim her homosexuality and acted as if she was the world's first lesbian."

With all this apparent fondness, I still didn't see how the two harmonized, no matter what the superficial attractions might be. Even as friends they seemed mismatched. "What do you two find to do together?" I asked rather bluntly.

"It isn't all what you think," she said, evidently thinking she was reading my mind. "We are good companions. I generally take the lead because I'm older. But Cindy likes to cook, so I let her."

"But neither of you is particularly the dependent type," I said tactfully, "and there may be clashes. Will your relationship survive these?"

She shrugged philosophically. "Who can say what will last?"

I essayed a comparison. "Did you think that Frankie would last?"

The unexpected reference to Frankie seemed to affect her emotionally. Her eyes moistened with the faintest suggestion of tears. "As lasting," she said, "as any relationship without bonds can be."

Swinging back to the present, I asked, "If you and Cindy should break up, what would happen to her?"

Her eyes opened wide and she regarded me evenly. "I would never do anything to hurt her." She appeared utterly sincere.

Despite her assurance, I got the impression that Cindy's stock was not quite as high as it had been, though Cindy herself might not be aware of her altered position.

I also was not quite sure why Bobbie had suggested the interview, since the relationship with Cindy, if anything, seemed less understandable now than before.

When we met Cindy later, she seemed moderately subdued. "I suppose I've been pretty well chopped up," she said, taking in the two of us with an appraising glance, as Bobbie perfunctorily kissed her on the cheek.

Bobbie gave her a piercing look. "Is baby feeling sorry for herself again?" she said, playfully flicking her hand under Cindy's chin.

Cindy tossed her head. "I'm twenty-four years old," she said testily.

"I know," Bobbie replied sweetly.

It seemed like a good time to say good-by. "See you in San Francisco," I said, shaking their hands.

Cindy sniffed half-heartedly, as Bobbie threw her a reprimanding glance.

"Now, be polite to the man," she said with faint irony, "and tell him how glad you were to meet him."

With Cindy strangely silent, we made arrangements for a future meeting.

Two weeks later I was waiting at my Bay area hotel, when they picked me up in their car. Cindy drove with breezy nonchalance, passing everything on the road. Bobbie pointed to the speedometer, but Cindy kept her foot down on the accelerator. They had seemed glad to see me but were clearly preoccupied with each other and Cindy's driving. On a steep up-grade, typical of San Francisco, Cindy shot through a corner stop sign. "Easy, girl," Bobbie said severely.

Petulance clouded the other girl's face. "Now," she said, "she's telling me how to drive."

Bobbie sighed a little wearily. "Let's pick up some ice cream," she said.

Cindy pulled over to a curb. "I suppose I'll have to get it," she said, scraping to a stop in front of a store.

The shop was closed.

"Couldn't you see there were no lights?" Bobbie said.

"Would I have gone in if I had?" Cindy rejoined. "Don't blame me because it's a holiday."

We finally halted before a small apartment building on a perpendicular hill. "This is it," Cindy said ironically. "Just Bobbie and me and kitty make three."

We climbed a couple of flights of stairs and the meow of a cat greeted us as Bobbie opened the door. As I stepped inside, a well-fed tabby rustled against my legs and followed me curiously into the living room. Then, as it turned from me indifferently, its curiosity satisfied, Bobbie quickly picked it up and planted an affectionate kiss on its nose. The cat purred.

As I looked around, I saw a pleasant room, comfortably furnished and quite cozy except for the dank, musty odor of cat and the cat hairs on the upholstery.

Cindy poured the tea. "It's all we have," she said, curtly.

"Nice girl." Bobbie beamed approvingly, as though unaware of her protégé's temper.

Cindy looked at her sharply. Bobbie, unconcerned, squatted comfortably on the floor, sipping her tea and stroking the purring cat.

Cindy seemed oddly abstracted.

"Have you been seeing your family lately?" I asked, trying to bring her into the conversation.

"As much as I want," she said, still tense.

Bobbie smiled benevolently. "Now, what kind of an answer is that?" She was apparently determined to treat Cindy as though there were nothing wrong. "Now, let's stop feeling sorry for ourselves," she said. She wagged an admonishing finger. "Remember what we said about self-pity."

Cindy scowled and looked away quickly, dabbing her eyes.

My eyes took in the snug little room. "Has your mother ever been here?" I asked Cindy.

She shook her head.

"Answer the man," Bobbie said in a teasing voice.

With eyes flashing, Cindy finally muttered sarcastically, "Hardly."

"Does she know about you and Bobbie?" I asked.

She looked at me a while before answering. "Somebody has been talking to her," she said gruffly. "You know, the usual well-meaning friend." She was suddenly loquacious.

Her mother's suspicions had been aroused, and the last time Cindy was home, her mother had grabbed her roughly by the shoulders and fiercely asked, "What's going on over there between you and that girl?"

Cindy had snorted. "All kinds of sex orgies, what do you think?"

The mother had refused to be lightly put aside. Furiously, she had shaken her daughter, demanding, "Are you queer?"

Cindy had turned away in confusion. "Yes," she repeated sarcastically, "I'm having a ball."

Her mother had not responded in kind. "You're my daughter," she had warned, "but if you're queer, I never want to see you again. Get that straight."

It had been a disagreeable experience, and just the thought of it brought tears to Cindy's eyes.

"Poor me," Bobbie said, gently mocking, "wants to be accepted."

"I told her, didn't I?" Cindy said defiantly. "I didn't hide it."

"Not really," I said, "because you acknowledged it in such a way that she wouldn't take your admission seriously."

Bobbie gave her a complacent look. "Exactly," she said, "just as I told you."

Cindy's good nature was worn thin. "What do you want of me?" she asked heatedly. "I'm doing the best I can."

"I want you to face things, not avoid issues as you did with your mother," Bobbie said evenly.

Cindy regarded her partner sullenly, as though she were seeing her with new eyes. "Why don't you say what you really mean, and get it over with?" she said.

Bobbie shook her head reprovingly. "Now, don't start putting things into your head," she said.

I had noticed the friction, of course, and thought that Cindy might be chafing at the unaccustomed role of being the secondary partner, or housewife. Or, as I looked at her narrowly, following the trim outline of her sensuous figure, it again struck me that she might be a lesbian only because she was avoiding a male relationship because of her unfortunate girlhood experiences.

"Actually," I said, "you might not be a lesbian at all, and are secretly pining to be somebody's bride."

She did not even think I was funny. "Oh, what do you know about it?" she said. She jabbed her hands deep into the pockets of her slacks. "Anyway," she said bitterly, as though to herself, "I won't have to go around worrying about my mother any more."

I looked up inquiringly.

Cindy appeared surprised. "Hasn't she told you?" she said, indicating Bobbie with a nod. "I'm moving to Los Angeles." She spoke shortly, biting her lip.

I turned to Bobbie. "Are you giving up this apartment?"

"Oh, I won't be moving right away," Bobbie said easily. She looked fondly across the room at the somber Cindy. "It'll give Cindy a chance to do things without my standing over her all the time." She laughed softly. "She's beginning to resent me, and"— she paused—"she has made friends there and won't be alone. She'll do fine."

"But you'll be coming down later?" Cindy's voice had a note of entreaty in it.

Bobbie smiled patiently. "Yes, dear, if I can work things out." She made an expressive gesture with her hands. "You know, I have my job and the apartment lease to settle first."

"But you will be down?" Cindy said. She was no longer rebellious, and a look of fear had crept into her eyes. She was like a small child appealing to its mother.

Bobbie was as calm and assured as ever. "You know, dear," she said with tenderness, "there is no security anywhere, except what we find and develop in ourselves. No other person can do it for us."

I turned to the stricken Cindy. "Isn't this rather sudden, your moving?"

She rallied bravely. "Bobbie thinks it might be best—for a while, anyway." She seemed near tears again.

Bobbie looked at her with an enigmatic smile. "Now," she said soothingly, "let's not feel sorry for ourselves. We're a big girl now."

As though annoyed with herself, Cindy impatiently brushed a tear from her cheek. "Aw, leave me alone," she said.

I was afraid she was going to bawl. "Who knows," I said to Cindy comfortingly as I rose to leave, "you might like Los Angeles."

"I'll certainly try," she said darkly.

Bobbie laughed and patted her hand approvingly. She seemed in strangely good spirits.

At the door, alone with Bobbie, I whispered, "You said you would do nothing to harm her."

Bobbie smiled good-naturedly. "She is ready to be on her own. I'm only holding her back here."

The door closed on me.

Two days later I was talking to a lesbian who, like Bobbie, worked with children. She had known Bobbie for years.

The subject of Cindy inevitably came up. "In a way," she said, "it's Frankie all over again."

"But Bobbie is still mad about Frankie," I said.

My lesbian authority laughed. "All that love stuff has nothing to do with a breakup. It gets down to basics, who's butch and who's femme, and how they're going to work things out together. It's not a matter of dress or haircut, either. It's attitude."

I still waited, not understanding fully.

She explained patiently, reverting to Bobbie's first relationship. "As time passed, Frankie's personality developed. She became more assertive and reliant, as she tried to express her natural self. She didn't accept the status quo any longer, but Bobbie remained the same, the would-be dominant figure—the butch, so to speak—and so an underlying conflict developed."

But how did Cindy fit into the equation?

"She was feminine sometimes, aggressive others," I pointed out.

My authority laughed. "She's only rebellious, and this stage will pass too." A reflective light came into her eyes. "She has a good many normal feminine instincts, including a bourgeois need for approval. She may even marry and have children someday, reviving natural instincts which have been suppressed by fears of sex. Basically, she's a square."

"But this was the lesbian romance that was going to last for all time: Bobbie and Cindy."

The lesbian smiled. "Who said that—Cindy?"

I nodded.

She shrugged. "We all knew it was only a question of time. Bobbie's too much of an intellectual snob to be wet-nursing any roommate very long, particularly one who's not quite dry behind the ears and always putting her foot in her mouth besides."

"But didn't she know all that when she first took her in?"

She smiled roguishly. "In case you don't know it, Cindy is a mighty attractive girl. I can't blame Bobbie for going after her."

"But Cindy actually was the aggressor," I pointed out, "and brought the relationship to a head in rather quick order."

The authority laughed. "There was quite an argument over that in Los Angeles, and Cindy got hell for blabbing her guts."

"What was all that about?" I inquired in some puzzlement.

"Bobbie was furious with her for telling you that it only took seven days for them to get together."

I was still puzzled. "What was so terrible about that?"

"It just made it look, under the circumstances, as though that was what the relationship was all about. It didn't do much for Bobbie's image as a super-intellectual, primarily interested in a partner's mind."

Recalling the wisdom of Laura, the soothing-syrup girl, I observed, "But I thought Cindy was a sort of educational project for Bobbie."

The authority laughed. "She was. The only trouble was that the teacher got bored."

18

THE BISEXUAL

"The girls told me to be careful about coming over here," she said with a wicked gleam in her eyes.

She had kicked off her shoes, doubled her legs under her, and was eying me as though I were some sort of spider.

She was thirty-five or so, tall and raw-boned, with a good figure and a bold, aquiline face, and she was obviously relaxed.

"Shall we adjourn to the pool?" I suggested. "There's not much smog for Los Angeles." I looked out the hotel window.

"I'm comfortable here," she said, smiling.

She studied me with a frown. "I have a problem, and maybe you can help me. I'm a little bit like the 'Lady and the Tiger': I don't know which way to turn. You know that I've been married and I have two kids. They're with my mother now." She looked up, and I nodded. "And I would like to see them brought up in a normal situation." Her eyes followed the curling spiral of smoke from her cigarette. "And so I'm considering marriage. He's much younger, only twenty-two, but he's gentle."

She kept flicking the ash off her cigarette. "On the other hand," she said slowly, "I have an offer from an old friend of mine, a professor I knew in college, to make my home there, all expenses paid, and with the children. It would be wonderful security."

"The professor isn't offering marriage?" I asked.

"Hardly." She laughed. "The professor is a woman." She peered at me from across a big coffee table. "And so that's the problem—shall I be a lesbian and take certain security, or be a wife and run the risk of another lousy marriage?"

I felt that this was a problem only a Solomon could decide. "I'm sure," I said, "that you'll make the right decision."

I had seen her twice previously, with other girls I knew to be lesbian, and had been rather surprised that she was one herself. "I've been married three times," she said, "and had any number of romances, and no man knew I was a lesbian unless I wanted him to know." She shrugged. "How could they?"

At times she talked like a man, moving her hands sharply for emphasis, swearing gruffly without the appearance of profanity, rasping out her words. On other occasions, she was coy, smiling winsomely, occasionally blushing, or self-consciously tugging her skirt down over her knees.

She was an advertising executive, and had been a copywriter, a schoolteacher, a probation worker, and even a clerk in a hardware store. "Anything but a secretary or a stenographer," she said, "taking dictation from some lug of a man whose mind works sixty miles an hour slower than mine." Her voice was tinged with scorn.

She was so thoroughly ambivalent that even her name reflected this ambivalence; it was Sidney. "Not Sid or Siddie, but Sidney—a nice, chaste, upper-class English girl's name." She grinned sardonically.

She had been visiting in Los Angeles for just the week. "If I get married again," she said, "I'll live in San Francisco, or somewhere near it. If I pick the professor, I'll be nearer L.A." She lit one cigarette from another. "Frankly, that's a consideration, since I really dig San Francisco. It doesn't have Disneyland, but it's still Fairyland, U.S.A."

As though still weighing the matter, she said with a frown, "Marriage means mothering some guy again, worrying about the bills and all that jazz—all kinds of responsibility. Whereas, if I take the other offer, she'll worry for all of us." She bit her lip. "The only trouble is the kids. I'd like them to have a chance."

I looked at her curiously. "Why can't you marry a man who'll take care of you?"

Her eyes suddenly became cold, and there was a chill in her voice. "There isn't such a man. They either beat the hell out of you, trying to show how masterful they are, or they're forever wanting you to wipe their noses for them."

"Perhaps you just haven't met the right kind?" I suggested.

She turned on me angrily. "How many men," she asked sarcastically, "do you have to know?"

The only men that she had known intimately who were kind to her had been homosexuals. "The rest," she said, "were filthy rotten, beginning with my father, who was the worst."

If anybody could be blamed for her lesbianism, she felt, it was Dad. He was a wealthy contracting executive, charming enough, except when he drank. "When he got sotted," she said contemptuously, "then his real character came out. He was an animal."

She seemed tense just thinking about it.

"Even as a child," she said, "I must have subconsciously known how he felt about me, but my mind couldn't accept it. It was so horrible."

Like many lesbians with a liberal education, she had virtually dissected every aspect of her life, sociologically, psychologically, even physiologically. And, while thinking may not have helped, it seemed to have made the problem clear. "When I was a kid growing up, he was bouncing me on his knee or picking me up or coming into my room when I was undressing, things like that."

"But that's not unusual, is it?" She seemed to be making mountains out of molehills.

"Not when that kid is thirteen years old," she snapped, "and as big and well formed then as she is today?" She threw out her chest to make her point. It was a good one.

At seventeen, she had come home from a date and found her father half reclining on the living-room couch, an empty whisky bottle on the floor beside him. He was apparently dead to the world.

Fifteen or twenty minutes later, after quickly showering and snuggling into bed, she had hazily sensed a foreign movement in the room and, half asleep, had made out a dim figure bending over her. She had screamed, and flicked on a light. Her father stood bleary-eyed, shaking his head, in apparent befuddlement. With a half-muttered excuse, he had turned and wobbled out of the room, not looking back.

She had felt sick in the pit of her stomach, as if a knot had formed there. She had tossed all night, not falling off to sleep until dawn poked its fingers through the blinds.

"In the morning," she said, "he was bright and cheerful, as though nothing had happened, but when he stooped over to kiss me, I couldn't help myself: I drew away. Everything that I had known subconsciously but didn't want to face had suddenly crystallized."

She had planned to go to college near home, but instead chose a school a full day's drive away. "It was just near enough so that Mother could drive up occasionally, and yet far enough so that I had an excuse for not getting home weekends."

Her feelings about her father were ambivalent—perhaps, she felt, accounting for her own ambivalence. She had a grudging respect for his toughness and success in the world of men, his competence in his own field, and after all these years, she thought that she understood his compulsive drinking. "In a way," she said, "he couldn't face himself—or me—unless he was grogged."

There had been no more midnight visitations. "But whenever he got drunk, which was often, he'd call me a whore, or a slut, or any choice epithet his dirty mind could think of. Every young man was a rival." Her mother's protests were weak and unavailing. "I think she knew the problem, but what could she do? She was the old-style wife, meek and obedient, and convinced deep-down that it was a woman's role to be long-suffering."

She regarded her mother as a saint, but felt she should have taken her and left home. At school, she was able to collect her thoughts and start wondering what she was going to do about herself. She had already had her first ambivalent feelings about men. But how could she be sure what she was?

She explored every book on homosexuality in the campus library. "I had all the symptoms"—she laughed—"including the beginner's lack of courage." And it required a great deal of persuasion to bring her out.

She was twenty when she finally had her first intimacy with a much older woman. "And I was in ecstasy for three weeks until I discovered that she was only using me to get somebody else jealous, and that disillusioned me about girls." She started dating young men again, though she felt no excitement with them.

She was still bruised over her deflating experience when she met the professor, who was then a young instructor. She had somehow made her interest known to Sidney without a word being spoken—just a touch, a look, a smile. But Sidney, leaping from the frying pan into the fire, had eloped instead with a young man she hardly knew. As she looked back now, her motivation was abundantly clear. She had felt a desperate need to get away from her father, and she had been resisting the professor and the forbidden world of lesbianism which she symbolized. Perhaps because she had sought normalcy so frantically it had eluded her. This was a dozen years ago, and one bad marriage had led to another. Now she could dismiss her husbands contemptuously, ticking them off on her fingers:

"The first was impotent, the second was a brute who enjoyed beating me, and the third was a cheat."

In view of her attitude, I wondered why she had kept on marrying.

"Maybe I just liked to suffer," she said with a shrug.

And had she not been interested in a woman during all those disillusioning years of marriage?

She inhaled deeply on her cigarette. "I was determined," she said, "after that one lesbianic incident to make a good wife of myself. Could I help it if I always picked the wrong man?" She stood up and stretched, revealing the clear outlines of her sweatered figure, and stared moodily out of the window. "I noticed pretty girls, of course, but I thought I had to be one thing or the other." She snuffed out her cigarette vigorously. "That's how little I knew about it then."

The first marriage had not lasted long and she had gone to work, teaching. Her children were born of the last two marriages; her former husbands had made no difficulty about yielding custody, nor did they in any way attempt to see the children. "They both tried to get out of their responsibilities, as usual," she said laconically, "and wound up claiming the kids weren't theirs."

"But wouldn't the courts make them pay support at least?" I asked.

Sidney shrugged. "I didn't want them messing around the kids, and I didn't want to see either of them again—ever."

She had mentioned her straitened circumstances. "But you could have had the financial support without them around."

She said morosely, "I didn't care at the time, and, anyway, it gave me great pleasure to throw it in their teeth."

"Throw what?" I asked.

"That the kids weren't theirs." She smiled.

I regarded her in some surprise. "But weren't the children really theirs?"

"They probably were," she said indifferently, "but it didn't matter that much. Every time they beat me or cheated on me, I'd get back at them with some guy I didn't even like." She sighed. "I was so promiscuous after a while that I lost all respect for myself. And"—she shrugged—"you can't respect anything unless you respect yourself."

She did not defend her promiscuity. "I was always searching for something," she said, "but of course there was no chance of finding it with men." She smiled bleakly. "Do you know in all those years, with all those men, I never consummated a single solitary relationship." She closed her eyes. "In all those years I never met a man who wasn't rough and inconsiderate in his haste to gratify himself."

I wanted to make sure that I understood her correctly. "You

mean that in all your years of marriage you never knew what it was to achieve a climax?" I had thought this symptomatic of nymphomania.

"If that's true," she said ironically, "a good many lesbians are nymphomaniacs."

The male bisexuals I had known had claimed that as their moods varied, they had enjoyed both sexes and not shuttled from one to the other out of dissatisfaction.

"What makes you think of yourself as bisexual?" I asked.

She arched her penciled eyebrows. "What am I, then?"

I pointed out that female bisexuals, like the male, apparently enjoy both sexes, and she seemed to enjoy neither.

"Since I met Tex," she said—he was the gentle young man who was a prospective Number Four—"I realize the shortcomings of all the other men I've known. He's so thoughtful and considerate at all times, putting my wants before his own." A dreamy note came into her voice and she smiled as she interpreted my questioning look correctly.

"Sexual wants," she said. "If I had met somebody like him when I was younger, I might never have looked at any other woman." Despite her fervor, I got the idea that she was trying to convince herself.

As it was, more than ten years had elapsed between her first and second experience with a woman. Because of her background, perhaps, she had always felt a conventional need for social approval, and thought any woman who was noticeably lesbian a fool.

Her introduction to the lesbian world came about quite inadvertently, though previous experience had undoubtedly ripened her for the plunge from conventionality. After her third divorce, she was commiserating with another divorcee about their common marital misadventures, conversing together on the divan, when she felt herself suddenly regarding the other woman with new interest. "Her boy-friend was impotent," Sidney said, "and I could feel myself identifying with her immediately." The girl lived in the same hotel and a rendezvous was simple. Nevertheless, Sidney's courage required fortification. "I had to get halfway through a bottle of whisky that time," Sidney recalled, "but from what I remember of it, it was worth it." She smiled. "It was certainly educational."

Through the other girl, Sidney's circle of friends widened and her higher education progressed.

She felt that her education—maritally—had stood her in good stead in the new pursuit of making friends and influencing people. "Knowing what happened to me as a thrice-married woman put me in a favorable position to recognize unhappily married women who might share my new interest," she said. "I could spot them right away, the type that was beginning to look a little dried up at thirty, because sex, instead of being a rewarding experience, was just another domestic frustration."

Just as she wondered why she had become a lesbian, so had she studied other women she knew. She was positive that the physical distinction had a major part in a woman's becoming a lesbian, since rape, incest, and other traumatic sexual experiences had occurred to many young girls without their turning to women. "The lesbian is constructed differently from other women," she maintained. "The clitoris is less sensitive initially, and I have a feeling it may even be in a different position." Without any awkwardness, she mentioned the importance of the clitoral stimulation in preliminary sex play among lesbians.

I acknowledged there might be a psychological difference stemming from the Freudian concept of an arrested psychosexual development in the adolescent, or clitoral, stage. "But as to a physical difference," I said, "doctors don't agree with you."

"I'm sure," she rejoined tartly, "that they were male doctors." She brooded a while, and said at last, "The male just doesn't realize the importance of this stimulation to the female, or else, typically, he doesn't care in his selfish concern for himself."

She smiled smugly. "Nobody can anticipate a woman like another woman. First, she knows from knowledge of her own anatomy exactly how to warm, kindle, and ignite her partner, how to be tender when tenderness is called for, and how else to be when the emotional peak is reached." A soft smile played about her lips. "There is nothing more exciting," she said, "than woman's love for woman, and nothing more gratifying."

Regardless of how Sidney once felt, it seemed obvious now that the male had been relegated to a secondary role in her life. "In view of everything," I said, "you will probably decide on the professor."

She looked startled for a moment and then, remembering the social dilemma she had postulated earlier, smiled congenially. "It might not work," she said seriously. "We're both a similar type. The perfect butch-femme combination is rare. I'm aggressive and she's used to giving orders, so it all might go up in a cloud of dissension." Her mood suddenly changed, and she looked at me in amusement. "Have you heard the 'frank' joke?"

I shook my head.

She told the story with gusto. "One lesbian was eying another lesbian at the bar, and finally got up the courage to move over and talk to her. 'I'm one of those people who like being frank . . .' she began, when the other girl abruptly cut her off. 'Forget it,' she said with a growl, 'I'm Frank.'"

Laughing, Sidney looked quite feminine. She had stood up and was now combing her hair, peering into a mirror to check her make-up. "Do you mind?" she said, touching up her lipstick and eye shadow. She was in a tight-fitting skirt almost as revealing as her sweater, and looked, I thought, much too feminine to be butch.

"I can be either," she said carelessly, patting her red hair into place and vigorously rubbing the color into her cheeks. "But basically I suppose I'm the butch."

It had struck me that a lesbian bisexual would be more femme than butch, since her bisexual role would then be merely an extension of the feminine role she was already playing.

Sidney looked doubtful. "Some of these clinging femme types are more caricatures of a woman than any butch," she said. She gave me a quizzical smile. "I haven't done bad lately with the wrong sex and I haven't been noticeably femme."

Her eyes gleamed reminiscently as she reviewed her relationship with young Tex. "That's why," she said, "I have been considering marriage. We do so well together."

They had known each other about a year. The young man had been her production assistant in an advertising agency, and she had first begun to admire him as an artistic genius. "You should see his designs. What imagination and ingenuity," she rhapsodized.

In the circumstances, his genius seemed beside the point. "Isn't twenty-two a little young for you?" I asked. She was ten years older, anyway.

"That's one of the obstacles," she conceded, "but we get along wonderfully. He likes to cook and clean and do things around the house, even to sewing and mending things, and that stuff is pretty much a drag for me."

She noted my surprise. "Oh, yes, we've been living together about six months, and it's working out fine. Hadn't I told you?"

"Then why not get married?" I asked.

"I want to be sure," she said.

Somehow Tex didn't strike me as very masculine. "Is he a homosexual?" I asked.

"Bisexual, like myself." She glared at me, instantly defensive. "Don't get the idea that homosexuals—bisexuals—aren't as manly as any other man. They're just different in some ways."

I looked at my watch. It had been a rather long session, and it certainly had not resolved her problem. She still had her "Lady and the Tiger" choice.

"By the time you get to San Francisco," she said, "I may have decided." She smiled. "Anyway, I'll take you for a whirl of the gay bars when you get there. It might be enlightening."

Sidney was as good as her word. When I turned up for our date, she picked me up at my hotel in metropolitan San Francisco. And in her small foreign car, which seemed several sizes too small for her, she carried me off for a night of adventure.

I had noticed immediately that she was not in a particularly good mood. When I asked whether she had come to a decision yet, she snapped, "I thought our conversation was confidential."

"I haven't told anybody but Winchell," I said.

She laughed, and her spirits seemed to rise. "I just don't want any of these dames around here to know what the hell I'm doing," she said. "They're miserable gossips."

Her car raced over the bridge and through a maze of side streets in the dark dreariness of Oakland. "The Front and a couple of other San Francisco bars have closed," she said, "and this place on the other side of the bridge is getting the trade."

As she scooted her little car up one street and down another, looking for the place, I asked about her children.

"They're all right," she said shortly. "They're with my mother."

"Have you seen them?"

She was vague. "I talked to them over the weekend. It was little Karen's birthday."

"Don't you miss them?" I asked.

Her brows knit in annoyance. "They're better off with Mother and Dad until I stop hopping around and make up my mind what I'm going to do." She paused. "I may go back to teaching just so I can give them the home they need." So far, she had mentioned neither Tex nor the professor, and appeared preoccupied with the problem of her children.

"How does your father react to them?" I asked.

"Fine. He'd like to adopt them, but I'm not about to agree."

"Why not?" I asked.

"I want them with me." She looked stonily ahead. "Nobody is going to mess up their lives if I can help it." She responded to my unspoken question as though reading my mind. "My father and I don't have much to say to each other these days," she said.

She stepped heavily on the gas, as if accenting her remarks, and in a few moments we ground to a halt before a dingy-looking bar with a store-front window.

There was a small sign with a pretentious name over the door. But the pretentiousness ended there. As we strode into the bleak barroom and looked around, a crop-headed girl behind the bare bar shot us a quick appraising glance. To the right of the bar, an open staircase led to a back room, from which girls were floating downstairs, in slacks, jeans, or shorts, to register complaints. "I've been trying to get Peggy to wait on me for an hour," a blond girl said, pouting.

The girl behind the bar nodded significantly in our direction. Her face was an inscrutable mask.

"I thought they knew you here," I whispered to Sidney.

She groaned. "I guess they don't recognize me in a dress."

I looked more closely around the bar. A grizzled old bum who looked as if he had stumbled in off the street was nursing a bottle of beer in one corner. Besides myself, he was the only man in the place. Sidney snorted. "If that tramp knew where he was, I'll bet he'd sober up fast."

Over the bar there was a blazing announcement of a mammoth Fourth of July blow-out. This was it.

So far we were being studiously ignored. "Can we get a couple of beers?" I said finally. The girl slowly brought out two bottles.

"How about joining the party?" Sidney asked, nodding upstairs.

The girl shrugged. "It's a private shindig."

Sidney's jaw was beginning to jut out. "Let's take a look around anyway," she said, moving toward the staircase.

As we clambered up the steps, the hubbub in the upstairs room suddenly subsided. Then, as we took a corner table in the hall-like room, girls dancing together to the blaring music of a juke box slowly returned to their tables. There were easily a hundred girls in the room, and they were all watching us now, either out of the corners of their eyes or with frankly curious stares.

I was the only male in the room, and Sidney was the only girl in a dress.

After looking around the room herself with an expression of deep resolve, Sidney got up and said, "I'm going downstairs and straighten things out." She was back in a few minutes, smiling. "Babe, the girl at the bar, apologized for not recognizing me. She thought we were cops." She paused, grinning. "I told her who you were, too."

"And who am I?" I said, somewhat amused.

She chuckled. "You're a big man out here. *The Sixth Man* was on the best-seller list for a long while—second only to the Bible."

In a few moments I had substantial evidence of my new distinction. Wearing an apologetic smile, Babe came trundling over with a tray loaded down with food. "Sorry about the mix-up," she said pleasantly, using my first name, "but we thought you were cops. Honest."

"You don't seem to be doing anything out of the way," I observed tactfully.

She shrugged. "You know how people are. They won't leave you alone."

With Babe's gesture of welcome, a more relaxed mood seemed to prevail throughout the room, and some couples got up and began dancing again. Now that we were no longer suspect, I could allow my glance to linger around the room. Most of the girls at the tables were young, between twenty and thirty, and some even younger, in their teens. But there were few noticeably attractive girls. Sidney took a practiced look around the room. "Hardly worth bothering about," she said. She seemed fidgety. "Do you mind if I change?" she asked, leaning across the table.

"Change what?"

"Change my clothes. I have a complete outfit in the car."

She was gone only a few minutes. When she returned, her mood had changed, along with her attire. She was beaming good-naturedly as she patted her gabardine slacks and tucked in her shirt. "Now," she said, "I can relax."

Her eyes swept to the dance floor, where three or four couples were doing the twist. "You notice," she whispered, "they're not dancing together. They're careful not to embrace, or anything like that. They run it like a straight place."

At the nearest table, a slim woman of thirty, chic in tailored slacks, was eying Sidney with curiosity. "I don't know what she's looking at me for," Sidney said, "she's butch." The girl with the butch was a beauty. She was no more than twenty at most, with a soft rounded face, upturned nose, and warm liquid eyes. Her dark hair flowed over her shoulders, and she moved with the sinuous grace of a leopard.

She was the magnet for many eyes. One girl in a sweatshirt sauntered over, said a few words to the butch, who nodded nonchalantly, and the beauty got up to dance. The butch's gaze followed her protégé carefully as she did the twist with the other girl. "It's the hair and the walk that gets her," Sidney decided. She smiled. "I like the large-busted type myself," she said. "And, anyway, she's too young." It was obvious to Sidney that the butch was sure enough of herself to let her partner dance with anybody in the place. "There's not much competition," said Sidney, looking around.

As the beautiful young femme resumed her seat, her butch friend expertly patted a few fallen tendrils of the girl's hair in place, and then casually hoisted her trousered legs and stretched them across the other's lap. Her glance meanwhile fell casually on our table.

With a laugh, Sidney bent forward to explain, "She's staking out her rights just in case anybody at this table gets any ideas."

Sidney was bored. "They're mostly squares here," she said. "Many of them are so unattractive they can't get a guy, so they decided they were lesbians." She was all for moving on. So, after paying our respects to proprietor Babe, we left the Fourth of July celebration without much more ado.

"That was a bust," Sidney said. Though it was late, she seemed rather restless. "I want to call Charlene," she said as we squeezed into her tiny car and started off.

"Is Charlene your professor friend?" I asked.

She seemed momentarily puzzled, and then a smile flickered across her face. "Oh, no, Charlene is the most beautiful young thing you ever wanted to see."

At a nearby corner, she pulled the car up and disappeared into a phone booth. When she reappeared, she looked out of sorts.

"Did you talk to Charlene?" I asked.

"No, the butch answered the phone." She laughed crossly. "You know the old saw: 'If a man answers, hang up,'" She flipped her cigarette out the car window. "I was hoping Charlene would answer, and then get out on some excuse or other." She grimaced. "That damn butch watches her, so that we've been able to meet for lunch only." She jammed on the brakes as we almost shot through a red light. "But we'll make it yet."

I looked at her curiously. The traces of femininity once so apparent seemed to have vanished. "You're very busy," I said, "what with the professor, your twenty-two-year-old fiancé, and now Charlene."

She flared up angrily. "Don't mention that faggot to me," she said. "I'm through coddling him. Let him play house with some nice boy."

This was her first reference to Tex. "What happened?" I asked. "I thought he was the perfect gentleman."

"Never mind what happened," she snapped. She looked at her watch, suddenly tired, and yawned. "Shall we call it a night?"

"Did he walk out on you?" I asked.

She turned on me in disgust. "Men are all the same," she said with withering contempt. "One day I came home in the middle of the afternoon and found the s.o.b. in my bed with another guy, and in my house. The ungrateful slob. He wasn't even paying rent."

With "Tiger" Tex out of the running, only one choice remained—the "Lady."

I did not see Sidney again. But without referring directly to the professor, I asked a pretty girl whom I had met with Sidney one night whether she felt Sidney would eventually settle down.

"Sidney?" she said incredulously. "Not Sidney. She's having too good a time."

I didn't quite understand.

The pretty blond femme smiled. "She's out to make a one-night stand with every pretty little thing she sees."

"Did you know she had children?"

"Vaguely, but Sidney isn't the family type. They must have been accidents."

I found it puzzling that Sidney should enjoy her relationship more with a male homosexual than with a more masculine male. But the blonde found this simple logic.

"They complemented each other," she explained. "Sidney was aggressive, the boy passive. She couldn't stand housework, he even liked to cook, and they both appeared to be AC-DC, gaited either way."

"But why," I asked, "should Sidney's relationship with the homosexual have been more rewarding physically than her relationships with the ordinary male?"

My lesbian authority shrugged. "I wouldn't know about it myself," she said, "but the woman in these relationships takes charge, and the gay boy does whatever she wants, when she wants, and aims to please at all times." She grinned impishly, and it was almost a leer. "Do I have to draw you a diagram? After all, the male homosexual doesn't have to change his pattern, particularly, to be the perfect lover—for a lesbian."

She was not impressed by Sidney's bisexuality. "The people who swing one way or the other are invariably so damn promiscuous," she said, "that their bisexuality may be only a reflection of their extreme promiscuity."

It seemed likely, then, that any course was open to Sidney. "She might get married again, then?" I asked.

"She might marry some fag," the blonde conceded, "and she could still knock around with lesbians all she wanted. But"—she held up an admonishing finger—"no self-respecting lesbian would put up with all that playing around." Her blue eyes twinkled. "Hell," she said, "she acts like a Goddamn man. The other day we were at a meeting and I was listening to a talk and she kept her knee in my back all through the damn speech." The knee in the back was apparently a crude overture.

I was still trying to appraise Sidney as a type. "Wouldn't there be less wear and tear," I asked, "for her to just go back to teaching and raise her family quietly?"

The femme chuckled. "You've got to judge people by what they want, not by what they say they want, and Sidney just couldn't get along now without the excitement of being a lesbian."

"How about marriage?" I asked.

She snorted. "She doesn't want a man."

"Then you don't really think she's bisexual?" I persisted.

The pretty blonde laughed. "If anything," she said, "she's trisexual. She'll try anything."

19

FAMILY TYPES

A woman with a heavy accent answered the phone. "Is Sophie there?" I asked.

"No," the woman said, "she's at a girl-friend's."

"Is she at Millie's?" I asked.

"Oh, yes," she said pleasantly, "she's there every night." Her voice held all the comfortable assurance of a mother who knew her daughter was safely occupied.

Sophie and Millie were only names to me—girls who had volunteered to talk to me after I had mentioned at a homosexual meeting the reluctance of so many secret lesbians to reveal themselves to the serious reporter. I noticed from the note sent on by the secretary of the homosexual group that the two girls lived near each other, and had assumed that they were friends.

When I phoned Millie, the voice that answered was guarded and noncommittal. "This is Millie," she said.

"Can you speak frankly?" I asked.

"Not very well," she said.

I asked whether she and Sophie could meet me.

"In the Grand Central area," she said, after a whispered consultation with Sophie. "We work near there."

The meeting was arranged.

They were not quite what I expected. Millie was a tall girl with austere features, long hair, and an aloof manner. Sophie was shorter, with a round face, and a male pompadour that was distinctly butch. She wore a heavy sheepskin coat, with the broad collar turned up.

She was surprised that I was able to pick them out among the people waiting outside the cocktail lounge.

"How did you know?" she asked.

"Radar," I said.

Both laughed uncertainly as we took a discreet table in the big room.

Millie looked around carefully before slipping off her coat. There were only a few people sitting around, mostly men and women raptly absorbed in each other. She seemed satisfied. But she was not sure she wanted a drink.

"Aw, go on and have something," Sophie said. "Be a sport for a change."

Millie ordered a Dubonnet on the rocks, while Sophie, who had obviously already been drinking, decided without hesitation on a Scotch. While neither seemed particularly uncomfortable, the conversation started slowly.

"Was that your mother I spoke to?" I asked Sophie.

"I guess so," she said. "It must have been."

"She spoke with an accent—was it Polish?"

She shook her head. "No, we're Finnish. She indicated her high cheekbones. "Can't you tell?"

Her mother had sounded very casual in referring me to the girl-friend. "I guess she doesn't know about you and Millie?" I asked.

She frowned. "I don't think so, though my brother sort of let the cat out of the bag once." She didn't elaborate.

Millie remained silent and detached, so distant that I wondered how she had agreed to sit down with a reporter, and then, surprisingly, I discovered that the meeting had been her suggestion. As usual, Sophie had gone along.

Sophie now explained sardonically, "I think Millie feels what you might call introspective."

The other girl's expression didn't change. "It's not that at all. I just thought I might learn something about myself." She nodded toward the other tables. "Shall we keep our voices down, and not advertise publicly what we're talking about?"

Sophie's lips curled. "There you are, always thinking about what other people think instead of what you think."

As they talked, I had opportunity to observe both closely. They were in their early thirties, and Sophie was clearly the butch type. Millie struck me as a lace-curtain lesbian. She was articulate and knowledgeable but often arbitrary and smacking of the text-books; however, her partner was obviously impressed by her manner.

The two didn't seem to go together. Millie held not only a master's degree but a doctor's degree in education, and was a medical researcher. She was well traveled, and came from a family that apparently had money.

In contrast, Sophie was bluff and hearty, and spoke with the breezy vernacular of the Bronx. After one year of college, she had quit to help out at home. She worked in a small office, and prided herself on getting along with everybody—men and women. "I don't hate anybody," she said, grinning. "I just like some more than others."

Finishing her drink, she smacked her lips, as Millie frowned at this breach of taste.

"Aw, go on with you," Sophie said, "I'm having a good time." She ordered another drink.

While Sophie jibed at her friend from time to time, Millie seemed primarily concerned that these jibes might be overheard. As she again looked around watchfully at the nearby tables, she said in a tone of quiet reproof, "I like being a lesbian, but I don't think it's anybody's business."

Looking at her, I wondered again why she had agreed to the interview; it didn't seem consistent with her air of bland superiority or her apparent obsession with privacy.

She replied rather obliquely. "I have thought about why *The Sixth Man* was successful," she observed, "when so many other books on homosexuality didn't do so well. Psychologists, sociologists, even homosexuals have written about it quite informatively, but your book was the only one that became a best-seller, and I have figured it out." She seemed quite pleased with herself.

I thought that, like so many homosexuals, she was going to attribute its comparative success to sensationalism. She surprised me. "You saw homosexuality through the eyes of the average person, and what you found interesting or revealing, so did they."

Somehow, as she said it, it was no compliment. But Sophie was quick to concur. "I didn't read it," she said, "but that Millie knows her books, if she doesn't know anything else." She laughed uproariously, as though she had said something very funny.

Avoiding the other girl's gaze, Millie apologized for her coldly. "She's got an odd sense of humor."

"There you go again," Sophie rejoined, "always belittling me."

Coolly, Millie turned her attention to me. While she was no beauty, she was attractive, and she would have been quite feminine had there been any animation or warmth in her face. As though peering into my mind, she said in a low voice, "Have you any idea why men show interest in me when I don't have the slightest interest in them?"

"If they think you're a lesbian," I said, "it's probably a subconscious challenge, and if they don't, it's just because you're an attractive woman."

"But I don't like men," she said. "Since I was a child I haven't been able to bear them, and I don't like the idea of a man touching me." She shivered slightly. "I don't even like to talk to them."

As I regarded her uncertainly, she gave the first glint of a smile. "It's strange," she said. "You're the first man I haven't minded talking to about anything that touches me closely."

Sophie had been following our conversation with interest, while downing another drink. Despite her serious drinking, I got the impression that she was listening at least as intently as I was. But so far she had seemed content to let Millie occupy the spotlight.

Millie seemed the kind of girl that any man would enjoy dating. She was tall and well formed, and had a Nordic good looks. Yet she had mentioned men only with repugnance. And so I asked, "Have you ever had a boy-friend?"

She didn't answer directly, but, looking across at her partner, she said somewhat enigmatically, "I feel that anybody who is bisexual isn't really a lesbian; they're just confused." She glanced over at Sophie.

Sophie apparently got the message. Her lips tightened, and she said sourly, "So I've balled with two or three men, so what?"

I could sense the electric tension but didn't quite understand what it was all about. I tried a safe question.

"Have you ever wondered," I asked Millie, "what made you a lesbian?"

"I haven't been able to stand men since I was eighteen months old," she said casually. It was obvious from her expression that she had enjoyably anticipated the impact of her remark.

Sophie, now sulking behind her drink, said with a mirthless laugh, adding to my bewilderment, "Tell him about the bronchoscope." She turned to me for support. "Millie is always trying to learn how it all happened, and I tell her that only *now* matters— don't look back. Isn't that right?" It was almost a plea.

Millie rarely resisted an appeal to talk about herself. "When I was a year and a half old," she said, in a monotonous voice, "the doctors stuck a bronchoscope with a light down my throat and for some time thereafter, whenever men came near me, I would start to wail and carry on."

I didn't see the significance.

"The doctors," she said tartly, "were all men."

I was still mystified.

Sophie appeared to be enjoying herself. Slapping the table, she jeered, "That old bronchoscope's the penis symbol, and she's been afraid of men ever since. How do you like them apples?"

As though she had not been interrupted, Millie calmly described another traumatic experience; this time she was nineteen. "I awakened one night," she said, "and walked down the hall, stretched out my hand in the darkness, and felt something clammy"—she grimaced—"and went into a swoon." Her family found her lying on the floor. She was hysterical for days, almost suffering a breakdown. She never did know what she had touched.

She fixed her expressionless eyes on me. "What do you make of that?" she asked.

I frankly didn't know what to make of it. It might have been a sex symbol, but who could say?

Millie grunted with satisfaction. "That's what the psychiatrist thought, too."

Sophie shook her head ruefully. "I tell her she ought to forget her complexes and think about other people for a change." She appealed to me. "Suppose it's another sex symbol; what good does it do to know?"

Ignoring the other girl, Millie turned the conversation to girls she had admired—from afar—and the type of girl she thought especially attractive. "I like the cool, poised kind," she said, "sleek and well turned out."

Sophie wore an injured air. "I don't know what she thinks of me," she complained, "when she's always talking about somebody else."

As though Sophie had not spoken, Millie explained for my benefit how she classified other girls. She thought of them as three distinct types. "There's the well-stacked, swinging type, who's very feminine but curious, the neat butch, who's quite sharp in her trim shirts and tailored slacks, slim and assured, and then"—she laughed bleakly—"the sexless wonders."

Sophie snorted. "Get her," she said sarcastically, "it's all in her mind."

I was interested in the "sexless wonders."

Millie's voice was filled with contempt. "You know, these fat, overgrown, plain girls who can't get a man or a woman so they become very officious, and usually wind up running clubs and committees"—she looked over at Sophie for confirmation—"like that girl who is so active with that homosexual group."

I thought her less than charitable, and the heavy-set Sophie, who evidently misread her meaning, said with a growl, "Don't go making any remarks about me. I'm not that hard to take." She was obviously upset. "Believe me," she said wearily, "I can't figure out what this girl wants. She's always talking about this or that girl, and I think she'd leave me at the drop of a hat if she thought she could latch on to somebody else."

Millie coolly flicked the ash off her cigarette. "I told you I'd like to go to California."

"Yeah," Sophie said, "and me with fifty dollars. Can you imagine how I'd look stranded out there by myself?"

Instead of reassuring her friend, Millie seemed to enjoy her uneasiness. "You don't have to worry," she said, without appearing to mean it.

Sophie hastily helped herself to another drink. "Jeez," she said, throwing up her hands, "how do you reach this one?"

With Sophie's movement, I noticed that the two girls wore identical rings, simple bands of gold. "Are those marriage rings?" I asked.

Sophie's laugh rang hollow. "That was the idea when I got them, but you might call them friendship rings now, if that. But I suppose I should consider myself lucky that she even wears one." She brooded darkly. "She doesn't know how to give; all she can do is take. She can't even tell me she loves me. I have to keep asking her." While she was speaking to me, her eyes were fastened on Millie.

Millie shrugged listlessly.

"You see?" Sophie exclaimed. "I can't even get a rise out of her. Nothing touches her, she's so wrapped up in herself."

I wondered how long they had been seeing each other.

"Two years," said Sophie with a look of disgust, "and it's no different now than before. She just wanted somebody to bring her out, and I was it."

Sophie was obviously drinking too much, and the more she drank, the more the other girl's coolness goaded her. But Millie sat sweetly unconcerned, in the splendor of her self-assurance and the strength of her detachment. She did not even appear to be touched by the revelation that had slipped from Sophie's loosened tongue.

As I studied them, they seemed such incongruous types, but, as a famous actor had once said of love, "It's like a cold: you catch it, and you don't want it, but you can't get it out of your system."

Millie's impassivity intrigued me even more than Sophie's fretfulness. I wondered if anything could reach her, however close it came. "And so Sophie was the first for you?" I said, observing her narrowly.

She remained coolly nonchalant. "I was interested in girls from the time I was eighteen," she said casually, "but I never had the courage. Several years ago—I must have been twenty-four—I kept thinking about this girl in my office, but I lost my nerve just as I was about to approach her in the ladies' room." She pursed her lips. "It was just as well, because that very afternoon she announced she was getting married to a boy in the office." The thought of a rebuff, and consequent exposure, had petrified her.

Sophie shook her head impatiently. "I keep telling her that a girl's being married makes little difference. Sometimes they're worse than the others. I used to like straight girls, and I'd find out by bringing the conversation around to fairies how they felt about homosexuality generally." She found the office ladies' room a convenient confrontation point, and if the girl didn't draw away, she might then suggest a drink or dinner. "Married or single," she said, "they're all curious."

It seemed terribly risky. "Was it worth it?" I asked.

"Sometimes," she said modestly, "but the girl might decide after a couple of weeks that it wasn't her cup of tea, and I wouldn't bother any more. They were usually just curious, like I said."

Struck by Millie's air of complete detachment, I suggested that perhaps she, too, had only been prompted by curiosity.

Millie perked up. "Do you really think so?" she said. "I've wondered about that myself at times."

Sophie gulped down another drink. "You don't know what you are or what you want—that's the trouble," she snapped. "You have no interest in anybody or anything but yourself, and you're the biggest mystery of all."

Even before this attack, delivered with almost savage fervor, Millie lost none of her aplomb.

I found her regarding me pleasantly, and I returned her look. She had a surprisingly good face, when you studied it: the high cheekbones of the sultry Scandinavian, the fair brow, clear skin, deep-set eyes, and good teeth. But, unfortunately, she looked as though she had never come alive. "You know, of course," I said, "that you're unusually attractive."

"Oh, she knows that," Sophie said derisively, "and she knows it's that aloof manner that gets them."

"You're sure," I said to Millie, "that you couldn't develop some interest in a man?"

She shrugged. "The only man I could ever stand was my brother."

"How about your father?" I asked.

"He's all right," she said grudgingly, "but he's always knuckled under to my mother. He has no mind of his own."

Sophie rallied to the father's defense.

"I wish I'd had a father like that, so friendly and good-natured, instead of that no-good s.o.b. of mine," she cut in bitterly. "The bum would come home drunk when we were kids and beat the hell out of us until we'd run up to the roof and stay there until he drank himself into a stupor." Suddenly, her face had become livid with anger. "When I was fifteen," she said, "I made up my mind that if that s.o.b. ever hit me or my mother again, I'd kill him."

There was no mistaking her sincerity. And a year or so thereafter, when he was drunk and disorderly, she had lifted her hands to him, pushing him roughly to the floor when he threatened her. He had crumpled up immediately, losing all his fight, and what vestige of respect she had for him had vanished. He was no longer a figure to be considered in the household.

It was a compelling story, as she told it, but Millie's mind appeared to be elsewhere. She wasn't even listening. She turned to me impatiently as Sophie concluded, and said, "You mentioned the other night at the meeting that you had attended the lesbian convention in California." She moistened her lips slightly. "What do you think of the girls out there?"

It seemed a rather broad question. "Exactly what do you mean?" I asked.

She hesitated. "Don't you get the impression, particularly in San Francisco, that the girls out there are smarter and more sophisticated?" She made it clear she was speaking of lesbians only.

I had been favorably impressed by the San Francisco chapter of the Daughters of Bilitis, especially the leaders, who seemed a stimulating, enterprising group living interesting, productive lives while seeking to do some good. "Many are quite unusual," I agreed.

"You see?" Millie said, looking triumphantly at the disgruntled Sophie. "I knew the girls out there had a lot more to them."

But Sophie obviously felt her partner's interest was more than elementary. She shook her head wearily. "She's like her mother; she doesn't think I'm good enough for her."

I looked up in some surprise. "Does her mother know about you two?"

Sophie smiled grimly. "Oh, sure"—she motioned across the table—"she had to tell her."

I turned to Millie. "Why did you have to do that?"

Her face still wore its same calm expression. "Oh, she kept asking questions, and I decided to satisfy her curiosity."

"You don't believe that?" I said.

She looked at me from under her long lashes. "Why not?"

"Why," I asked, "were you trying to hurt her?"

She was still toying with her drink. "I don't like her particularly, but I have no reason to hurt her. I'm not that interested." She gave her mirthless smile. "A psychiatrist told me that my mother tried to seduce me, and that was why I resented her." Again, she seemed to enjoy dropping a little bomb.

Sophie snorted. "If you'd stay away from those psychiatrists, you'd be better off."

"Where did the psychiatrist get that idea?" I asked Millie.

She lit a cigarette, and said carelessly, "I had told him about my mother trying to kiss me while I was in the bath, and how when I tried to push her off, she still kept trying, as though it was something she had to do." She was then nineteen or twenty, and had been undergoing treatment since her disastrous dream experience.

But she had not been impressed by the psychiatrist. "The next time I went to him, he said, 'Now, you were telling me about your mother trying to seduce you.'" She had never gone back. "I didn't like him putting his words in my mouth."

She still hadn't told me how she had happened to break the news to her mother.

She looked over at Sophie. "We had been seeing each other for a while," she said, "and had finally planned to go away for the weekend that was supposed to change my whole life." Her voice was faintly ironic.

They had decided on Montauk, a bleak fishing resort on the extreme tip of Long Island. All that week Millie had been simmering with excitement, not so much at the thought of getting to know Sophie intimately, but in anticipation of a decisive step that might overnight change her life.

Her mother, never quite approving of Sophie, couldn't understand why they should be planning a weekend together. She had confronted her daughter.

Millie smiled as she recalled the scene. "She asked me what it was all about, and I told her."

The mother hadn't believed her. "It can't be true," she said imperiously. "No daughter of mine could do anything like that."

Millie had taunted her. "What's the matter, Mother, are you jealous?"

"Jealous?" The older woman was horrified.

"Why, yes, Mother," the daughter had replied. "You've wanted to swallow me up ever since I could remember."

"You don't make sense," the mother had said. "This is another one of your little games."

Nevertheless, she had studied her daughter closely when she got back from the weekend. "It was as if she expected to see some sort of scarlet letter engraved on my forehead," Millie said. There was a gleam in her eyes now. "But I didn't have to say a word to her. She knew right away that things were different." She laughed harshly. "And she never asked me another question."

Sophie had listened intently, not even touching her drink. Then she tossed off another Scotch and wiped her mouth. "She never thought I was good enough for Millie. She's an intellectual snob." Her voice was sharply edged with sarcasm. "Like her daughter."

Millie's father had had no suspicions. "He never knows what's going on," Millie said.

Sophie's eyes flashed at the indifference in Millie's tone. "You're lucky to have a father like that," she said. "My old man made two hundred dollars a week all during the Depression and we never had any food on the table, because the s.o.b. drank all the dough away. He was a real no-goodnik."

Millie apparently thought it was time for an intermission. Picking up her bag, she looked around for the ladies' room. And as she got up, revealing a strong, sinuous figure and long, shapely legs, many masculine eyes turned to follow her appreciatively all the way out of the room.

Sophie, who seemed to be bearing up well, considering the alcoholic intake, ordered another drink and glumly shook her head. "I have all the bad luck," she said. "I either go for somebody who takes me over the coals, or a cold fish like that one." She looked at me, hesitated, and then said with a nervous laugh, "Incidentally, I'd like to get something straight. I've had maybe a dozen affairs with men, not two or three, like I said, but she doesn't think you can be a lesbian and like men, so I don't let on as a rule." Her voice had become a confidential whisper.

One point intrigued me. She had mentioned earlier, almost in passing, that she didn't like anybody doing anything to her, accounting for her always being the butch. "I don't like that passive role," she said, "it doesn't suit my personality."

So how then could she enjoy any of her relationships with males?

She had the good grace to blush. "Whatever there is," she said with a grimace, "I do."

Taking advantage of Millie's absence, I probed the puzzling relationship between the two. Frankness seemed the best approach. "How long do you think you two will stay together?" I asked.

She shrugged, suddenly morose, "Who knows?" she said grimly.

I took another tack. "Do you think Millie could ever accept a boy-friend?" I asked. "She's a very attractive girl."

Sophie turned her heavy-lidded eyes on me. "You think so, heh?" she said, and laughed gratingly. She had apparently thought of the possibility before, for the question didn't surprise her. But she considered it unlikely.

"She's so wrapped up in her own feelings she can't think of anybody else."

If the relationship was as unrewarding as it seemed, it seemed odd that Sophie should bother with it.

"I guess I'm a masochist or something," she said with a grimace. "Anyway, she's under my skin, and she knows it."

Despite her male haircut, Sophie had struck me at times as the more feminine of the two. She was certainly more demonstrative. "Have you thought of reversing the roles?" I asked.

"You mean 'kiki?'" She frowned. "Sometimes I think she's more butch, but, like I told you, I can't stand anybody touching me."

"Are you going to California together?" I asked.

She shrugged. "If she wants, but I have the feeling that she's looking all the time for something more—for some new thrill or kick."

"Suppose she were to start going out with a man?" I asked.

She shrugged. "I wouldn't mind that as much as a girl. I'd raise hell then."

"You have had other girls," I pointed out.

"Only two or three seriously," she said, "and not any since I met this beaut."

She had always gone overboard for anybody she liked. One girl she supported for nearly a year and even took her into her family's home to live when she was down on her luck. Eventually, it had been the cause of a family breach. "My brother got a little sweet on the girl," Sophie explained, "and made a pitch. But when she was drinking one day she told him she was already taken—by me."

That finished the girl-friend as a house guest, and broke up the romance in the bargain. There were further repercussions. One night at the dinner table as Sophie lightly discussed a possible vacation in California, her brother had sneered, "That's a good place for you, out there with all those queers."

Her mother had looked up, startled, at the hostility in her son's voice, but had apparently not caught the innuendo.

It was months before Sophie got involved again. Immediately prior to Millie, there had been another serious romance. Sophie was still friendly with Marian, despite the breakup. "She walked off, too," Sophie said, "as soon as I stopped with the handouts." But the "friendship" had continued. Only that week they had all gone together to a jam session in the Bronx, Marian and her new girl-friend, a light-skinned Negro, and Millie and Sophie. "They were mostly Negro there," Sophie said, "but we had lots of fun. They don't have all the inhibitions we do." Sophie spoke of the Negro girl admiringly, even though she had replaced her in Marian's affections. "She's usually the liveliest one at our parties. Nobody thinks of her color. She's a dream."

Paradoxically, her father's own narrow-mindedness had made her broad-minded. Whenever he was drunk, Sophie's father had ranted against Negroes and Jews, and she had felt a compensating regard for both races. There was another factor. "I guess," she said, "I feel a lot in common with other minorities."

We had covered quite a bit of ground before Millie got back to the table, freshly powdered and lipsticked, and looking as though she had just stepped out of a bandbox.

"I suppose you were talking about me," she said with a half-serious smile.

"Wouldn't you like to think so?" Sophie said gruffly.

I mentioned that we had been discussing dancing in the Bronx.

Her face immediately brightened. "Those jam sessions are the greatest," she said, in mock imitation of the current hep set.

"Those Negro kids are the mostest. They give themselves over completely to the music and laughter, and what comes after." She seemed pleased with the unconscious rhyming that had slipped out. "I'll tell you what it is," she said. "I don't think they're rooted in all that phony tradition that bogs us down, and makes us conform and do things we don't want to do."

Sophie gave her a sharp glance, but the other girl only smiled blandly. "What," asked Sophie, "do you want to do that you're not doing?"

Millie yawned. "Oh, nothing," she said, stretching sinuously, and checking the big clock on the wall. "I got to get going," she said, "or Mother will be phoning the neighbors."

We discussed another meeting. "Why don't you come out with us one night?" Millie said. "We're planning to visit a new spot in Long Island. It's mostly a suburban crowd—you know, discontented wives, unhappy girl-friends, and kids like I used to be. It's nothing fancy. They kick their shoes off, sit around on the floor, drink beer, play the juke box, and dance."

The crowd was supposed to be a smart one. "None of the beatniks and the obvious lezzes, but the Island's avant-garde," Millie explained.

Reportorially, it seemed interesting.

Sophie looked uncertainly at Millie. "Maybe they won't let him in," she said.

"We don't know if they permit men," Millie said, "but we'll find out."

I would be away two or three weeks but would call when I got back.

Both girls seemed pleased at the way the discussion had gone. As I paid the check, Sophie protested. "I've been doing most of the drinking—let me pay for Millie and myself."

She was placated only when I pointed out that I was in their debt for the information they had given me.

"All right, then," she said grudgingly. She shook my hand. "I want you to know how much we enjoyed the meeting," and then she added in a burst of generosity, "When you get back, maybe we can take you to some house parties with us; you'll meet the kind of lesbians you never see in bars."

I dropped them at the subway, and we parted great friends—I thought.

Three weeks later, back in town, I called Millie. Her voice was guarded on the phone, but no more so than the first time I had called. "Have you talked to Sophie?" she asked.

I mentioned that I had misplaced her number. She gave it to me. "You'd better talk to her first," she said.

Sophie, too, seemed surprisingly distant when she came to the phone. She seemed hazy about the tentative date we had made. "We don't think bars are very important," she said, "unless you're only interested in sensationalism." Her voice was a million miles away.

I pointed out that the proposed visit had been their idea.

"I know," she said, "but we got to talking about it later and decided that you didn't have a serious approach to the over-all problem."

"That isn't true at all," I said.

"Well, frankly," she said, "Millie was disappointed in you. She had the idea that you would be more scholarly."

"She knew what to expect," I said. "She read *The Sixth Man*."

"Yeah," she said, "but we got to talking about the book with a few homosexuals, and they said it didn't add much. They knew everything that was in the book."

"If I were to write about a prison," I pointed out, "I wouldn't write it for the prisoners but for a public which knew little or nothing about prison life."

She grunted a grudging assent, but then said, "Anything we tell you isn't going to influence you. Anyway, how can you judge people by a single interview?"

I pointed out that while I would like to see them again, "I only have to see a swallow once to know it's a bird." I still couldn't understand her change of attitude. "You seemed friendly enough last time," I said.

There was a short silence. "Well, I was drinking quite a bit. I had about seven or eight shots before I even saw you." But the next day the whisky had apparently worn off. "When we thought about it," she said, "we decided we didn't like your remarks about the lesbian group here." This was a new tack.

I reminded her that I had only agreed with them that the membership seemed too small to accomplish great things.

"That's how much you know," she snapped. "There may be only five or six members openly, but you should have seen the party in Philadelphia last week. There were two hundred there, and everybody had a helluva time."

I turned the conversation to Millie. "How are you two getting on?" I asked.

"Fine," she said, "and nobody is going to break us up." She obviously was volunteering no information.

While it seemed a lost cause, I still tried to point out that as a reporter I could probably do a more objective job than the most scholarly investigator. "I think," I said, "that a reporter is a little more flexible than a psychologist or a sociologist who already has a point of view based on his special orientation."

She sneered. "Don't hand me those big words. You've got a mind like an elastic band: it'll stretch a little and then snap right back."

I really didn't know what was bothering her.

"Didn't Millie say anything to you?" she demanded brusquely.

"She just suggested that I call you."

"Well, she's got a good mind and she knows what's going on," she said harshly. "Nobody's pulling any wool over her eyes."

"If she's interested in the scholarly approach," I said, "then she must know that many psychologists, including Freud, think that homosexuality often results from arrested psychosexual development."

"There you go insulting us now," she growled, "telling us we're retarded."

Her voice grated unpleasantly. "How could you get anything out of us," she said, "when you did all the talking that night, trying to make an impression?"

I still didn't know what she was getting at.

"Listen, buddy," she said, "all you newspaper people are the same. All you're interested in is the buck—you don't give a damn about us."

I was still puzzled. "Did you want to be paid for your story?" I said. "You should have said so, then." I pointed out that many researchers had shied away from a subject so obviously fraught with difficulty, and that I had many times thought of abandoning the project. "Even women investigators have kept clear of it," I said, "for one reason or another."

She picked me up on only one point. "Who'd listen to anything that a woman had to say?" she remarked bitterly.

I couldn't help laughing. "I have," I said, "for what appears to be eternity."

"You haven't minded it at all," she said, "so don't give me that." Her voice was rasping.

I didn't understand.

"Not much you don't," she said. "Listen here, buddy"—her voice rose stridently—"we're wise to you. We know what you're after, and you're only sore because you didn't get it from some dumb lesbian here or in California."

I took a second take before I realized the full import of her insinuation. "What makes you say that?" I asked, not terribly surprised at anything at this point.

"Aw, you're like every other guy," she said. "You're all the same."

It was obvious that there was no purpose in continuing the conversation. But as I put down the phone, I felt only regret that I had been unable to dent this unassailable wall of hostility.

I brooded about the incident for days. And then, still not having the slightest idea why an apparently amiable relationship had deteriorated disastrously, I revealed the story to a young lesbian friend as an example of the baffling complexities of the lesbian mind.

Though she was only nineteen, my pretty confidante had considerable first-hand experience with lesbian thinking and a bizarre sense of the ridiculous. By the time I had finished, she was almost doubled up in laughter.

"Complex!" she howled. "It's as simple as the ABCs. Can't you just see that queen sitting there that night, enjoying all that attention, and then teasing the butch later about how interested you were in her?" The tears streamed down her face. "And that poor butch already worried about getting the gate, thinking of you as another rival." She wiped her eyes. "That Millie telling you how you were the first man she felt like talking to—boy, did that ever hit the butch between the eyes after she got to thinking about it the next day."

I wondered how she could be so sure.

She gave me a mischievous look. "Don't you know yet that just as the John feels that every pretty lesbian is a challenge, the attractive femme thinks that she could have any man if she didn't want a girl more."

It seemed incredible that Millie had been playing this game.

My young informant shrugged. "It's done every day in the year, a million times."

But still, why twist everything I had said?

She made a little face. "Because they're a little twisted themselves—that's the kind of lesbians they are."

I looked at her with sudden curiosity. "And what kind of lesbian are you?"

She smiled; it was almost a grin. "I'm the kind," she said, "that can't stand the family type—the good old stay-at-homes—they're much too phony for me."

20

THE RECKONING

The rise of female homosexuality may very well be only one phase of the continuing drive of women all over to share a place in the sun with the male.

In a drastically changing world, the roles of male and female are changing drastically, too. "The men," one homosexual pointed out, "are getting more like women every day, and the women more like men." Women hail cabs, order meals, tip waiters, bawl out underlings. They run businesses, boss men around, make up payrolls, and sway major elections. Their influence is widening every day. But, even more importantly, they no longer think of themselves as the lesser sex. As they look around, they see other women doing the things they would like to be doing, and they are impressed by their own sex in their competition with men.

This new respect of women by women, some lesbians have observed, makes it simpler for women with no apparent homosexual traits to develop attachments for other women. "She looks at other females," one psychologist told me, "as somebody to be cultivated and looked up to, not just as a convenient repository of gossip or a casual companion for a dull afternoon."

As women have gained new authority, men have correspondingly yielded traditional prestige and powers. Even in questioning her secondary position, the woman has already broken with the concept of male supremacy, and is in open rebellion against male downgrading of the female intellect.

Established in business and the professions, no longer is the woman dependent on the male for financial support; but, more significant, she no longer requires his approval or acceptance, psychologically or otherwise. "We are proving every day," a typical working wife observed, "that we can do whatever a man can."

In discovering herself, the woman has become aware of a new power, which, it might very well be, she has not yet learned to properly use in pursuit of her own happiness. While she still clings vaguely to feminine privilege, she insists on flexing her muscle like a man, and this may be why, some experts say, she flounders around at times in a world of ambivalence.

"It is obviously difficult for the working woman to think like a man from nine to five, and then change her thinking with a dab of face powder and a touch of perfume," a well-known psychologist points out. "It is also unrealistic for a woman earning her own way to defer to the male, when she is more successful and manages things better."

And nowhere, of course, is this more evident than in Hollywood, where women have reached the pinnacle of fame and fortune, and arrogantly queen it over males subservient to their success.

Throughout contemporary life, the mundane as well as the glamorous, the female pressure for equality—or superiority—keeps mounting. It makes itself felt in countless little ways, trivial in themselves. "Nine out of ten men come in here with their wives," a men's clothing-store salesman reported, "and their wives tell them what to buy."

Femininity sometimes seems a lost art. In a television repair shop, for instance, a proprietor observes ruefully, "The man comes in nice-like to complain about a set, but the wife takes over and starts bellowing like a truck driver."

In the same way, some speculated that the modern woman's

widespread use of slacks might be an indication of subconscious wish fulfillment.

Often scoffing at marriage, once the great female dream, young women now insist upon putting their right to "self-expression" above traditional wifely duties. "Why," career girls ask, "should I work all day and then come home to chores while my husband plays the lord and master?"

In this climate, it is not surprising, perhaps, that the growing ambivalence of the female should often manifest itself in lesbianism, experimental or otherwise. Many experimented out of curiosity, and put it away out of caution; others maintained a double life, and still more, the complete rebels, chose the lesbian life, maintaining only enough secrecy to keep jobs and homes safe.

There were many obvious reasons for increased homosexuality, male and female, in which the changing role of the woman was clearly associated. There was the growing pattern of the broken home, the rise of Momism with the virtual abdication of the male as the dominating factor in the home, lack of a strong parental image for the impressionable child. And with all this there was a corresponding decline of public morality, replaced by a fuzzy amorality in which the breach of virtually all inhibitions was carelessly tolerated.

Often younger lesbians seemed so amoral that their very amorality closed them off from the pangs of guilt which plagued earlier generations with more stable standards.

But homosexuality began and ended with individuals, and affected all individuals differently. There were many anomalies. Often it seemed to repeat itself in families, and yet in the same family some children were homosexual and others not.

Apparently, the tendencies to homosexuality, like other weaknesses, could be passed from parents to children, laying dormant until they were triggered by some traumatic event. But not all children in a family inherited the same qualities or susceptibilities; nor were all affected similarly by their home environment. "The attitudes of parents vary toward their children in accordance with variations in the parents' age and physical and emotional well-being," one authority told me. "A father, healthy and energetic at thirty, might be a stabilizing influence on a child. That same father, a parent ten years later, might be an entirely different individual, soured by reverses, impatient with the stress of parenthood, not even wanting a child he would have welcomed ten years before." As it did for the father, the same held true for Mom.

Medical evidence supported the theory that the tendency to homosexuality, like that to weak lungs or poor eyesight, could be a family legacy. Making a survey of adolescent drug addicts, Dr. Robert W. Baird, a distinguished gland specialist, discovered that many of the girls, who were also lesbians, came from homes where the fathers were homosexual, and the children knew it. "They may have either inherited the weaknesses that had made their fathers susceptible to homosexuality," Dr. Baird pointed out, "or they may have been influenced by a weak paternal image —or both."

As an endocrine specialist, Dr. Baird felt that the individual was composed in part of a harmonious blend of temperament-forming male and female psychological genes inherited from both parents. Where these genes were more strongly disposed one way or the other, there might be a resulting imbalance, resulting in vulnerability to homosexuality. In keeping with this theory, many people were so genetically balanced that they could never become confirmed homosexuals, even if exposed temporarily to situations encouraging homosexuality. Still others, the doctor pointed out, were so vulnerable that improper parental identification might induce their homosexuality, while some, less vulnerable genetically, might require the additional trigger of a traumatic sexual experience—an attempted rape, or homosexual assault when young. "If young women should enjoy the homosexual contact," he said, "in a formative stage of their lives, it might then fix their sexual pattern, arresting the normal development of their feelings toward the opposite sex."

What Dr. Baird had theorized seemed to coincide with others' experience. But it didn't, of course, account for the spread of lesbianism and male homosexuality—not to a point where homosexuals talked of concentrating in sparsely settled sections of the country where numbers alone could make them a potent political force. In northern California, for instance, there was a campaign by some homosexuals to get their "brethren"—male and female—to move to neighboring Nevada, the most thinly populated state on the mainland. "The general idea," a lesbian related, "was that homosexuals would then be able to elect U.S. senators, congressmen, and even legislators on a statewide level, this gaining spokesmen and influencing legislation favorable to homosexuals."

Perhaps because they have less problems with society, few lesbians took the proposal seriously. "All we have to do is let down our hair," one lesbian observed facetiously, "and we can pass. Besides, it was preposterous, like so many homosexual projects which flaunt convention."

Like the male homosexuals, many lesbians converged on the big cities, where they could get safely lost. But, just as lesbianism cut across class, racial, and religious lines, it had no geographical boundaries. I had talked to lesbians from virtually every state of the union. And regardless of origin, their reactions were as diverse as other women's, except for a morbid preoccupation at times with their own homosexuality. "The trouble with being a lesbian," one woman told me, "is that even if other people don't know it, you do." However, because lesbianism often seemed a mere projection of their affectionate natures, they seemed less disturbed generally by an occasional trespass than the male homosexual.

And by and large, the lesbians dwelt less on their homosexuality than the male counterpart did. Though I had encountered a good deal of hostility, especially among the younger fry, I was also aware that many well-adjusted lesbians preferred to remain unnoticed and had not the slightest interest in lesbianism as a cause. They were mostly interested in getting by.

Most of the lesbians I met were proud, defensive, and supersensitive. Once they had acknowledged their lesbianism, they studied the researcher narrowly, noting each word, gesture, and expression in their effort to decide how prejudiced he was. "We know you've got to be prejudiced as a male," one lesbian told me. "We're just wondering how much."

But even the most conservative were occasionally goaded by a desire to flaunt their homosexuality, for in being furtive about their lesbianism, they felt they were using society's brush to stigmatize themselves. The visits to the lesbian bars were often an expression of this reaction, providing some with their only opportunity to openly express themselves as lesbians.

In their bravado, some bombastically dismissed fears at being recognized in these bars. "If anybody questions *me*," a pretty airline hostess said with a shrug, "I'll question *them*."

The bars themselves were obviously not representative of the lesbian swarm. Most lesbians never ventured into a lesbian bar, either because they had no need for these contacts or because they feared being branded lesbians. And in many communities where there were plenty of lesbians, there were no lesbian bars.

More than anything else, perhaps, the lesbian bars reflected the surging juvenile rebellion, with baby butches and young femmes conspicuously flexing their muscles as they registered their "right" to self-expression. Possibly because they were more delinquent than lesbianic, it was with the youngsters touring these lesbian bars that the Daughters of Bilitis seemed to score their greatest success.

"All we try to do," a highly respected D.O.B. member had told me, "is to help the individual recognize his own worth as a human being, and thus direct the wasted energies of antisocial hostility toward more productive goals."

But there was more to it than that. One convert, transformed from a ranting butch to a lady-like type in months, was a living testimonial to the possibilities of group therapy. "As I attended the meetings," she said, "I was able to identify with members whom I had come to respect for their wisdom, character, and standing in the community. They didn't even look the way I thought lesbians should look, and I began to take stock of my own appearance. And above all, I realized that if these women whom I had come to respect for themselves could be lesbians, there was nothing shameful about being a lesbian."

After this thought occurred to her, a whole new world seemed to open up. "I even felt glad that I was a lesbian and that I shared something—a sort of feeling of belonging—with these women who were able to keep their heads high."

Having been through the rebellious stage themselves, D.O.B. members were able to discuss the motives of the novices, and make them understand they were primarily hurting themselves in blindly revolting. Yet, if lesbianism was not a sickness, as some insisted, but only a variation of behavior, many lesbians still had consuming personality problems.

"The defiance, disillusionment, and despair we all know," observed D.O.B.'s Jaye Bell, "lie under the mask of gaiety which the habituals at the bars put on. Some have been so long on the underside of the coin that they are afraid of the side toward the sun. But for those who want the sunny side, let's try showing it to them. And while there are many we won't be able to reach, we can at least stop some of this antagonism toward society, which profits nobody."

Everybody, she felt, could enjoy a place in society, regardless of sexual preference, "when she learns that home life and public life mix like oil and water, and will do so for a long time to come."

Like an iceberg, the lesbian floats mostly undersurface. However, the rising prominence of the lesbian is often reflected by the male's growing suspicion of her as a competitor. And many a swain who once curiously visited lesbian bars has learned to stay clear of these bars or go stag. Recently, for instance, a Broadway playboy was sitting with his nineteen-year-old date in a Greenwich Village club when a tall blonde sauntered over and asked the girl to dance. She looked in confusion at her escort. He nodded, amused. But as the girls returned to the table, he overheard the blonde saying, "Keep away from these men, honey; they only want one thing."

He glared at the blonde. "And what," he snapped, "do you want?"

On his next visit to the club—alone—he had his answer. He saw two familiar figures on the tiny dance floor, locked in tight embrace: the hard-faced blonde and his former date.

An even more unsettling experience befell a middle-aged Cleveland bachelor. With a male friend and two girls, he had made up a foursome for dinner and the theater. They were halfway through the meal, when the wife of a prominent surgeon walked in the restaurant and sat down. "She smiled at the girls," the bachelor recalled, "and they got up to say hello. The next thing we knew, all three of them were walking out the door without even saying good-by."

Smarting over the incident, the bachelor looked up one of the girls a week later. She expressed her regrets and then explained, "We're her love slaves. Whatever she tells us, we must do."

He compared notes with other bachelors and discovered that they had had similar experiences. "How," he asked, "can such a thing be?" It was too much for his uncomplicated male mind.

While I was writing this book, the most frequent question from heterosexual friends was, "How many of *them* are there?"

Only oblique comparisons were possible. In New York City, the police had estimated four hundred thousand male homosexuals; in Los Angeles, some one hundred and fifty thousand—or approximately one out of every six male adults. The percentages varied in other large cities, but male homosexual organizations insisted they could appeal to twelve million homosexual voters across the nation. There were no similar estimates for the lesbians, but it seemed reasonable that just as the laws of natural selection allocated approximately one male for every female—or vice versa —so too this social law governed the equal distribution of the homosexual—male and female. Or, as one lesbian put it far more eloquently, "For every one of them, there's got to be one of us."

And so it seemed to the close observer. Female homosexuality was noticeably simmering just under the surface. Nearly every pretty girl—models, actresses, secretaries—all very straight, had at one time or another been the object of a lesbian advance, but because of the subtlety of the advance, often did not recognize it until later. One raven-haired model, for instance, reported meeting a girl in a restaurant rest room who promptly struck up a conversation on modeling. This girl later stopped by the table, chatted with the model's male date, and invited the two to her apartment for an after-dinner drink. When the model declined, though her date was willing, the invitation was quickly withdrawn.

In a well-known night club, the feature singer embraced a pretty acquaintance sitting at a ringside table and whispered, "I'm singing my next song only to you." The girl didn't think too much about it until the number was announced. It was, "I'm in the Mood for Love."

In many factories and offices, lesbian nests have developed unnoticed, until a sudden, revealing development. In Southern California, when two telephone girls eloped together, the managers of a telephone exchange discovered why so many of their girls had been so businesslike with the flirtatious office male. It was a dubious victory for virtue.

While wealth and social distinction often protected lesbians from gossip, these same lesbians, because of their prominence, had a sharp impact on their surroundings. One group, known as The Graces (more from their benevolences than from their given names), developed one of the finest residential districts in New York City, and were a vital force in the cultural progress of the community. Yet only a few in their circle knew of their sexual preference.

Secretive as they were, lesbians, I found, had almost radarlike communication with each other, and seemed able to spot, not only other lesbians on sight, but potential lesbians as well.

In this competition, even the most discerning male was at a disadvantage. Strolling in Central Park, a jaunty impresario with an eye for beauty noticed a young woman sunning herself on a park bench, amusing herself with a toy poodle she had on a leash. He wanted to stop but feared a rebuff. But thinking of the girl's beauty after he had gone on a while, he suddenly retraced his steps.

But the girl was talking with two girls, masculinely attired, who also had poodles. They were eagerly comparing notes about their dogs. The impresario retreated philosophically. "How," he asked, "can any man compete with a woman who can start talking with any girl she sees?"

In their growing independence, many housewives often made it clear, subtly, what their preferences were, while clinging to the male as the home provider. In the city or suburbia, the domestic scene was changing. In a small diner on Long Island, two couples strode in—two short-haired girls and two long-haired girls—holding hands. "They're in here every night," the counterman confided to a customer, "playing the juke box, having their coffee, and griping about the old man."

Then, turning to one of the women, an attractive matronly type in her thirties, he asked slyly, "How are love and a film the same?"

She was annoyed. "You and your jokes," she said tartly.

Undaunted, he provided his own answer. "Because they're both developed in the dark." He cackled at his own joke.

Nobody else laughed, and a girl with a modified butch-type haircut leaned over the counter and hissed, "Maybe *your* dirty kind of love is in the dark."

As her three companions regarded her approvingly, the counterman grumbled to himself, "And to think some poor sap is supporting all that."

Actually, as some psychologists pointed out, it didn't matter so much whether there were five, ten, or twenty million secret lesbians as it did that the problem was increasing without any organized effort to sift its causes and corrections.

To even begin to understand the problem, it was first necessary to know the lesbian—her thoughts and actions—and then try to comprehend what made her tick.

What motivated her and where was she going? Though the answers often eluded the lesbian herself, it was obvious that her sexual deviation was only an expression of her difference, not the difference itself.

Whatever made her different also made sex with a male less enjoyable than with a female. Freud's contention that the homosexual had been arrested psychosexually at the adolescent stage had its supporters. But what did the Freudians mean by psychosexual arrestment? Did they mean the lesbian had stopped developing emotionally at the age of, say, fifteen or sixteen, without a comparable mental arrestment? Quite obviously they *did*, since the homosexual was often intellectually superior in the arts, sciences, diplomacy, and business.

Where the lesbian's behavior appeared infantile, as it often did in her own summation of her problems, it may have been an infantilism developing indirectly through a Freudian-like block that likewise caused her to shun the emotional demands of making a home.

Though influenced by factors in early childhood, this psychosexual arrestment apparently didn't make itself felt until the potential lesbian was old enough to experience the first symptoms of sexuality—the yearnings, fears, and confusions of adolescence. "When I first realized that I was different from boys and that they expected something of me just because I was different," a teenaged lesbian told me, "I drew back in horror. And when a boy told me that was how I had been born, I didn't believe my mother and father could have been guilty of something so ugly." It was shattering to learn the boy had been right. For in this desert of unenlightened Puritanism, no one had ever troubled to tell her of the beauty of sex accompanied by love.

Although the vast majority of lesbians had experienced an intimacy with a male, some psychologists saw the lesbian as a perennial virgin at heart, never actually surrendering herself to a man even in her phony transports of love. Regardless of the psychologists, I met very few lesbians who thought of themselves as virgins—even when they were virgins. They regarded virginity, for the most part, as a dubious commodity, and would have cheerfully exchanged it for something useful. "I would do anything with a man for love or gain," a pretty teen-aged lesbian told me, knowing that if she did have a relationship with a man, she would not give of herself any more than the prostitute does, and for the same reasons.

In her frequent sorties into prostitution, the self-acknowledged lesbian had the dual interest of not only financing a lesbian relationship but of degrading the male with her phony transports of love. There was little chance of her giving anything of herself. "Like the male homosexual," one authority pointed out, "lesbians generally fly from a mature relationship."

Actually, the virginity of a lesbian was significant only as it highlighted her personality. Meeting hundreds of lesbians, checking on hundreds of others, I discovered that nine out of ten had had some physical relationship with a man. The lesbian virgin was an inconsiderable minority. Ridden by fear, she was motivated, not by any moral consideration, but by an exaggerated need to shield herself from the male. "Why," one girl asked, "should I give a man something that means so much to him?" Actually, she feared him more than she hated him.

As an extreme of both the male and the female, the lesbian was difficult to fit into any set pattern. For, while some lesbians shrank from the touch of a male, others were indifferent, or grudgingly acknowledged a liking for some males but based their liking entirely on the individual's charm, wit, and intellect—not specifically masculine attributes.

Most significantly, perhaps, I do not recall a single lesbian who thought of the male as the superior sex.

The lesbian often beguiled herself about her own motivations, reaching out for whatever reasons that best gratified her vanity as she rationalized her behavior. Many of the younger lesbians, the baby butches, for instance, were caught up in a fantasy of excitement that served to becloud the fact that they were actually avoiding a responsible relationship that might take them to the altar—what they scornfully chose to call conformity.

Even married with children, unsuccessful wives turned to lesbians as an escape from unwanted responsibility, while professing a variety of reasons ranging from boredom to a husband's alleged infidelity. "In reality," a psychologist pointed out, "the complexities of married life were too much for her. She fled a situation in which she had to bolster her man, while at the same time subordinating herself to him."

Actually, lesbians often deliberately chose male relationships which—consciously or subconsciously—they knew had little chance of lasting. And then, as a remarkably well-informed lesbian psychologist pointed out, they were able to say they had tried matrimony or something less, and had found that it was not their cup of tea. "Having chosen a male partner who could never work out for them," the psychologist stated, "they were able to throw off the blame on him, and at the same time give themselves an excuse for turning away from men."

Even their children, when they had them, became more like possessions than responsibilities. If the lesbian was careful about her furniture, she usually took good care of the children. However, if she was careless about the house, the child too was neglected. Even though the butch Dottie thought her husband a "slob," she still permitted him to bring up their child, because the girl's presence would have cramped her relationship with her lesbian partner. Yet, as she preferred to see it, she was thinking solely of her daughter's welfare in keeping her from a lesbian atmosphere. "Had she felt a normal maternalism," a psychologist observed, "she would have kept the child and changed the atmosphere."

Even lesbian couples who adopted children were apparently indulging irresponsible whims. "They certainly weren't thinking of a fatherless child who was bound to have two strikes against him before he got started," the physchologist said. "They were more like children playing with dolls."

I made a few other discoveries—disagreeing even with the vaunted Golden Mean of Sex.

The lesbian revolt against conformity did not always make her more of an individual, regardless of lesbian insistence that conformity stifles creative functions. For all too often the failure to conform was not a positive force but a pretext not to grapple with reality on any front that would test the individual's mettle. Bisexuality was advocated by some as an outlet that provided not only greater satisfaction to the creative but bridged the gulf between the sexes. Under observation, it did neither of these things.

In bisexuality, the lesbian found no serenity in any direction and her bisexuality seemed only a reflection of her own sexual confusion. "I'd go from one affair with a woman to another with a man," one bisexual reported, "always trying to escape what I was doing, but in the end I felt in tune with neither men nor women. I was as much alone as when I first discovered I was a lesbian."

The fact that she was so often unhappy did nothing to deter the lesbian from lesbianism. With all the lesbian's idiosyncrasies, complexities, and mysteries, it was obvious that lesbianism was not only here to stay but, on a tidal wave of new feminine self-appreciation, might one day be openly professed by the countless who lurk in the shadows of a clandestine world.

The acknowledged lesbian seems her own worst enemy, partly through her failure to cope with existing taboos, partly because of limited social horizons. "It is not always society that isolates the homosexual," a D.O.B. official pointed out. "It can also be a homosexual's view of himself."

In some ways, the lesbian is an incorrigible optimist, or perhaps she is again indulging in a mirage of self-delusion. But with the homosexual problem growing as numbers and influence mount, many lesbians see acceptance by the heterosexual world as inevitable, as was the case so long ago in ancient Rome and Greece. And non-homosexuals wonder whether this rising prevalence and acceptance of homosexuality may be the mark of a similar decline in culture.

But millions of lesbians and male homosexuals, lesbians contend, cannot be treated as second-rate citizens without society suffering irretrievably from lost productivity. And the homosexual, they insist, must function openly and naturally, without fear of retribution, if she is to make her needed contribution to society.

"Society must come to realize," so the D.O.B. summed up, "that the stereotyped image of the homosexual is but a half-truth, and that condemnation for simply *being* is not about to solve anything. For society to ignore the problem by continuance of the outmoded methods of closing gay bars, thus denying him (or her) the right to congregate in a public place; of denying employment to the homosexual when his inclinations are discovered; of casting aspersions upon anyone who would help or do research on the homosexual, is to commit socio-cide."

Accepted by society, the lesbian could concentrate on the positive instead of dribbling away her creative powers in a distillery of hate and resentment. And then there would be no socio-cide—so said the D.O.B., speaking for millions of uncounted lesbians who dared not raise their heads.

Some, not as directly involved, take a different view. "Homosexuality," one psychologist told me, "is a reflection of a sick moral climate. Once we make the individual conscious of his responsibility to family and society, as well as to himself, homosexuality will begin to disappear. A whole child," he stressed, "can develop only out of a whole home, in a whole community, in a whole nation—and no homosexual is a whole person."

And how was all this to be accomplished with a world in ferment teetering on the brink of suicide—not socio-cide—from day to day, flirting with a war which was in itself a mark of a cancerous society.

The psychologist had no ready solution. "But," he said grimly, "if homosexuality continues at the present rate, it may simplify its own problem, and the world's, too."

I did not understand.

He smiled dourly. "If nothing else," he said, "with time it should end the population problem, and then, ironically, homosexuality will also have solved the problem of the homosexual."